STUDIES IN INTERNATIONAL ORDER

The International REGULATION OF FRONTIER DISPUTES

The International
REGULATION OF FRONTIER DISPUTES

Edited by
EVAN LUARD

LONDON
THAMES AND HUDSON

Mr Luard has recently been appointed as Parliamentary Under-Secretary in the Foreign and Commonwealth Office. This book was already completed before that appointment took place, and the views he expresses in it are entirely his own.

Printed in Great Britain by
The Camelot Press Ltd, London and Southampton

ISBN 0 500 25025 1

CONTENTS

1 FRONTIER DISPUTES IN MODERN INTERNATIONAL RELATIONS

Evan Luard

Frontier disputes are a subject of special importance in the study of international relations and one that has perhaps been insufficiently explored.

It is a commonplace that territory has a psychological importance for nations that is quite out of proportion to its intrinsic value, strategic or economic. Sentiments of national pride and national honour are aroused by threats to territory more rapidly and more intensely perhaps than over any other type of issue. Long-standing resentments and long-cherished desires to recover territory may be harboured, whether the territory in question represents an economic asset or an economic burden, and whether it is inhabited by ethnically related people or not.[1] In consequence, disputes over territory have been perhaps the most important single cause of war between states in the last two or three centuries.

This remains true to a considerable extent even in modern times. It is sometimes suggested that wars in the modern world are no longer territorial. They are said to be mainly ideological or colonial conflicts, or civil wars within fixed frontiers. It is true that the majority of conflicts in the modern world are not *mainly* about territory; and are often internal rather than external. But there continue to be a large number of wars, and an even greater number of disputes, whose cause is purely territorial. Indeed in absolute numbers, there may be as many as in any previous time.

Of the sixty principal wars since 1945, nine have been colonial; that is arising from movements for independence, whether or not widely representative movements, within colonial territories (Indonesia, Syria and Lebanon, Philippines, Indo-China, Malaya, Kenya, Cyprus, Algeria, and Angola). There have been twenty-seven civil wars, including sometimes some element of external intervention (eleven mainly ideological, involving Communist or extreme left-wing groups, eight political, not involving Communist or left-wing groups, and seven involving minorities).[2] Of the external wars, there have been six which were not merely about local frontiers but represented attempts to win control of the whole or a large area of another territory (Korea, Guatemala, Egypt, Hungary, Goa and Czechoslovakia).

But there have also been thirteen cases of armed action (not always involving casualties), and in one or two cases unofficial rather than official action, resulting from disputes over territory. These were the following:

Eire–Northern Ireland (1945–60)
Afghanistan–Pakistan (1950–62)
Saudi Arabia–Abu Dhabi and Muscat (1952–56)
Cambodia–Thailand (1953–62)
China–India (1954–62)
China–Burma (1956–60)
Nicaragua–Honduras (1957–61)
Egypt–Sudan (1958)
Iraq–Kuwait (1962)
Morocco–Algeria (1962)
China–USSR (1963–)
Somalia–Kenya (1963–67)
Somalia–Ethiopia (1963–67)
Argentina–Chile (1965)
Yemen–Aden (sporadic)

There were also five important cases of armed conflict, arising largely over frontiers, as the immediate consequence of the establishment of new states:

India–Pakistan (1947–49)
India–Hyderabad (1947)
Arab States–Israel (1948–49, 1956, 1967)
Indonesia–Malaysia (1963)
Pakistan–Kashmir (1965)

Classifications of this kind can never be entirely satisfactory, because sometimes a number of motives may be at work, or different nations involved may have different motives in particular conflicts (as over the three-power attack on Egypt in 1956). In some cases too the degree of armed force employed may have been minimal. All of these last eighteen cases nonetheless represent armed conflicts of a kind over frontiers.

While disputes over territory remain intense, however, there has been a significant change in their character over the last thirty years or so. In part this reflects the change in the character of wars in general: they have been generally limited in scope and aim. In the eighteenth and nineteenth centuries most wars were, in one degree or another, territorial. But they were then aimed often at the total conquest of another state, and the wresting away by these means of considerable territories, sometimes entire territorial units, whether in Europe or overseas. In some cases the *result* of such wars was a fairly marginal exchange of territory, but the original objective was wider. Even in the inter-war years the aggressions that took place – over Manchuria, Ethiopia, Austria, Albania, Poland, Finland, the Baltic States, and West Europe – were aimed at wholesale conquest rather than marginal border areas.

But since 1945, except in the last five cases mentioned above, two of which were cases of national reunification, territorial conflicts have usually concerned relatively restricted frontier areas. They have also mainly been conducted with limited aims and by limited means. It is true that attempts to win control of whole territories have partly been replaced by forms of proxy warfare: by the provision of assistance to rebels in other states to win control there by indirect means. Nonetheless the change is significant. It perhaps represents a genuine advance, even a change in motivation: consolidation rather than expansion. Territorial wars have been waged not so much to change the map, as to define it. Conquest of new lands, and the advancement of national power or glory that results from it, are less often the aim than the *defence* of territory often held on both sides to be justly theirs.

There is another difference between the period since 1945 and that before. Of the cases mentioned in the period between 1918 and 1939, seven out of the eight were undertaken in Europe, or at least by European powers. Since 1945, every case has occurred *outside* Europe. This is partly a reflection of the fact that *new* states have emerged entirely outside Europe, and frontier disputes are naturally particularly likely to occur where new states arise. But it also reflects the greater stability of European politics as a whole, the firm balance of power established in Europe, which is not always available elsewhere, the clearer definition of the frontiers of Europe, whether or not they are accepted as final (and it is the lack of definition of frontiers, as much as conflicting claims, which frequently gives rise to conflict), above all the lack of powerful forces hostile to the status quo.

Disputes of this kind do not always involve war. Besides those cases where armed action, on a greater or lesser scale, have occurred, there are a very much larger number of *disputes* over frontiers, where mutually conflicting claims have been put forward, leading often to a war of words and continuing tensions, rather than armed clashes. A number could still lead to armed conflict in the future. Sometimes such claims are loudly and repeatedly proclaimed at every possible opportunity. In other cases they have been allowed to lie almost dormant, and been put forward only where necessary, as a matter of form, to reserve rights. Principal examples of frontier disputes, not prosecuted by armed force on any significant scale, are the following:

Spain–Gibraltar
Greece–Albania
Bulgaria–Yugoslavia

Germany–Poland
Morocco–Mauritania
Iran–Bahrain
Iran–Gulf States
Iran–Iraq
Sahara, various
Syria–Turkey
Morocco, Mauritania–Spanish Sahara
Niger–Dahomey
Malawi–Tanzania, Zambia, Mozambique
Philippines–Malaysia
Japan–USSR
South Vietnam–Cambodia
Guatemala, Mexico–British Honduras
Argentina–Falkland Islands
Venezuela–Guyana
Ecuador–Peru
Antarctica–various

This list does not claim to be comprehensive, but, taken with the list of conflicts, it shows how far frontiers, while undoubtedly more firmly and unchallengeably established than in any earlier time, even in the modern world remain contested, and possible sources of future wars.

Let us next look at some of the reasons for the large number of disputes that exist.

There are easily understandable causes why there have been a particularly large number of conflicts and claims concerning frontiers over the past twenty-five years.

The first, and most obvious, is the end of the period of colonialism, and the emergence to independence of many states previously dependent. This has brought about claims of a number of kinds. Sometimes colonialism has suppressed certain claims, which have risen to the surface again only after the colonial power was removed. This, for example, was the case with Morocco's claim to Mauritania, the Philippines' against Malaysia, Thailand's against Cambodia and others. In other cases the claims arise from the very fact of colonialism: the claim has been directed against occupation of the territory by the colonial power itself, though it will be equally upheld against any independent state that replaces it: this, for example, is the case with the Spanish claim against Gibraltar, the Argentine's against the Falkland Islands, Guatemala's against British Honduras, or Iraq's against Kuwait. Sometimes the claim arises not when the colonial power itself is there, but only when it prepares to hand over the territory to an independent sovereignty, and is directed above all against the illogicality of colonialism's boundaries. This was true of Somalia's claim against Kenya and Ethiopia, and Indonesia's against the Borneo territories. Finally, disputes can emerge from the form in which independence was given or comes about: the dispute between India and Pakistan over Kashmir, or of Eire against Northern Ireland, have been of this type, and the Arab–Israel dispute, though somewhat more than a frontier conflict, is of the same kind.

Another reason for the prevalence of frontier disputes in the modern age is simply the penetration of administration to the remotest areas, and the demand for more accurately defined borders than existed before. In many cases there had been a certain ambiguity about the exact demarcation of borders in the past. Only in recent times has it become necessary for administration from the centre to be established in frontier areas, and thus for a precise delineation of the border to be laid down. Resources may become known near the border. The disputes between China and India over the north-east and north-west borders of India, between Algeria and Morocco, and between Chile and Argentina were basically of this type.

A final reason why there have emerged a relatively large number of frontier disputes in the modern world is that there are a greater number of opportunities for asserting claims than before. In the past, two nations might for long harbour conflicting claims without even being aware of the fact, and certainly without feeling it necessary perpetually to reiterate them. Today in international organizations, both world-wide and regional, legal rights must be reserved. Such bodies also provide ideal opportunities for the waging of verbal battle over territories of this kind. Even nations that cannot afford a physical battle may value the chance to open fire with less costly verbal ammunition in world forums. Organs of the press and nationalist parties serve to inflame sentiment, and make it necessary for the government to reassert their claims in the appropriate body. Nationalist feeling is intense. Political leaders may deliberately make use of such claims to arouse public opinion on their side: Indonesia's claim against Malaysia, and Spain's against Gibraltar, among others, have probably been used partly for this purpose.

Whatever the real reasons for such claims, there exist a large number of legal or other grounds which nations can cite to *justify* them. Often they are justified by a period of occupation long in the past. In considering the case between Norway and Denmark concerning Greenland in the inter-war period, the Permanent Court of International Justice examined evidence going back to the tenth century. Indonesia's claim to North Borneo was based on the extent of a medieval Javanese empire. Iran's claim to Bahrain is based on a period of occupation in the eighteenth century. As we shall see in a moment, claims are doubtful under international law unless they have been maintained and reasserted continuously throughout the period of foreign occupation, but this has not deterred some countries from resurrecting claims that had been long forgotten. Here the dispute is concerned with which period of occupation has most significance. In other cases claims to territory are based on the contention that the original settlement was based on coercion (China has spoken for decades of the 'unequal treaties'), or accepted at the time only by a government that was not truly legitimate or representative.

Again, claims may be justified simply on considerations of natural justice, because it is held that ethnic, linguistic or geographical ties join the territory naturally to another country.

Spain's claim to Gibraltar, or Somalia's to territory in Kenya and Ethiopia are of this sort.

Often, however, the criteria used by two different claimants diverge. France could claim Alsace-Lorraine on the basis of culture, and Germany on the basis of language. Spain claims Gibraltar on the basis of natural geographical ties, while Britain and Gibraltar resist on the basis of self-determination.

Perhaps the most widely used of all the justifications for frontier claims is self-determination. At the end of the First World War this concept became the foundation used for determining the frontiers of a number of states. It was invoked once again in the demands for independence by many colonial territories after the Second World War. But it is important to stress that the word was used in a quite different sense in the two cases. After the First World War, frontiers were *changed* in order to conform roughly with ethnic ties (though the principle was never applied so generously in favour of the defeated powers). In some cases peoples were given the chance to choose their new sovereignty in referenda. After the Second World War such choices were rarely given. 'Self-determination' was merely used as an equivalent for 'independence'. Sovereignty was always given within existing boundaries, however illogical, from an ethnic or linguistic point of view, these might be, and however much they might conflict with self-determination in the normal sense. Often the two were in total conflict (as in the Somali cases). And this fact itself became, in some instances, another cause of frontier disputes.

The boundary disputes that have arisen in the modern world may be divided into four main types. There are those where there exists no recognized boundary, whether delimited or demarcated, and no mutually agreed treaty, so that the conflict is between traditional, or quite arbitrary, claims on either side. There are those where there exists a de facto frontier, either *delimited* in a treaty or map, or even *demarcated* on the ground, but the entire legitimacy of the frontier is challenged by one party or the other.

There are those where there exist two rival delimitations, sometimes deriving from different treaties, and the conflict concerns which is the legitimate line. And there are those where there exists a mutually agreed delimitation of the frontier, but there is a dispute about the demarcation on the ground. Not every dispute can be neatly classified into one of these groups – some overlap more than one – but they represent the basic categories with which we are concerned in this book.

The first of these types, where no recognized boundary, either delimited or demarcated, exists, was probably at one time the most common of all kinds of territorial dispute. The conflicts between European powers in Asia, Africa and elsewhere arose through two or more powers competing for land that was regarded as belonging legally to nobody, or over which sovereignty was so tenuous and so disputed that it was regarded as open to appropriation by any nation. Often non-European areas, with one or two notable exceptions, such as China, were not thought to have any special sovereignty of their own. Disputes normally arose through a challenge by external powers on the basis of power alone, rather than of treaty or prescriptive rights. Such cases are comparatively rare now because virtually the whole area of the globe is held, and is administered, or at least claimed, by some power. But one or two modern disputes do belong to this category; that between Saudi Arabia on the one hand, and Abu Dhabi and Muscat on the other, was of this kind, since here the evidence on either side related to the allegiance of tribes and traditional 'control', rather than to the terms of a treaty or adjudication. There are a number of other boundary disputes, for example in the Antarctic and in the Persian Gulf area, of which the same thing is largely true. Perhaps the classic cases of this kind today concern the continental shelf and the sea-bed.

Far more common are disputes of the second kind, where there exists a de facto boundary, which may be firmly established and defended, but the whole basis of which is challenged by another. Of this kind, for example, were the disputes between Germany and Czechoslovakia, and Germany and Poland before the war, or between Somalia and her neighbours, or Indonesia and Malaysia since. Disputes of this type have been particularly common since the end of colonialism, for there will often be a well-defined frontier inherited from the colonial power, which one party accepts and the other rejects. The same situation may occur where one power accepts the result of a previous armed conflict and the other rejects it: as between the Arab States and Israel. In some cases of this type *both* parties may dispute the existing de facto boundary: this is the case today with the conflict between India and Pakistan over Kashmir. Sometimes the challenge to the existing boundary comes not from governments, but from movements often without official support: this was the case with the attempts by the IRA in Ireland to eliminate the political frontier between Northern Ireland and Eire. This is perhaps the most difficult of all types of frontier dispute to resolve, except through some political decision or bilateral agreement. For example, there can be no legal adjudication in these cases, since the main object of one party is often to challenge the basis of the existing law.

The third type of boundary dispute also remains common in modern times. This arises where there exist two rival claims concerning the correct delimitation of the frontier. The dispute between China and India concerning their mutual boundaries in the north-east and the north-west of India was of this kind. Here both sides accepted that there existed treaties determining the border, and there was no major conflict of interpretation of these treaties; but the two sides differed as to which treaties were applicable. Sometimes these disputes may be not so much between two treaties as between two principles of international law: for example, between the principle of discovery and occupation and that of prescription, or between occupation and cession, or between subjugation and self-determination. The dispute between Norway and Denmark over Eastern Greenland, considered by the Permanent International Court of Justice in the inter-war years, was one of this kind. Most of those disputes concerning which period of occupation in the past is significant are of this type.

Finally there are the cases, now increasingly frequent, where the dispute is not over which agreement is valid, nor the general provisions of such agreements, but concerns the exact interpretation on the ground of an agreement that is mutually accepted: the *demarcation* of the frontier. Of this kind, since 1945, have been the disputes between Cambodia and Thailand over the Preah Vihear Temple, the boundary disputes between Belgium and the Netherlands and that between Chile and Argentina, among others. These may be easier to resolve than some of the other kinds already considered, especially if the territory involved is small and of little economic or strategic value. The procedure used in the Argentina–Chile dispute for arbitration by Britain, described in a later chapter of this book, is an example of the international measures that can be taken in such cases. But there remain a large number of frontiers which are delimited in treaties, but not yet demarcated on the ground, or not fully demarcated, and there is thus room for the emergence of a considerable number of disputes or conflicts over such issues in the years to come. When demarcation does take place, small variations are often permitted from the line as delimited on the map, to comply with local features, to prevent the splitting of villages or of cultivation from villages, or to follow natural boundaries more accurately, and this too may lead to disputes. There can thus be a very long time-lag between the signature of a frontier agreement and the final settlement of all demarcation disputes. The territorial settlement between Chile and Argentina was signed in 1882, but the problems of demarcation on the ground are still not yet finally resolved. The boundary between Canada and the U S, which was theoretically settled in 1782, had to be the subject of at least seventeen treaties, conventions and protocols, and a number of mixed commissions, lasting almost a century and a half between 1782 and 1925. It will thus be seen that even if treaties governing all world frontiers were signed and sealed, which is far from being the case at present, there would remain room for many conflicts.

It may also be useful, as a preliminary, to examine the provisions of international law in relation to frontiers.

Textbooks on international law usually recognize five modes by which a nation can acquire territory: occupation (of territory not itself sovereign or owned by any sovereign power); prescription (effective possession over a period); cession; accretion (through a change in the shape of land by natural processes); and subjugation (conquest).

Occupation occurs where a state intentionally acquires sovereignty over a territory not at the time under the sovereignty of another state. This occupation must be by and for a state: international law no longer holds that ownership by individuals, for example, can be taken as evidence of occupation by a state, and therefore of sovereignty (thus occupation and administration by a body such as the East India Company, or by the Brook family in Sarawak, would no longer be accepted as evidence in itself concerning national sovereignty). Occupation must also be effective occupation; the evidence required of this is usually held to be both possession and administration. Possession requires some settlement within the territory, with the intention of asserting and acquiring sovereignty: thus the planting of a flag does not represent occupation unless there is some permanent occupation to maintain the flag. Administration must include some permanent form of government from the home state: informal agreement with native peoples without this will not be taken as evidence of occupation. Discovery of a territory alone no longer affords any sovereignty, though it may be held to confer a title which bars other states for a period, until discovery is made good by effective occupation. The act of occupation brings the territory concerned within the territory of the occupying state, and therefore within the law of nations. Unless the occupying power withdraws, other states cannot therefore acquire sovereignty except by cession or by conquest.

Prescription is a form of occupation which may occur through possession and administration for a certain length of time, even if there is doubt whether there was a previously existing sovereignty. There is no general rule as to what length of time is involved, and this has therefore been the subject of numerous disputes. The essential point is that occupation should not be challenged during that time by any other state. Even if unlawfully occupied in the first place, a territory may be held to become the sovereign territory of the occupying power so long as no other state protests or asserts its own sovereignty for a sufficiently long period.[3] Complementary to this, therefore, is the doctrine of estoppel, under which a nation is precluded from putting forward a claim to a territory if, by its previous conduct, it has appeared to acquiesce in the sovereignty of another nation in that territory. This doctrine, as we shall see, has been of importance in a number of contemporary territorial disputes.[4]

Cession is the one means of acquiring territory that is derivative rather than original: in other words it is by virtue of the act of another state. International law recognizes that sovereignty over a territory can be legally transferred from one state to another by an act of cession. It can only take place between states, and cessions made only by private persons or corporations do not fall within the sphere of international law. Cession must be effected through an agreement embodied in a treaty, whether peacefully negotiated or as a result of a war, and with or without compensation. In theory international law accords the right to a third party to refuse recognition of a cession contrary to international law, for example because of 'unlawful resort to war'. International law even asserts that third parties have no duty to 'acquiesce in such cessions as endanger the balance of power or are otherwise of vital importance'.[5] It is scarcely surprising that in practice these rights are rarely exercised. How many cessions would survive if they were? Third nations do of course sometimes refuse to acknowledge acquisitions of territory, whether or not these are claimed to have been illegally acquired: for example, in the doctrine of 'non-recognition' used by the US in relation to the acquisition of Manchuria by Japan and of Ethiopia by Italy, and in the refusal of many Western powers even today to acknowledge formally the annexation of the Baltic States by the Soviet Union in 1940. But in general other nations normally tend to accept settlements made between two parties as a result of a conflict, without inquiring too carefully whether the acquisition was through a 'lawful' or 'unlawful' act of war. The most important cases of refusal to accept cessions are of course those where the nation compelled to cede itself subsequently refuses to acknowledge the act as final or permanent: this may be seen in the refusal of many in France to accept the permanent loss of Alsace-Lorraine after 1871, or of some in Japan today to regard Habomai and Shikotan as lost to the Soviet Union (which has signed no treaty).

Accretion occurs where the shape of a frontier is changed by natural processes: for example, through the washing up of soil by the river or the sea, the extension of deltas or the formation of islands, or through changes in the course of a river. International law lays down detailed rules about such matters that are not usually of much practical significance. Changes of this kind could scarcely be the subject of inordinate numbers of boundary disputes, though at least one such dispute in recent years, between the US and Mexico concerning their legal boundary, resulted from changes in the course of a river. In most cases where changes of this kind occur, it is self-evident where sovereignty belongs: in the only doubtful case, where a river leaves its bed and totally changes its course, international law not unnaturally lays down that the frontier continues to run along the old river-bed.

The final mode of acquiring territory is through *subjugation.* In international law conquest itself, that is military occupation in time of war, provides no right to sovereignty. Only if conquest of a state is followed by formal annexation does subjugation take place and sovereignty is then transferred (when only part of a territory is taken, the conquered state normally enters into a treaty and acquisition is by cession). Even a part of a state may be subjugated if the conquered state refuses finally to cede it. Until transferred in this way, territory, even though occupied, remains under the sovereignty of the conquered state. It is thus formal annexation which turns the conquest into subjugation. When the US, the Soviet Union, Britain and France together declared their assumption of supreme authority in Germany in June 1945, they expressly declared that this did not entail the annexation of Germany, or, therefore, any change in sovereignty. Permanent boundaries, it was declared, would be determined at a future date. But only in 1954 did the three Western powers agree to a full restoration of sovereignty to the West German Government in those territories controlled by them; even then sovereignty was restricted in certain important ways. According to some authorities, the Charter of the UN and other international instruments now 'probably render invalid' conquests by a state which has resorted to war contrary to its obligations.[6] But in practice, as in the case of cession, outside governments have normally acknowledged faits accomplis without any too squeamish concern over the legality of the act by which the territory was acquired. Most outside nations acknowledge the Soviet Union's sovereignty in the Baltic states, India's in Goa, the Hungarian Government's in Hungary, or Algeria's in the areas it controls, whatever their views of the legality of the process by which those territories were obtained.

Even if these various and complex provisions of international law were everywhere acknowledged and everywhere observed (and even if international lawyers were themselves agreed), they could not prevent disputes or wars arising through differences in *interpretation.* A nation may claim to acquire territory through occupation, yet find that another nation claims already to have acquired sovereignty there, through previous discovery and occupation: this is what happened between Britain and France in India in the eighteenth century, and between a number of countries in parts of Africa during the nineteenth century; it was the subject of the dispute between Norway and Denmark over Greenland in the inter-war period and has underlain disputes between Britain and France over the Minquier Islands, or between Britain and Argentina over the Falklands, and a number of other disputes in modern times. Even if a claim by occupation was once regarded as legal and unchallenged, the inhabitants of the territory may themselves challenge sovereignty, as many colonial peoples in Africa and elsewhere have done in recent times, and as such territories as Anguilla, Biafra, Nagaland and others do in turn today, on the basis of 'self-determination' which is acknowledged in the UN Charter. Territory may be claimed on the ground of prescription by one country, and challenged by another: this was the basis of the dispute between the US and the Netherlands over the island of Palmas and between the US and Mexico over Chamizal, and of rival claims to the Antarctic in recent years. Territory may be ceded by one government to another and effectively occupied, yet the cession may be challenged by a subsequent government which repudiates its predecessor (as China has claimed territory ceded to Russia in the nineteenth century). Even territory acquired by accretion may, however carefully the law is drafted, be the subject of disputes; as that between the US and Mexico, which lasted for fifty years before it was finally settled in 1963. Finally, even territory acquired through subjugation may arouse disputes, either because there is doubt about the extent of the territory acquired or because the entire conquest is challenged: this applies to the West German refusal to acknowledge the Oder-Neisse frontier, or attempts by the Arabs to overturn the frontiers established by Israel, or Israel's 'annexation' in Jerusalem.

Thus the provisions of international law, though they provide some kind of framework, or body of authority, to assist in the resolution of frontier disputes, certainly do not in themselves go far to prevent their occurrence or even to determine unchallengeably their settlement. For it is sometimes ambiguous; even more often disobeyed.

Finally, it may be worth looking briefly at the principal types of *procedure* available to the international community for resolving frontier conflicts.

The oldest, simplest and perhaps the quickest procedure available is war. The likelihood of this method being chosen clearly depends on a number of factors: the psychological value of the territory concerned to each of the two parties; the strategic and economic value of the territory in question; the relative armed strength available to each side; the availability of peaceful international procedures for a settlement, and especially the awareness of the parties of this availability, together with their assessment of a favourable outcome through their use. It will also depend to a considerable extent on the degree to which the frontiers have been stabilized, or how recently they have been established and how widely disputed (compare Europe between and after the wars).

If one considers the frontier disputes of recent times, it seems that war is especially likely to be chosen as a procedure for settlement where there seemed to be a reasonable chance of securing a quick and total victory, and so presenting the antagonist with a fait accompli (China–India, Algeria–Morocco); or where the frontier concerned is remote and inaccessible (Bolivia–Paraguay; China–India; Saudi Arabia–Muscat, Abu Dhabi). In other cases in this category the object of armed conflict may be to harass and annoy, and give vent to a feeling of resentment rather than to win back the area concerned (Somalia–Ethiopia, Kenya; Indonesia–Malaysia). Conversely, peaceful procedures seem more likely to be used when the parties to the conflict already have close and friendly relations (France–Britain, Netherlands–Germany, Netherlands–Belgium, China–Mongolia, Mexico–U S). This is especially so where one party is much weaker militarily than the other. There is also obviously a greater chance of a peaceful settlement where the territory concerned is small and not intrinsically valuable.

The next procedure which may be used to resolve such disputes is bilateral negotiation. In most cases this is attempted at some point. Sometimes it is used, as recommended in Article 33 of the Charter, only as a first step to reach a settlement before other procedures are resorted to. This is what happened over the Cambodia–Thailand case, where diplomatic discussions first took place between the two parties. Only when these had already broken down were there attempts at mediation (through a representative appointed by the Secretary General), and finally adjudication (by the International Court). But in a number of other cases, bilateral negotiations alone have been sufficient to resolve the dispute. Since 1945 this method has been successfully used between China and a number of her neighbours (Burma, Nepal, Pakistan, Afghanistan and Mongolia), between the Netherlands and West Germany, between the US and Mexico, between Mali and Mauritania, and in a number of other cases. Sometimes bilateral negotiations may be used to settle not merely the demarcation or delimitation of a frontier, but other questions connected with the control of that frontier. Bilateral negotiations between Austria and Hungary led to an agreement concerning mutual control of the frontier between them.

The next form of procedure available in cases of this kind is the use of 'good offices' by another power to resolve the matter. The definition of 'good offices' is not exact. But it is usually used in relation to the efforts of a third party to bring two disputants together or to act as a go-between, without trying to suggest a solution to the dispute in question: it must therefore be distinguished from 'mediation', which implies an attempt by a third party through negotiations to *resolve* a dispute. The 'good offices' of a third power were frequently used in the nineteenth century to start the process of reconciliation between two powers and so the resolution of particular disputes. For example, the 'good offices' of the British Government were used to resolve the dispute between Portugal and Brazil over Brazilian independence in 1825 and between the US and France over the interpretation of the Treaty of Paris, while France in turn used her 'good offices' to resolve a dispute between Britain and Greece in 1849–50. In the declaration of Paris of 1856, it was stated that

> States between which any misunderstanding might arise should, before appealing to arms, have recourse so far as circumstances might allow to the good offices of a friendly power.

In recent times this function has been more frequently filled by some international personage, such as a representative of the UN Secretary General. As we have seen, a representative of the Secretary General took the first steps in resolving the frontier dispute between Cambodia and Thailand in the late fifties: as a result of his efforts, diplomatic relations between the two countries were restored, and subsequently the issue was submitted to the International Court of Justice. Over the dispute between Indonesia and Malaysia, the Secretary General dispatched a mission to ascertain the wishes of the people of North Borneo concerning their frontier. The Secretary General also appointed a special representative to look into the dispute in which Muscat's sovereignty over certain areas was contested by other Arab powers. Good offices may therefore represent a half-way house to an agreed resolution of the frontier dispute itself.

Mediation involves a request by both parties to another government to assist them to resolve some dispute. It does not involve any commitment in advance to accept the recommendations of the mediating power, and in this it differs from arbitration and judicial settlement. Mediation has been fairly frequently used in the resolution of frontier disputes during the past century. At the Hague Conferences of 1899 and 1907, it was provided that any power should be entitled to offer good offices or mediation to powers who are in dispute and that this should not be regarded by either party as an unfriendly act. Since 1945, mediation was attempted over the dispute between Guatemala on the one hand and British Honduras (Belize) on the other. In an informal sense, Zambia successfully mediated between Somalia and her neighbours over their frontier conflict in 1967. Sometimes a form of collective mediation takes place. For example the Colombo powers sought unsuccessfully to mediate between China and India over their frontier dispute (their solution was accepted by India but rejected by China). The OAU attempted a form of collective mediation over the Algeria–Morocco dispute. Again mediators have often been appointed by the Secretary General, sometimes at the request of the two governments. Thus the Secretary General appointed a series of mediators to resolve the dispute between India and Pakistan over Kashmir and another to seek to resolve the Arab–Israel conflict. Mediation is discussed in the chapter by Miss Schwiesow.

The next form of procedure available in such cases is that of *arbitration*. This is the submission of the dispute to an arbitrator, or a body of arbitrators, to be determined according to the principles of international law. It differs from judicial settlement (submission to the International Court) in that the choice of arbitrators is to some extent within the control of the individual parties. Arbitration has been a favourite method of resolving frontier disputes since the early-nineteenth century, and even earlier. It was common at this time to ask foreign sovereigns to adjudicate: the King of the Netherlands arbitrated between Britain and the US on the North-East Boundary question (1831); the Tsar of Russia between France and the Netherlands over the border of the Guianas (1891); the King of Spain between Britain and Germany over the Walvis Bay dispute (1909); and the King of Italy between Britain and Brazil over the border of British Guiana (1904). In other cases a commission, with one or two judges appointed by each party and a neutral chairman, was appointed: this was the procedure used in the British Guiana–Venezuela dispute in 1899. Between the wars a whole series of arbitration treaties between individual powers was entered into, and arbitration took place in a number of cases, including the Chaco dispute between Paraguay and Bolivia, where the Presidents of six American states arbitrated, in this case on the basis of equity rather than law. Since 1945, Britain has been asked to arbitrate between Chile and Argentina over one section of their mutual border, and arbitration took place by a commission between India and Pakistan over the Rann of Kutch dispute. Normally the task is the interpretation of a previous written agreement with reference to the actual location of the frontier, or of some general principle, such as the *uti possidetis* principle adopted in Latin America; only very rarely is there a request for 'express delimitation', that is for a judgment on external grounds of where the boundary should lie. Although one of the main objects of an arbitration is to provide a judgment that both parties agree to accept, awards are sometimes rejected: the US rejected the arbitration award made by the King of the Netherlands on the North-East Frontier in 1831 because of objections from Maine and Massachusetts. In some cases an award has been rejected at first and only finally accepted at a much later date: this happened with the arbitration on the Chamizal case between the US and Mexico, which the US rejected when it was made in 1911 and only finally accepted in 1963. This procedure is discussed by Mrs Fox in Chapter 6 below.

The next procedure available for the resolution of these disputes is *judicial settlement*: submission to an international judicial body for decision. The second Hague Conference in 1907 set up a Permanent Court of Arbitration which was to be available for the settlement, according to the principles of international law, of any disputes which the parties might submit to them. The Permanent Court of Arbitration was used to arbitrate a frontier dispute between Norway and Sweden in 1909, and between Portugal and the Netherlands in 1914, but has rarely been used since. In 1923 the Central American states set up the International Central American Tribunal, and undertook to submit to it 'all controversies which now exist between them or which may hereafter arise'. Arbitration by the Permanent International Court of Justice was requested by Denmark and Norway to resolve their dispute concerning sovereignty in Eastern Greenland in 1933. *Advisory* opinions (which have no binding force on the parties) were given by the Permanent International Court of Justice in the case of the boundary between Czechoslovakia and Poland (1923) and between Iraq and Turkey (1923). Since 1945 the International Court has given judgment in the case of the Minquier and Ecrehos Islands (1953), the dispute between the Netherlands and Belgium (1959), the case between Honduras and Nicaragua (1960) and that between Thailand and Cambodia (1962). The effectiveness of its action in these cases is discussed in Chapter 7 by Mr Darwin.

Finally, there are those procedures that involve action by a collective organization, regional or international. Regional organizations have quite often been used to assist in resolving frontier disputes. In 1929 the International Conference of American States set up a Commission of Investigation and Conciliation, which succeeded in moderating for a time the conflict between Paraguay and Bolivia over central Chaco. Since the Organization of American States was founded in 1947, its council or other bodies have discussed the boundary dispute between Equador and Peru (1955), the dispute between Honduras and Nicaragua twice (1957 and 1961), when it induced the two parties to submit their dispute to arbitration, and the Rio Lauca dispute between Bolivia and Chile (1962). The Organization of African Unity sought to use its influence over the conflict between Algeria and Morocco in 1963–64. A military commission was set up of officers of Ethiopia, Mali, Algeria and Morocco, to delimit a neutral zone along the border; and later the foreign ministers of the OAU set up a seven-nation commission of arbitration and conciliation. The OAU also discussed the conflict between Somalia on the one hand and Kenya and Ethiopia on the other from 1964 onwards, and was associated with the successful mediation finally effected by the government of Zambia. The OAU have also discussed the establishment of a permanent Commission of Mediation, Conciliation and Arbitration, which might be used to discuss such disputes. The success of the efforts of regional organizations in this field are discussed in the chapter by Dr Lyon.

At the international level, the League of Nations discussed a considerable number of frontier problems. In a few cases it succeeded in resolving the question at issue. Indeed its record in this respect is in some ways considerably more successful than that of its successor. These efforts are described in the chapter by Mr Windass. The UN has also on occasion dealt with questions of this kind. The problem of Kashmir was discussed over a long period, and a UN mediator appointed to deal with it. The Agreement on Trieste between Yugoslavia and Italy, though reached through negotiation with the Big Four, was accomplished under the auspices of the UN, and finally endorsed by it. The frontier dispute between Venezuela and British Guiana was raised by Venezuela in the UN before Guyana's independence, but the UN decided to take no action pending bilateral discussions. The disputes between Thailand and Cambodia, and between Indonesia and Malaysia, since they involved the problem of sovereignty in particular areas, represented frontier disputes of a kind, and were also discussed in the UN. In the former case a representative of the Secretary General was again appointed, and his report did something to reduce controversy over the issue. The UN has also discussed a number of conflicts in which a colonial territory has become the subject of a claim before it reached independence: Gibraltar, the Falkland Islands and British Honduras. The success of the UN over these various kinds of dispute is discussed in the chapter by Dr James. On the whole, it is perhaps significant that so few of the frontier disputes of the age have even been considered within the UN. Even fewer have been successfully resolved.

These then are the main types of procedure available for the resolution of disputes of this kind. One of the main objects of the chapters which follow is to assess in greater detail the effectiveness of each.

TEXT REFERENCES

1. This of course is not to accept that there exists among men some type of *innate* 'territorial imperative'. All the evidence – particularly the lack of importance of borders among primitive peoples – suggests that sentiments about frontiers are *culturally* promoted by the traditions and customs of the prevailing international culture.

2. For more complete details of all these wars and disputes in the period since 1945, see Evan Luard, *Conflict and Peace in the Modern International System*, Boston 1968.

3. Prescription is defined by Oppenheim as:

> the acquisition of sovereignty over a territory through continuous and undisturbed exercise of sovereignty over it during such a period as is necessary to create, under the influence of historical development, a general conviction that the present condition of things is in conformity with international order.

Oppenheim, L., *International Law*, London 1955, vol. 1, p. 576.

4. See below, Chapter 6, pp. 183–84.
5. Oppenheim, L., *International Law*, London 1955, vol. 1, p. 550.
6. Oppenheim, L., *International Law*, London 1955.

BIBLIOGRAPHY

Adami, V., *National Frontiers in relation to International Law*, Rome 1919.
Boggs, S. W., *International Boundaries*, New York 1940.
Cukwurah, A. O., *The Settlement of Boundary Disputes in International Law*, Manchester 1947.
Hill, N., *Claims to Territory in International Law and Relations*, London 1945.
Holdich, Sir T. H., *Political Frontiers and Boundary-making*, London 1916.
Jennings, R. G., *The acquisition of Territory in International Law*, Manchester 1963.
Jones, G. B., *Boundary-making*, Washington 1945.
Wyman, W. D. and Kroeber, C. D., *The Frontier in Perspective*, Madison 1957.
Young, O., *The Intermediaries: Third Parties in International Crises*, Princeton 1967.

2 THE LEAGUE AND TERRITORIAL DISPUTES

Stan Windass

The Treaty of Versailles and the other peace treaties associated with the end of the First World War involved a reshaping of territorial structures throughout Europe and the Middle East on a scale unparalleled since the collapse of the Roman Empire.

Germany was partially dismembered, and reduced from her dominant position in central Europe. The Austrian Empire, which for centuries had enjoyed supremacy in Europe under the Hapsburgs, was reduced to a small republic of six million inhabitants. Turkey lost her extensive domains in the Middle East together with most of her Balkan territories. At the same time Russia, in the throes of revolutionary ardour, loosened her grip on the Tsarist Empire in eastern Europe, where nationalist movements were already strong.

Out of the remains of the great empires new entities arose – as a century before new entities had arisen out of the collapse of the Spanish Empire in Latin-America. From the Russian Empire came Finland, Lithuania, Estonia, Latvia. Poland was reformed from part of Germany and part of Russia, and Czechoslovakia from Germany and Austria-Hungary. The Balkan States were rearranged, and Egypt, the Sudan, Cyprus, Palestine, Syria, Mesopotamia and Arabia emerged from the Ottoman Empire.

This massive reorganization of territorial structures was to be presided over by the League of Nations – man's first tentative effort to create a world political organization. It is hardly surprising that a ship launched on such stormy waters should eventually suffer shipwreck. What is surprising is not that the efforts of the new world organization eventually collapsed in the stress of war, but rather that it survived so long. During the fifteen or more years when the League was afloat, it accumulated a wealth of experience in the field of international relations from which we still have many lessons to learn. This is perhaps particularly true in the case of frontier disputes.

In theory, the only guiding principle of law which was written into the League Covenant for the resolution of territorial disputes was the conservative principle of territorial integrity. Under Article 10, members undertook 'to respect and preserve as against external aggression the territorial integrity and existing political independence of all members of the League'. Lord Robert Cecil had tried to introduce into the Covenant a flexibility clause, giving the Assembly power to recommend territorial adjustments. In this suggestion he may have been ahead of his time – we are still far from reaching a stage of international organization where we are willing to hand over to an international body a general power to recommend boundary changes. In any case, Cecil's proposals were not accepted, and the nations bound themselves only to preserving the status quo.

Nevertheless, there was one very active principle which influenced the League in many of its initiatives, even though it was not formally written into the Covenant – and this was the principle of self-determination. The war, in a sense, was about self-determination. It began with the assassination of the Archduke Ferdinand of Austria by his subject Serbian nationalists at Sarajevo. The incident was a symptom of the general conflict between rising forces of nationalism and the autocratic power of a historic empire trying to maintain and extend its dominion. This does not mean, of course, that the allies who were drawn into the war against Austria and Germany were fighting for nationalism (avowedly, they were fighting for the principle of territorial integrity). Nevertheless, once the crust of the old order was broken, and the empires of central and eastern Europe descended into the melting-pot of war, it soon became clear that the force of national liberation movements was of strategic importance. The Sykes–Picot agreement of May 1916 guaranteed freedom to the Arabs from the Red Sea to Damascus, as the price of their active support in overthrowing the Turks. When Czechoslovakia was promised self-government whole regiments deserted the forces of their Austrian overlords to join the Russian and other allied armies, and Rumania joined forces with the allies in response to a similar guarantee.

Increasingly, towards the end of the war, respect for the principle of self-determination in some form became prominent among the explicit war-aims of the states at war with Austria, Germany and Turkey. By tentative advances, the allies added to their war-aims the liberation of races long ago absorbed into the system of the great military empires. On 10 January 1917, the allies defined their war-aims in a joint statement to President Wilson, and these included a reorganization of Europe based on 'respect for the principle of nationalities', the restoration of territories formerly torn from the allies by force 'against the wishes of the inhabitants', the 'setting free of populations subject to the bloody tyranny of the Turks'. The tentative commitment by the allies to the principle of self-determination was pushed two steps further by the post-revolutionary Russian statement in 1917, which, in the first rush of revolutionary enthusiasm, cut all roots with the imperial past, and proclaimed the purpose of giving a new sovereign identity to any national group which freely expressed such a desire.

Principles arising out of political stress tend to have a life of their own, which can go beyond the intentions of those who originally formulated them. This is especially true of the principle of self-determination, which, though never an overriding consideration, provides an important connecting motif in the League's handling of the disputes we shall consider in this chapter. The principle of self-determination was the one thoroughly respectable principle on the basis of which all states could argue in the international forum which the League provided.

Articles 12–16 of the League Covenant laid down procedures for the resolution of international disputes.

Briefly, members were bound to submit disputes to arbitration or to judicial settlement, or to inquiry by the League Council. In the event of a dispute being referred to the Council, the partners would each submit a statement of their case, and the Council would endeavour to effect a peaceful settlement. If the Council did not succeed in this, then it would publish a report giving its recommendation for a settlement. If the report was unanimous (not counting the votes of the parties to the dispute), it would have the effect of condemning as an aggressor any state making war against another state which complied with the report.

A procedure was thus provided for identifying the international criminal-state, and under Article 16 provision was made for punishment and coercion of the offender, in the form of economic and political sanctions and military action by the law-abiding members of the League.

In fact the League was never cut out to be the stern guardian of the world's peace, preserving the boundaries of all members and punishing aggression. The League never succeeded in growing any teeth – as we shall see in the Leticia dispute – and when ultimately confronted by determined aggression it was unable to function at all. Article 16 anticipated a degree of international order which did not exist.

On the other hand, the disputes with which the League was presented in its early years were not cases of simple territorial aggression, but were rather disputes arising from situations of indeterminacy resulting directly from the decay of old empires, the settlement of new lands. This applied as much to the European as to the Latin-American cases, where problems of definition caused by the withdrawal of Spain a century before had never been finally resolved. In such situations the principle of territorial integrity did not have clear and unambiguous application, though it was one of the principles which had to be taken into account; and in such cases the League certainly had a valid part to play, and the procedures laid down in Articles 12–15 provided a satisfactory framework of action.

In the 1920s and early 1930s, the European states were unwilling to relapse into the chaos of war, and the League for a time enjoyed the transitory prestige of the untried and untested. It was during this period that the League was presented with the series of frontier conflicts which we are to examine in the following pages.

THE AALAND ISLANDS

Geographically speaking, the Aaland Islands were predestined to be an object of territorial conflict. They are situated in a narrow gap between the two land masses of Sweden and Finland. They command the entrance to the Gulf of Bothnia, and are therefore strategically vital in any naval conflict; and, whichever of the neighbouring states is in occupation, the Aaland Islands are 'like a dagger aimed at the heart' of the opposing power.

Throughout the Middle Ages there was no territorial problem in the Aalands, since both sides of the Gulf were part of the Swedish Empire. The Aaland Islands were, however, racially and linguistically much more closely united to the Swedes than to the Finns.

In 1809, Russia, after a successful war against Sweden, imposed on her the Treaty of Frederikshavn, which divided the territory on one side of the Gulf of Bothnia from the territory on the other. The Swedish negotiators were given instructions to cede Finland if necessary to Russia, but not the Aaland Islands. However, the victors were able to impose their will, and the Aalands, together with Finland, became part of the Russian Empire.

Throughout the nineteenth century Finland, including the Aalands, existed as a partially autonomous Grand Duchy within the Russian Empire, having its own formally constituted Diet responsible for all internal matters, but never claiming independence in external affairs.

Towards the end of the nineteenth century, Russia embarked on her programme of 'Russification' of subordinate peoples, and Finland was treated as an ordinary province of the Russian Empire. Attempts were made to suppress Finnish culture and Finnish traditions. At the same time, Finnish nationalism acquired new vitality, and pressures increased for total separation from Russia.

In 1917, as a result of the Bolshevik revolution in Russia, a very confused situation arose. One of the first acts of the Bolshevik government was to issue a manifesto proclaiming the right of self-determination of all peoples within the Russian Empire who were not of Russian race. On the same date, 15 November 1917, the Finnish Diet assumed supreme power, constituted a national government, and issued an appeal to the Finnish people exhorting them to make every effort to enable Finland to take her place as an independent and sovereign nation. The new state was recognized by Russia in January 1918, and immediately afterwards by a number of other states.

The internal progress of Finland was, however, by no means as orderly as the external events suggest. The declaration of statehood by the Finnish Diet was the beginning of a civil war. The authority of the Diet was violently disputed by a pro-Russian revolutionary party, and Red Russian troops soon joined in the fray in an effort to supplant the new government. For a period there was serious disorder, and the government had to leave the capital.

Meanwhile, in the Aaland Islands a new sense of identity was taking shape – or rather, the ancient sense of identity with Sweden was being fiercely revived. In August 1917, when the break from Russia began to seem imminent, the delegates of the Aaland communes assembled at Finstrom passed a resolution expressing their keen desire to be reunited to Sweden, and communicated their resolution to the King of Sweden.

The civil war which followed Finland's breakaway, and the

serious threat of a Bolshevik takeover, naturally increased the determination of the Aalanders to take charge of their own affairs. In December a plebiscite was organized in the Aalands which expressed the wish of an overwhelming majority of the islanders Jo return to Sweden, and another more extensive plebiscite in tune confirmed this result. The King of Sweden supported the Aalanders, and in February 1920 a Swedish military expedition was sent to the islands, at the request of the inhabitants, to secure the withdrawal of both White and Red Guards during a period of disturbance when the government of Finland seemed unable to exercise effective control. Naturally, this greatly heightened the sense of solidarity with Sweden.

The Aalanders did everything within their power to make their case known internationally. They set up a centralized representative body to give coherence to the expression of the popular will. Repulsed by the Finnish Senate, they sent a delegation to the Peace Conference in 1919, and appealed to the Council of the League in 1920.

The Finns meanwhile opposed the claims of the Aalanders, and refused to enter into discussion with them about the future of the islands. They first attempted to control the situation by using threats and warnings; and when these proved ineffective, they tried to pacify the islanders by passing a special law which would give them considerable autonomy within the Finnish state. The islanders refused even to discuss this law, and feeling ran high on both sides. The Peace Conference left the matter unsettled, but by early 1920 there seemed to be a serious possibility of a military clash between Finland and Sweden over this issue.

At this point the British government called upon the League Council to take up the question; and in June 1920, at a special meeting called in London, the two opposing states argued their case for the first time before a tribunal of the world community.

The case of the Aalanders was crystal-clear. They claimed the right of self-determination, one of the main principles on which the peace treaties were based. There was no doubt as to what the

Aalanders wanted; and what they wanted was, on the face of it, perfectly practicable.

Finland's case, however, was equally clear. She claimed that the Aaland Islands had been part of Finland for over a hundred years. In 1917, Finland had become an independent state and had been recognized as such by the international community. There was no doubt about what constituted this new independent Finland. The Aaland Islands were part of it, as they had always been, and the destiny of the Aaland Islands was a purely internal domestic matter concerning Finland alone. The international community had no authority to intervene.

This sharp clash of principles is of great interest for the development of international law. The conflict of views between Finland and the Aalanders involved the whole question of the right of self-determination, and, on an even wider scale, the problem of stability and change in the international community – a conflict which has not yet been resolved.

The Council of course could not even approach the problem without investigating Finland's preliminary objection. Accordingly, a Commission of Jurists was appointed to consider whether the dispute was a matter in which the Council had a right to intervene, or whether it was a domestic matter pertaining to Finland alone.

The difficulty was, of course, that what looked like a simple problem of jurisdiction was in fact very closely related to the main issue, and legally speaking it was very difficult to give an opinion about the question of jurisdiction without at the same time prejudging the whole dispute. Lawyers are trained to define situations: either a territory belongs to one country, or it does not. Finland's claim was that the Aalands belonged to her; if they did, then clearly the whole matter was at an end, and the Finnish case was won. If, on the other hand, the Aalands did *not* belong to Finland, then Finland had no right over them, and the Aalanders' case was won.

It is very much to the credit of the Commission of Jurists that they did not fall into this trap of definition. They refused to confine themselves to their legal textbooks, and they faced squarely the real political complexities of the situation. They concluded, as was certainly the case, that here was a situation of doubt and ambiguity concerned with the break-up of nations; that, as such, it was a problem of great concern to the international community, and of great importance for the growth of international law. For this reason, they concluded, the Council was competent to adjudicate.

The philosophy of political change and growth elaborated by the jurists in their report is worth quoting in full, for it retains its validity today:

> From the point of view of both domestic and international law, the formation, transformation and dismemberment of States as a result of revolutions and wars creates situations of fact which, to a large extent, cannot be met by the application of the normal rules of positive law. This amounts to a statement that if the essential basis of these rules – that is to say, territorial sovereignty – is lacking, either because the State is not yet fully formed or because it is undergoing transformation or dissolution, the situation is obscure and uncertain, from a legal point of view, and will not become clear until the period of development is completed and a definite new situation, which is normal in respect to territorial sovereignty, has been established.
>
> This transition from a de facto situation to a normal situation de jure cannot be considered as confined entirely within the domestic jurisdiction of a State. It tends to lead to readjustments between the members of the international community and to alterations in their territorial and legal status; consequently, this transition interests the community of States very deeply both from political and legal standpoints.

Having defined the 'area of significant doubt' in these terms, the jurists went on to consider what new principles of international order could be applied in such situations:

> Under such circumstances, the *principle of self-determination of peoples* may be called into play. New aspirations of certain sections of a

nation, which are sometimes based on old traditions or on a common language and civilization, may come to the surface and produce effects which must be taken into account in the interests of the internal and external peace of nations.

While clearly indicating support for the principle of self-determination, however, the jurists did not prejudge the issue in favour of the Aalands. They said that the principle of self-determination had to be balanced against other principles, and that a compromise solution on the lines of minority guarantees might prove to be the best solution.

The Council accepted the jurists' opinion, and decided therefore to send a Commission of Rapporteurs to the Baltic to make recommendations concerning the future of the Aalands.

In April 1921, having sifted through all the material concerning the dispute, the Commission gave its opinion; and this was that the islands should remain part of Finland.

The argument was basically very simple. The Commission cast no doubt at all on the spontaneity and vigour of the movement in the Aaland Islands for union with Sweden. On the basis of the principle of self-determination, the destiny of the islands would be clear; they should be assigned to Sweden.

On the other hand, the Commission was equally clear that, legally speaking, the Aalands had long been, and were still, part of Finland. Throughout its union with Russia, Finland did not suffer any partition of her territory. She governed herself in internal matters as a semi-autonomous Grand Duchy within the Russian Empire, and resisted efforts at Russification. This clearly identifiable unit acquired its independence 'en bloc' and was recognized by most powers as a defined unit. Although independence was followed by civil strife, this was not such as to cause any radical discontinuity – the Finnish Government continued to exist and to exercise its authority throughout the period of disturbance. In consequence of all this, the Commission considered that 'to detach the Aaland Islands from Finland would be . . . an alteration of its status, depriving this country of a part of that which belongs to it'.

What then of the principle of self-determination? When the 'fact' of Finnish sovereignty had been established in this way, clearly the argument of self-determination did not stand much chance. The arguments of the Commission are, however, important. First, they pointed out that the right of self-determination was not, properly speaking, a rule of international law. but a general principle expressed in a vague formula. It certainly would not apply to 'fractions of states' (like the Aalands) in the same way that it applied to 'a people with a defined national life' (like the Finns). To apply it in this way would be to invite international anarchy. . . . 'To concede to minorities, either of race or religion, or to any fractions of a population, the right of withdrawing from the community to which they belong, because it is their good will or good pleasure, would be to destroy order and stability within states and to inaugurate anarchy in international life; it would be to uphold a theory incompatible with the very idea of the State as a territorial and political unity.'

The argument seems irresistible; and yet the divergence between the views of the Commission of Rapporteurs and the earlier views of the jurists is striking. The jurists had said that there was a situation of doubt regarding sovereignty; the Commission said that Finland had always clearly possessed sovereignty. In a sense, the Commission had ruled that it was not competent to make a ruling – because if Finland was sovereign, the whole dispute lay within her own domestic jurisdiction.

The conflict of views was, however, more technical than real – more a conflict of language than a conflict of substance. The jurists had stated that the Aaland dispute arose out of a state of uncertainty resulting directly from the dissolution of Empire; they had stated that the international community was deeply concerned in the resolution of such conflicts – and their opinion was certainly a sound one. In stressing the role of the principle of self-determination they made a gesture towards the future. The Rapporteurs decided that the time was not ripe for such a gesture, and they resolved the problem in safe, traditional and conservative terms, rooted in the past rather than in the future. They too were probably right according to their premises.

That is not to say by any means that the Aalanders' rights were neglected by the Commission's report. Far from it. In spite of the fact that they had technically ruled that they had no jurisdiction, the Commission recommended that Finland should be obliged to give a number of guarantees to the Aalanders, designed to preserve their national culture and identity. These guarantees were very far-reaching, and amounted in fact to a considerable diminution of Finnish sovereignty. They gave the Aalanders right of pre-emption on land in the Aalands; they required five years minimum residence as a qualification for the franchise; they excluded Finnish from the schools in favour of Swedish, they ensured that governors would never be appointed against the wish of the people. All in all, the Aalanders were to be accorded a highly privileged position within the Finnish state.

Even more was asked of Finland. The Aalanders, to be safe, must have a right of recourse to the Council of the League. Finally, if Finland did not agree to these measures, then – in spite of the fact that the Aaland Islands were part of Finland – they must pass to Sweden. The degree of international legislation implied in those recommendations was startling, and perhaps reflects the over-confidence of the first years of the League.

As it happens, no drastic measures were needed. In June, the Council endorsed the verdict of the Commission of Rapporteurs. Finland, though sorely aggrieved at this interference with her private problems, was quite willing to give the required guarantees. Sweden, though she challenged the whole principle of subordinating the wishes of a whole population to 'legal niceties', was also ultimately prepared to accept the League's decision.

The political costs of opposing the first major exercise of authority of the new international organization would have been far too high a price to pay for what was, after all, a peripheral issue.

The territorial dispute was therefore resolved, and relationships between Finland and Sweden were soon back on an even keel.

The League's first experiment in international peace-making had been successful. This was partly because it demanded no change in the status quo. But there were harder tasks ahead.

VILNA

Like the problem of the Aaland Islands, the dispute over the possession of Vilna followed upon the dissolution of the Russian Empire, and related to former Russian possessions.

In the thirteenth and fourteenth centuries Lithuania was a vigorous and independent state, and indeed showed signs of expanding into a major European empire. At this time Vilna became the capital of the country. The fifteenth century saw a close union between Lithuania and Poland, and the two countries eventually cohered into one united kingdom in 1569. Poland was the dominant partner in the union, but the 'Grand Duchy' of Lithuania retained much autonomy, and Lithuanian peasants retained their language and traditions.

The racial structure of the Grand Duchy was, however, very complex. At the end of the eighteenth century, just before the Russian conquest, the population of Lithuania was 37 per cent Byelorussian, 26 per cent Polish, 20 per cent Lithuanian, 10 per cent Jewish, and 7 per cent small minority groups.

The expansion of the Russian Empire at the end of the eighteenth century eventually absorbed the whole of Poland–Lithuania, and at the Congress of Vienna in 1815 the Russian Tsar became also King of Poland and Grand Duke of Lithuania. Vilna remained part of the Grand Duchy of Lithuania.

The repressive policy of the Tsars, however, stimulated national resistance. A Polish–Lithuanian uprising in 1863 was savagely suppressed, but this did not prevent the growth of the nationalist independence movement both in Poland and in Lithuania. After 1905 the Russian policy became more liberal; national languages were no longer suppressed and Lithuanian and Polish newspapers appeared. At the end of 1905 a Lithuanian congress was held at Vilna, which was still regarded as the natural capital. This congress called for an autonomous Lithuanian state with frontiers drawn according to the wishes of the people.

By the beginning of the war in 1914 Lithuania was a ripe fruit ready to fall from the Russian tree. In 1915, the Germans, now at war with Russia, occupied Vilna. Just as it was in the Allies' interests to foster national independence movements which helped to dissolve the Austro-Hungarian and Turkish Empires, so it was in the interests of the Germans to foster similar movements which helped to dissolve the Russian Empire. In 1917 the Germans authorized a national congress at Vilna which called for an independent Lithuania with its capital at Vilna. An independent Lithuanian state was in fact proclaimed in February 1918, and in March 1918 was recognized by Germany with the proviso of a 'perpetual alliance' between Lithuania and the German Reich. A government was formed by the first President of Lithuania on 11 November 1918 – less than two months before the victorious Red Army returned to occupy Vilna, and the whole of the eastern part of Lithuania.

Meanwhile Poland had substantially won its struggle for national identity, having risen in revolt against the occupying German forces. But the conclusion of the armistice on 11 November 1918 was by no means the end of hostilities in this part of Europe. As the German armies withdrew, the Red Army advanced, hoping no doubt to establish a revolutionary regime in the new Poland. The Russians, however, were still just Russians to the Poles, and throughout 1919 and 1920 fighting continued between Polish and Russian forces, during the course of which Vilna was occupied alternately by Russians, Poles, and Russians again. In July 1920, when Vilna was coming under Russian occupation for the last time, Lithuania concluded the Moscow Treaty with Russia, by which the Soviet Union ceded to her Vilna, Lida and Grodno, providing, however, that the settlement of territories between Lithuania and Poland should be confirmed by subsequent negotiations between these two countries. After the final victory of the Polish forces over the Russians, the Red Army left Vilna at the end of August 1920, and Lithuanian troops moved in.

The Lithuanians considered that by virtue of the Treaty of Moscow her territory was now defined. But in fact Poland refused to accept the Moscow Treaty. As the Russian troops retreated from Poland and Lithuania, so the Polish advanced – and crossed into the territory of Lithuania as defined at Moscow. At this point, understandably, they met with fierce resistance from the Lithuanians – and on 5 September 1920, the Warsaw government appealed to the Council to restrain the Lithuanians and prevent the outbreak of war between the two countries.

The Polish government argued before the Council that the dispute arose because of the presence of Lithuanian troops to the west of the frontier provisionally assigned to Poland by the declaration of the Supreme Council on 8 December 1919. They argued, moreover, that Lithuania was abusing her neutrality in the Russo–Polish war by allowing Soviet troops into Lithuania and in denying access to Polish troops. It was indeed true that the clashes had occurred to the west of the military demarcation line. The Lithuanians, however, argued that the demarcation line fixed by the Allies was not binding on Lithuania, and that a new boundary-line had subsequently been fixed by agreement with Russia.

Behind the legal difficulties there was of course a serious and substantial dispute. The intermingling of nationalities in the territory claimed by Lithuania was great; and the definition of the new boundaries was bound to raise conflicts with neighbours. During the course of the violent clash between Poland and Russia in 1919–20, Lithuania had drawn closer to Russia, with whom she had concluded a favourable treaty, than to Poland, which seemed to present a greater threat; and Russia for her part favoured Lithuania as a more manageable 'satellite'. The Lithuanians had actually engaged themselves, by a protocol to the Treaty of Moscow, to allow Russian troops on grounds of strategic necessity to cross their frontiers and occupy part of their territories.

Poland, a new and undefined state in the process of rebirth from the old Tsarist Empire, had an enormous and pressing frontier problem due to the intermixture of nationalities in neighbouring territories; and nowhere was this frontier problem more complex than with Lithuania, which had been so closely linked to Poland for most of its history. There were large Polish populations within the territories which Lithuania now claimed; and – what was most crucial – within the city of Vilna itself, the ancient Lithuanian capital and the focus of Lithuanian aspirations, there were far more Poles than Lithuanians, the latter accounting for little more than 20 per cent of the population. On the principle of self-determination, the Poles had a good claim to the Lithuanian capital.

If the Lithuanians objected violently to Polish troops moving across the boundary fixed at Moscow, it was because they suspected – quite rightly – that the military movement was inseparable from the territorial claim; and since, like Poland, they were struggling for their new identity, it was inevitable that there should be conflict where the rival forces met.

The Council's immediate problem was to prevent a war between Lithuania and Poland. The problem seemed at first a very difficult one; but, oddly enough, after hearing the opposing claims of the two countries, the Council was able quite easily to arrive at a resolution agreed by both sides which seemed to provide some guarantee against an extension of the war. Lithuania agreed to accept the frontiers fixed by the Supreme Council of the Allies in December 1919 as provisional demarcation lines on the understanding that this was without prejudice to her territorial claims which were to be worked out subsequently through negotiations with Poland. Poland agreed to respect the neutrality of Lithuania provided Lithuania would secure this respect also from the Soviet authorities. The government of the Soviets for its part agreed readily to the withdrawal of all her troops from Lithuania, provided that Poland guaranteed respect for the neutrality of Lithuania. A League Commission was to be entrusted with the duty of supervising on the spot the observation of the terms of the agreement.

In fact the ease in reaching this agreement was deceptive, since the substantive problem had not been raised – the disputing claims of Poland and Lithuania to the city of Vilna. Poland had in fact gained a point by having the presence of her troops 'legitimized' in some of the territory claimed by Lithuania – to the west of the military demarcation line; and she had also secured a promise of Russian withdrawal from Lithuania. Lithuania had perhaps gained little except a non-aggression guarantee, but then Lithuania was both militarily and diplomatically far weaker.

The proposed League Commission was duly dispatched, and arrived at Suwalki on 5 October. On 7 October an agreement was signed there by representatives of both Poland and Lithuania, defining the line of demarcation and binding each side to observe the agreement until all outstanding disputes between them had been settled.

This agreement too was deceptive. The new Polish government under Pilsudski, supported by an efficient and patriotic army which had just defeated and expelled their former Russian overlords, were not going to allow the Lithuanians to establish their new capital in 'Polish' Vilna while long-drawn-out negotiations were carried on. Within a few hours of the signing of the Suwalki agreements the Polish General Zeligowsky advanced on Vilna; the Lithuanian government withdrew hastily, and Vilna was occupied by the Poles with hardly a shot having been fired.

The Polish government immediately disclaimed responsibility for Zeligowsky's actions. He was, they insisted, acting on his own initiative, and in defiance of the League.

In fact the occupation of Vilna was a carefully planned and deliberate manœuvre. Zeligowsky had acted under direct orders from Pilsudski, the Polish head of state. Even when disclaiming responsibility for his action, the Polish government took the opportunity to point out that Zeligowsky and many of his men were natives of Vilna; that they were regarded as national heroes in Poland; that they had been received with joy into the city of Vilna – and that for all these reasons disciplinary action against the general was out of the question. Military force, it was implied, was being used along the lines of moral right, if not of legal right, and military force had certainly altered the situation substantially in favour of Poland.

Lithuania demanded the immediate intervention of the Council; but Léon Bourgeois, the President of the Council, decided to wait until the scheduled meeting on 20 October at Brussels. By this time, the Russo-Polish war had come to an end; the frontier with Russia was fixed far to the east of the territory disputed between Poland and Lithuania, and Russia declared (in contradiction to the former Moscow Treaty) that the frontier between Poland and Lithuania was a matter entirely for those two countries to settle between themselves.

The Council sessions in which the dispute was debated were heated. It was the first time that the League had been openly defied. Ashkenazy, the Polish delegate, was on the defensive, and had to do a great deal of logical gymnastics to defend the Polish position. He claimed that an entirely new situation had arisen since the September meeting of the Council – the war with Russia had ended and a new treaty been signed, and General Zeligowsky had set up a de facto government of 'Central Lithuania'. Because a new situation had arisen the September resolutions were now extinct. Zeligowsky was, technically speaking, a rebel – but the Polish government would take no action against him, since he was regarded as a hero by the Polish nation.

Legally speaking, the Polish arguments were untenable. Zeligowsky was manifestly an aggressor. Yet underlying their arguments there was a much more tenable position, based squarely on the principle of self-determination. Zeligowsky and '90 per cent of his men' were from the Vilna region; if he was receiving reinforcements, it was from people returning to their own territory – and you cannot stop men going home. It was no use insisting on Zeligowsky's men leaving Vilna before a plebiscite, because they were entitled to be there and to vote. Lithuanians represented 'only 1 per cent of the population'.

It was impossible for either side to reject the principle of self-determination. Accordingly this formed the basis of agreement in the resolution presented by the President of the Council and accepted by both contesting governments. The Council was to organize and supervise a plebiscite in the area which the Council judged to be in dispute. The Council would have full responsibility for deciding upon the withdrawal or disarmament of troops in the area, and would be enabled to take control immediately of means of transport to the areas in question. The Military Commission would continue to exercise responsibility for the settlement of local difficulties.

It was one thing to agree to a plan, however, and quite another to put it into effect. A state of war existed between Lithuania and Poland, and no progress could be made towards a plebiscite until the war was subdued. The Polish army under Zeligowsky tried to extend its control beyond Vilna, and throughout November 1920 there were clashes between the opposing armies.

The League Commission did make progress; it got both sides to agree to an armistice and established a neutral zone between them; but still Zeligowsky remained in possession of Vilna, and the Lithuanians insisted, with perfect justice, that no plebiscite could be held until the Poles withdrew.

All the arrangements went ahead, with no one quite seeing what the final outcome would be. Contingents for an international force were promised by Belgium, Britain, France, Spain, Italy, Denmark, Norway and Greece; and the plans were worked out under Marshal Foch and General Weygand for the support and deployment of this force. Arrangements for the plebiscite were drawn up, and a civilian commission was sent to Vilna to prepare the voting. Yet none could see whether Poland was going to give way.

Then, at a certain point, the situation was completely reversed. For some reason it became clear to both Poland and Lithuania that a plebiscite was very likely to go in favour of Poland – and it made little sense in this case for Poland to be obstructive to a plebiscite, while Lithuania was co-operative.

Within weeks the roles changed. In February 1921 Poland assured Bourgeois that all Polish troops would be withdrawn as soon as the international force arrived; but at the same time, Lithuania, through her representative Valdemaras, found many reasons for postponing the plebiscite, and for restricting the area of its application. Lithuania, he suggested, had only agreed to a plebiscite in areas which she considered to be in dispute – and this did not include Vilna. He argued (with some justice) that the vote could not be fair until Lithuania had equal status with Poland as a full member of the League, and was recognized de jure by the Allies; and he argued, with even more justice, that the Polish forces occupying Vilna had been able to exert 'undue influence' on the population, which would prejudice the results of a plebiscite in their favour.

These objections could all have been overcome, and Lithuania would probably have been held forcibly to acceptance of the results of a fair plebiscite – had not Russia suddenly intervened diplomatically in Lithuania's favour. We have already noted the rapport which had been established between Lithuania and Russia, and communications between the two governments were close. There may well have been some collusion therefore in the threatening note which Russia sent to the Lithuanian government at Kovno, saying that she considered Vilna to be part of Lithuanian territory, until such time as Poland and Lithuania 'negotiated an agreement to the contrary'; that it was Lithuania's responsibility and hers alone, to send Zeligowsky's troops packing – and that if any foreign troops were sent to Lithuanian territory by the League of Nations, this would be considered a threat to the security of

Russia. Whether or not Lithuania was implicated in the sending of this note, the threat from Russia was sufficient to deter the League force from ever entering into the disputed area – for the participating governments were certainly not prepared to risk becoming involved in a League war. Russia, in fact, had exercised her first veto in an international organization.

The plebiscite solution was therefore effectively blocked, since it was agreed that there could be no plebiscite without League protection. With the solution on the basis of principle rejected, there was no other course for the Council but to try to arrive at some kind of compromise solution through meetings of the parties.

On 3 March 1921 the Council of the League passed a resolution asking Poland and Lithuania to enter into direct negotiations with a view to solving the dispute. A Polish–Lithuanian conference was held accordingly, under the chairmanship of Hymans, the Belgian representative on the League Council.

This conference produced a compromise plan, suggesting that Lithuania should be organized into two autonomous cantons – Kovno and Vilna – and at the same time a close military and economic treaty should be established between Poland and Lithuania which would guarantee the rights of the Polish population in Vilna, and the future of Polish culture. The proposal was similar to that which had secured the rights of the Swedish Aaland Islanders, while awarding their territory to Finland.

The Hymans proposals were accepted by Poland, but not by Lithuania. On 28 June 1921 the League Council approved the Hymans scheme and recommended that Poland and Lithuania should take it as a basis for further discussion. Meanwhile, Zeligowsky remained in possession.

No further progress towards a settlement was made in 1921, and on 13 January 1922, in view of the opposition of both parties, the League Council decided not to intervene any further in the negotiations for a final settlement. The matter thus became the sole responsibility of the parties and of the Conference of Ambassadors, who as agents of the Principal and Allied Powers were entrusted with the fixing of the eastern frontiers of Poland under the Treaty of Versailles.

Nevertheless, the League still had a role to play. After the clash between the Lithuanians and General Zeligowsky, a neutral zone had been established to the north-west of Vilna to separate the two armies. Within the zone a Military Commission of the League had originally maintained order, but on the dissolution of the Commission in February 1922 the zone fell into a state of disorder, policed by both Polish and Lithuanian militia and providing a battleground for conflicting nationalist pressures.

In order to put an end to this intolerable situation, the Council of the League resolved in May 1922 to send a Commission to the neutral zone to recommend a provisional line of demarcation. The Commission was sent, and reported back in February 1923 with recommendations for a compromise demarcation line drawn within the neutral zone and determined largely on ethnic lines, and in accord with the principle of self-determination.

Inevitably, Lithuania opposed the fixing of a provisional line – and with good reason. In theory, the ultimate fate of Vilna, which of course lay well to the Polish side of the demarcation line, was not prejudged. But clearly any international agreement about any demarcation line, however provisional, which left Vilna in provisional Polish territory, could not but contribute towards a consolidation of the Polish position.

Lithuanian apprehensions were fully justified. Shortly after the League Council had approved the recommendation of its Commission concerning the demarcation line, Poland appealed to the Allied Powers to exercise their right under the Peace Treaty to establish the eastern frontiers of Poland; and in March 1923 the Conference of Ambassadors accepted the provisional demarcation line as the frontier between Lithuania and Poland, thus awarding Vilna to the Polish forces which had effectively occupied it ever since Zeligowsky's takeover three years previously.

It was perhaps unfortunate that what might have been a victory of principle appeared as a victory of force. But in this, as in so many cases, the assertion of force was difficult to disentangle from the assertion of principle. If Zeligowsky took and ruled Vilna, it was in part because Vilna was predominantly Polish. If Lithuania refused a plebiscite, it was because Zeligowsky was in occupation, and because this occupation would inevitably bias any expression of opinion. If the Ambassadors simply accepted the status quo, it was because the status quo had in it an element of justice. What was left behind was a long legacy of resentment between Poland and Lithuania, the state of war between the two countries being formally ended only in 1927, without any progress having been made towards resolving the underlying conflict.

MOSUL

The Mosul dispute arose out of a fluid situation on the Turkish frontier at the conclusion of the war in 1918; and this situation itself must be seen in the context of the general disintegration of the Ottoman Empire, which was already well under way before the war started, but was greatly accelerated by the international conflict.

The Mosul was the northernmost part of three 'vilayets' or regions which now comprise Iraq. Iraq had been nominally part of the Turkish Empire since 1500, and had been closely ruled by Turkey throughout the nineteenth century; early in the twentieth century, the nationalist independence movement began to take shape in Iraq as it did in other Arab states. The successful revolution of the Young Turks in 1908 and their liberal proclamations stimulated nationalist aspirations – and the desire for independence increased further when the Young Turks failed to live up to their promises.

War was declared between Britain and Turkey in November 1914, and an Anglo-Indian expeditionary force landed at the southernmost point of Iraq. Throughout the war these forces advanced northwards through Iraq, occupying Baghdad in 1917, and approaching to within fourteen miles of Mosul when the armistice which ended the war with Turkey was signed in October 1918. After the armistice, however – and, according to the British view, in agreement with certain terms of it – the allied forces continued to advance, and occupied Mosul on 7 November in the face of indignant Turkish protests.

The allies, as we have said earlier, favoured nationalist independence movements for a mixture of idealistic and strategic reasons. Arab nationalism thrived in Iraq under this apparent encouragement. An Anglo-French Declaration published in Baghdad in 1918, after the defeat of the Turks, stated that 'France and Great Britain have in view . . . the establishment of national governments and administrations drawing their authority from the initiative and free choice of indigenous populations'. This declaration seemed to be in harmony with Wilson's fourteen points, and hopes in Iraq ran high, as did British popularity – for a while.

Turkey was not prepared to dispute the establishment of an independent Iraq, but she was prepared to dispute the inclusion in Iraq of the Mosul vilayet. Territorial dilemmas are bound to arise from such situations, so long as arguments are based only on the old structures. It was beyond question that the disputed area was for centuries under Turkish rule – beyond doubt, legally, that Turkey retained her sovereignty until she chose to renounce it. On the other hand, it was equally a fact that Turkish sovereignty over the Mosul had long been exercised by the Pashas of Baghdad – and that Baghdad was now the centre of a new entity, Iraq, which could equally claim the Mosul on grounds of 'historical coherence'. When old structures collapse, new ones must emerge – structures which are not necessarily precontained in the old order. These will emerge either by a trial of force – or by an agreement of principle – or by a combination of the two.

At the same time the vilayet of Mosul was of great importance to both countries, economically, politically and militarily. It dominated the overland routes to India, and would be of crucial strategic importance against a possible Russian attack from the north or east, or against a Turkish attack from the west. For the Turks, it lay at the intersection of all the roads connecting the southern parts of Anatolia, and therefore was of vital importance for the economic life and security of the region.

In addition, there were probably large quantities of oil to be discovered in the vilayet, and French, English and American oil concerns were waging private battle for priority rights for future exploration. The battle for oil, and the interest of the rival governments in securing the income from royalties formed a largely unspoken accompaniment to the political and diplomatic contest between the rival powers.

In 1920, Turkey and Britain signed the Treaty of Sèvres, in which the Mosul was awarded to Iraq. This treaty, however, never came into effect; and subsequently the Treaty of Lausanne was negotiated between Britain and the new Turkish government of Mustafa Kemal.

There was a general will to reach agreement at Lausanne, and all outstanding disputes were settled – except for the question of the future of the Mosul. On this issue both sides were adamant. Lord Curzon argued strongly that the matter should be referred immediately to the League of Nations – and emphasized to the Turks that in the League the unanimity rule prevailed, and no settlement could therefore be forced against the will of the Turks. It was finally provided in the Treaty that the dispute should be settled by direct negotiation between the two powers, but that if such negotiations failed, the matter should be 'referred to' the Council of the League of Nations.

The parties did not come to an agreement by direct negotiation, and the matter was duly referred to the Council of the League in September 1924. Before the Council, both sides argued their case; and both sides, having to find a respectable basis in principle for their claims, took their stand on the principle of self-determination. The inhabitants of the Mosul, according to the Turks, retained their loyalty to Turkey; according to Britain, they preferred to remain in the new Arab kingdom.

The underlying agreement on principle was promising; and it was not difficult on the basis of the principle for the Council to arrive at an agreed procedure for resolving the dispute. Both sides – though after some hesitation on the Turkish side – agreed to accept whatever decision the Council should make about the future of the Mosul. Both sides agreed to a halt in operations pending the decision of the Council, and to do nothing to alter the status quo. The Council then decided to set up a Commission, with the purpose of investigating all matters relevant to a determination of the frontier – but primarily to assess the wishes of the population.

Meanwhile the military situation remained fluid. Though both sides had agreed to respect the status quo, it was not really clear what the status quo was. On 9 October the frontier incidents became so serious that Britain issued an ultimatum to Turkey demanding that she withdraw all troops from the Mosul or face military action. The Turks then appealed to the Council for a definition of the status quo line; and at an emergency meeting in Brussels a demarcation line was laid down and agreed to by both parties. Thus the 'trial of force' was brought to an end, and the way seemed clear for a settlement on grounds of principle.

A commission was duly appointed by the Council, great care being taken to ensure its complete neutrality; it consisted of a Swede, a Belgian and a Hungarian.

As soon as the Commission arrived in Mosul, however, it was confronted with a dispute between the British-Iraqi and the Turkish authorities as to how the people of Mosul should be consulted. The Turks favoured a one-man one-vote plebiscite; only such a plebiscite could have the 'incontestable authority' necessary for the determination of the fate of a large population; they took as their own premise that 'no population can be transferred to another against its will'. As to the method of procedure, the Turks insisted that *before* the plebiscite was taken the districts must be placed firmly 'in the hands of the people themselves'. The Commission would have to make sure that the proportion of different elements in the public forces should correspond with the proportion in the population, and government officials should be temporarily replaced by persons elected by the local people or by their Councils of Elders. All foreign occupying forces would, of course, have to be withdrawn.

The logic of the Turkish view was clear. The British objections, however, were forceful and practical. First there was the general objection to plebiscites in a primitive population – 'Except in communities which have attained a high state of education and civilization, and which are perfectly organized, the result of a plebiscite is necessarily influenced chiefly by purely political and ethnological factors or temporary and local considerations, such as a land dispute, the imposition of a new tax, or a propaganda campaign which there would be neither time nor opportunity to counteract.' If a plebiscite were decided on for the purpose of fixing the frontier between Turkey and Iraq, that would mean that the uneducated voter would not attach sufficient importance to strategic, geographical, economic and administrative factors.

So far as procedure was concerned, the British fully agreed that all local forces would have to be organized to ensure that no 'undue influence' was exerted; but they felt that nothing short of a complete replacement of all local forces by a new neutral force would suffice. They then argued that it would be virtually impossible to provide such forces from outside which would be able to maintain order in these difficult regions during the turbulence which would accompany a plebiscite. The British therefore rejected the idea of a plebiscite, and favoured a selective consultation of local leaders.

The Commission began by supporting the Turkish view; but in the course of their early investigations they became convinced that the procedural objections raised by the British were crucial – that only the formation of a provisional neutral government and neutral force could ensure the genuineness of a plebiscite, and that such a government and such a force could not be formed. They also recognized the validity of the British objections to consulting through plebiscites a people of only rudimentary education, likely in any case only to follow the views of local chiefs or landowners who would themselves be influenced by personal quarrels, rivalries and feuds.

Accordingly, the Commission consulted about eight hundred witnesses, selected largely from lists submitted by Turkish and British assessors, and tried to piece together from these consultations a coherent picture of the wishes of the population. The consultations were held in secret. Even so, the dangers of the plebiscite situation still made themselves felt. Fear of reprisals from existing authorities was strong and widespread. Sometimes witnesses spoke in a private whisper in favour of Turkey, and then loudly proclaimed loyalty to Iraq for the benefit of those outside the room. Some had no idea what the question was about; many simply referred the matter to a chief or village-owner. Some wanted to know how their 'enemies' had voted so that they could vote for the other side – many reversed their opinion when consulted a second time.

The judgment which emerged from the consultation was not simple. The population of the Mosul was mixed. The largest group, the Kurds, were beginning to develop a powerful national Kurdish consciousness and were enamoured neither of the Arabs nor of the Turks. They would have much preferred their own independent state, but, if forced to a choice, about half would opt for Iraq, half for Turkey. Among the rest of the population, there was no nationalist feeling in favour of Iraq, and not much in favour of Turkey – but there was a general preference for British administration. This was hardly surprising, since under the very brief period of rule by British officials (acting on behalf of Iraq), extensive developments had taken place in the field of education, public health and security.

The 'wishes of the people' therefore indicated a preference for Iraq, but for practical rather than nationalist reasons; and the Commission's careful analysis of geographical, economic and strategic considerations pointed in the same direction. The final recommendation of the Commission therefore was that the Mosul should go to Iraq, the boundary between Iraq and Turkey running along the Brussels demarcation line – but only on condition that Iraq continued under British mandate for twenty-five years. If that condition was refused, then the whole territory should go to Turkey.

The report of the Commission was not particularly welcome to any of the three parties concerned. The Iraqi government had looked forward to complete independence in the near future; Britain had little desire to continue the mandate for so long a period; and Turkey had lost her case. The report, however, was endorsed by the League Council.

Britain and Iraq then worked out a procedural compromise, by which the mandate was nominally extended for twenty-five years, but on the understanding that Iraq could apply for admission to the League before that date and thus invite the League to end the mandate. Britain and Iraq therefore complied with the condition, and communicated their compliance to the Council – asking at the same time for an extra slice of territory for Iraq on the Turkish side of the Brussels line. This request was rejected, and the Council decided that the Brussels line should henceforth be the boundary between Turkey and Iraq.

Turkey, in spite of her prior commitment to accept the Council's decision, found it much harder to do so when the decision went against her. She raised procedural difficulties, arguing that the League unanimity rule must apply, and that the Council had no authority to settle the dispute without the consent of the parties. The matter was referred to the International Court of Justice; and the Court's advisory opinion was that the Council had power in the circumstances to make a decision binding upon the parties without their votes being taken into account.

Meanwhile, Turkey had moved in the military and political field. The day after the decision of the League on the Mosul, Turkey and Russia signed a non-aggression pact. The following day, Mustafa Kemal called an extraordinary cabinet meeting, and the Turkish government announced its readiness to meet 'every situation' in the Mosul. Clearly military action was contemplated.

Turkey was not, however, in a strong military position, and could only hope to secure any advantage against Britain by allowing Russian troops into Turkey, with all the risks which that implied. The Turkish military council weighed up the situation and rejected the possibility of war.

The government of Mustafa Kemal was realistic enough to accept that, if there was no war, there might as well be peace. Negotiations with Britain were opened, and on 5 June 1926 a treaty was concluded between the two powers which recognized the mandate of Iraq, and accepted the decision of the League Council in regard to the Mosul.

The agreement, however, did not represent a complete capitulation on the part of Turkey. Iraq was to pay Turkey a 10 per cent royalty on all oil rights in the Mosul – or alternatively settle for a lump sum of £500,000. The lump sum was paid and accepted in the same year, and the political aspect of the Mosul dispute was virtually at an end.

Again the League's peace-making activities seemed to have reached a successful conclusion; though again, it is equally clear that the conclusion reached was in accord with the realities of the power structure.

ALBANIA

Like the dispute over the Mosul, the Albanian frontier disputes, which occupied the League of Nations in 1920 and 1921, arose out of the collapse of the Turkish Empire, and the conflicts of power and nationality involved in the establishment of new territorial units.

The Turks had taken possession of the region at present known as Albania in the fourteenth century, and it was administered for five centuries as an integral part of the Turkish Empire. During the nineteenth century, however, the Turkish power declined, and the Balkans became a ferment of self-assertive local groups and a focus of conflict between the neighbouring empires of Russia, Turkey and Austro-Hungary.

Under the rearrangement of Balkan territories proposed by Russia, Austria and Britain at the Congress of Berlin, which ended the Russo-Turkish war in 1878, parts of Turkish Albania were to be transferred to Montenegro, a small country which had throughout the Middle Ages remained independent of the great empires. The proposed transfer provoked vigorous armed resistance in Albania – not because Albanians wanted to remain part of Turkey but because they wanted full independence. Though they were defeated, their struggle both against Turkey and against Montenegro was a stimulus to militant nationalism. In 1908 the 'bloodless' revolution of the Young Turks added fuel to the flames, and in 1912, after a massive national uprising, the Albanians occupied the key town of Skopje and forced Turkey to acknowledge their independence.

No sooner was the existence of Albania proclaimed, however, than the Serbs advanced towards Danazzo to claim their share; Greece declared her aim of annexing southern Albania, and Italy and Montenegro also expressed an interest in acquiring parts of the upstart state.

In order to prevent what looked like becoming a general conflagration, Sir Edward Grey called a conference of all the powers concerned in London. As the result of this conference, the Treaty of London was concluded in 1913 between Turkey on the one hand and Greece, Bulgaria, Montenegro and Serbia on the other. The principle of an independent Albania was accepted; and 'the delimitation of frontiers, and all other questions related to Albania' were referred to the European Concert of Great Powers – Germany, Austria-Hungary, France, Great Britain, Russia and Italy.

Carrying out their responsibilities under this treaty, the Concert powers in July 1913 defined Albania as an 'autonomous principality'. Its neutrality was guaranteed, its civil and financial administration was referred to a Commission, on which would sit delegates of the six powers and one Albanian; and responsibility for public order and safety was entrusted to foreign officers.

The delimitation of the boundaries of the new state was peculiarly difficult owing to the intermixture of tribes and nationalities, and the self-interest of the existing states. In the final outcome, Serbia retained an area in the north which included perhaps 800,000 'Albanians', and the southern boundary with Greece, an even more difficult problem, was referred to an International Boundary Commission.

There was much dispute with Greece over the procedure to be adopted by the Commission – Greece favouring a general cultural historical survey plus the principle of self-determination, and the Commission favouring a simple linguistic test. The Commission finally defined the boundary by means of the linguistic test, and awarded the disputed areas to Albania. Greece registered her formal protests and proposed that the question of the Koritza territory should be reopened – but nevertheless agreed to evacuate the areas assigned to Albania.

When the Greeks withdrew, the district of Northern Epirus, which Greece had claimed on the grounds of cultural affinity, rose in revolt (whether with or without Greek assistance is not clear), and established an independent administration. In May 1914 the governing commission of Albania was obliged to negotiate with this administration and agree to an autonomous status for Northern Epirus.

Such was the extremely confused situation in Albania when the war broke out in 1914. The territory soon became a battleground. The hardly established authority of the central government dwindled; and the allied powers, now primarily concerned with winning the war, clearly regarded Albania as an unimportant pawn in a serious game, and a weak element in a militarily vital area.

In October 1914 Britain asked Greece to reoccupy Northern Epirus in order to maintain order, and this district was then successively occupied during the war by Italy, Greece and France. In the north, Serbian troops occupied a further substantial area.

In November 1914, the Entente powers offered Northern Epirus to Greece, as the price of her support in the war. By another treaty in 1915, the allies conceded areas to Italy, and suggested that other districts might eventually be assigned to Montenegro and Serbia. It was clear that the allies now regarded themselves as having authority to dispose as they wished of Albanian territory.

It is surprising that Albania ever emerged from this melting pot as an independent entity after the end of the war. But emerge she did, and one of the factors in this emergence was the existence of the League of Nations, and of the ideals which were embodied in the League and therefore part of the world of political reality.

In 1919 Albania, through her legitimate representatives, appealed to the Peace Conference in Paris to define her territory. There was no other body to which she could appeal. Similarly, in 1920 she concluded an agreement with Greece to refer boundary problems between Greece and Albania to the Peace Conference in Paris.

On the face of it, this did not seem a very promising move for the future integrity of Albania. The general view of the major powers seemed to be that Albania's existence was in question. A Commission on Greek and Albanian Affairs was established by the Supreme Council of the Peace Conference, and the British and French delegations expressed their view that the 1913 agreements had 'never received the approval of the populations concerned', and that Argirocastro and Koritza should be incorporated in Greece. President Harding expressed the same view on behalf of the United States, and Italy and Greece, both eager to stake their claim, conducted their own negotiations about the fate of south Albania. Greek troops remained in Northern Epirus, and Serbian troops continued to occupy one-sixth of Albanian territory in the north. After long-drawn-out discussions the Paris Conference closed without a final solution to the problem, and the responsibility was passed on from the Peace Conference to the so-called

'Conference of Ambassadors', set up by the Allies to implement the peace treaties. In all these proceedings Albania as such had no part to play, nor was she directly represented.

Meanwhile, the Albanian national spirit reasserted itself. A national congress was held in 1920 in the town of Lushnje, in an Italian occupied area. The Albanians formed a government and set up a temporary capital at Tirana. Allied troops in Shkoder and Korce handed over to the new national government, and a popular rising in Vlone forced the Italians to withdraw.

It was at this point that another avenue was opened for Albania to pursue its case internationally for the integrity of her pre-1914 frontiers. The first Assembly of the League of Nations, in the latter part of 1920, received a petition from Albania – together with twelve other states – for membership of the new international body; and at the end of 1920, in the midst of her struggle for existence, and with a large section of her territory occupied and claimed by neighbouring states, she was admitted as a full member of the League.

No case for admission was more difficult than that of Albania; and the reasons for this were basically the same as the reasons for her difficulties with her neighbours. There was doubt about her status, her territory – about her very existence as a sovereign independent state.

The Albanian case for admission was referred, according to the usual procedure, to the Fifth Committee of the League. From there it was referred to a special sub-committee, which after thorough consideration decided that there was too much doubt about the status of Albania, and that the question of her admission should be postponed. There was doubt about whether she possessed a stable government; there was doubt about whether she was recognized either de jure or de facto as a sovereign state by any League member; and there was doubt about the definition of her territories. The Committee therefore recommended against admission. The Committee's view was presented to the Assembly; yet, astonishingly enough, the Assembly decided to reject its

Committee's advice and unanimously voted for the acceptance of Albania as a full member of the League.

The reasons for this dramatic acceptance of the new state are not perfectly clear – and yet this was a vital stage in the settlement of the dispute, for whatever pressures influenced the Assembly to accept Albania's membership must also have been influential in supporting her integrity against the states which had an interest in her dismemberment.

Certainly, Lord Robert Cecil, the leader of the British delegation, had a strong influence on the Assembly's decision; and from his powerful speech in the Assembly on the occasion of Albania's admission we can get some clue as to the mood of the occasion.

He argued first that whether or not Albania was recognized now as a state, it certainly had been recognized by six great powers in 1913, and had not been conquered or extinguished in any way since; therefore it continued to exist. But beyond the legal problem, there was the vital force of nationalism. 'There is no greater fact than the fact of nationality. There is no greater aspiration than the aspiration to national freedom. It is in the name of nationality and national freedom that I venture to appeal to this great Assembly to do justice and right to the people of Albania.'

Sir Ali Imam of India spoke in a similar vein, expressing his wish that 'The League of Nations will appear before the world as an impartial body, ready to support the weaker nations of the earth.'

The admission of Albania was, as F. P. Walters put it, 'in essence a notification by the League to the Supreme Council to hasten its decision concerning her frontiers, and to her neighbours not to try to appropriate part of her territory in the meantime'. Respect for the principle of nationality, and for the integrity of small states in Europe, was indeed one of the principal foundations of League idealism, and the League was in its first year of life. There could be no more effective appeal than through this principle to the support of the League, and legal scruples could be overridden if these principles were at stake.

The principles had of course their political foundation. It was partly by wedding the principle of nationality that the allies had enlisted the support of breakaway groups in the crumbling empires of Austria-Hungary and Turkey; and it was generally accepted that respect for national aspiration was not only a fine ideal, but a sound basis for peace. The League brought a new factor into the situation, however, for these ideals were now embodied in an organization which was not completely determined by the foreign policies of its founder allies.

The problem of Albania's frontiers was, nevertheless, still left with the Conference of Ambassadors, since it had been entrusted to them by the Peace Conference.

When the Second Assembly of the League met in 1921, the ambassadors had made little progress towards resolving the conflict. Meanwhile, Greek troops remained in the south, and Yugoslavs in the north. Skirmishes were frequent, as was to be expected in such a tense situation, and in April and June 1921 Albania used her new status in the League to appeal to the Council to resolve the territorial conflict and to 'free its territory from occupation'. The Council were persuaded, however – mainly by the Greek and Yugoslav delegates – to leave the matter in the hands of the Conference of Ambassadors.

In September, therefore, Albania seized the opportunity to bring the matter up before the Assembly. In the Assembly a strong conflict developed between the 'spectators', mainly smaller states, who felt that the principle of nationalities and the integrity of a small state was being threatened, and the powers most closely involved in the Albanian question – Greece and Yugoslavia and Britain, France and Italy. The 'spectator' group were indignant at the dilatoriness of the Ambassadors, and pressed for the matter to be taken in hand by the League; the involved powers gave repeated assurances that the Ambassadors were about to give their decision, and that the only right course was to wait for this decision. They made light of the Albanian reports of continuous frontier clashes, on the grounds that 'incidents were bound to happen'.

The Assembly accepted the assurances of the involved powers that a decision was about to emerge from the Conference of Ambassadors. But it did not disband without asking the Council to send a Commission of Inquiry to Albania to make sure that the decisions were peacefully carried out. This the Council promptly did, at the beginning of October.

Whether through the pressures generated at the Assembly or not, the next two months saw a complete resolution of the Albanian problem, a resolution strongly favouring Albania's claims.

On 9 November the Conference of Ambassadors made known its final decision – which was that the Albanian frontiers should remain as they had been settled by the Concert Powers in 1913 – with only three small rectifications in favour of Yugoslavia. This decision resolved all the procedural complications, and gave to the League a clearly defined responsibility to supervise, through the Commission, the withdrawal of Greek and Yugoslav troops from Albanian territory – a responsibility fully in accord with the League's sympathy for its youngest member.

The second crucial event was a dramatic change of attitude in London. H. A. L. Fisher, the British representative, had said in the Assembly in October that Albanian reports of Yugoslav aggression were exaggerated, and that 'incidents were bound to happen'. On 8 November, however, the day before the Conference of Ambassadors announced its ruling in favour of Albania, the Secretary General of the League received a telegram from the British Prime Minister, Lloyd George, demanding an immediate meeting of the Council in order to force Yugoslavia, under pain of sanctions, to observe her obligations under the Covenant with regard to Albania.

Between October and 8 November the British government had evidently become concerned that there was a real danger of war in the Balkans, and that Yugoslavia did have aggressive designs against Albania; and peace in the Balkans was more important to Britain than the friendship of Yugoslavia.

The decision of the Ambassadors reinforced by the trumpet blast from Lloyd George, was quite sufficient to bring about a rapid withdrawal of both Yugoslavia and Greece to their own agreed confines. The Commission therefore had little to do on its arrival other than observe a peaceful and orderly takeover by Albania of practically the whole of her 1913 territory. Following this apparent triumph of international organization, the League and its officials enjoyed a high prestige in Albania for more than a decade, and were able to assist in many ways in the country's development.

CHACO

The Chaco dispute, which kept Bolivia and Paraguay at war from 1928 to 1938, concerned the ownership of a vast tract of 100,000 sq. miles of territory in South America known as the Chaco Boreal. The area lay between the two contesting states, and was largely unexplored and uninhabited, except for scattered Indian settlements.

After the break-up of the Spanish Empire in South America, the newly-independent states had arrived at a general understanding that their boundaries should correspond with the administrative boundaries of their former overlords. In modern Africa the same rule of convenience has been adopted, and it is essential to have such a rule if the whole area is not to be submerged in the melting-pot of war. But the rule of convenience, then as now, was no cure for all ills.

The reason for this was not so much that the colonial boundaries cut across tribal boundaries – for all the dominant groups in Latin America were of the same Iberian stock – but that the Spanish administrative units had not always been clearly defined. Much of the continent was unsettled and undeveloped, and the administrative and judicial units and sub-units sometimes overlapped; nor was it clear in all cases which particular administrative unit, whether province or district, was to become a state – this depended inevitably on the nature of the independence struggle and the dynamics of self-determination.

In the case of the Chaco, both sides could claim some vestigial rights deriving from the Spanish administration. Paraguay claimed that the Chaco had always been included in the jurisdiction of the Governor in the Paraguayan capital of Asuncion; Bolivia claimed that the Chaco had been included in the jurisdiction of the 'Audencia' of Charcas in Upper Peru (which later became Bolivia).

The fact was, however, that as both states developed their national consciousness and their ambition during the latter part of the nineteenth century – and as both suffered defeats and losses at the hands of their more powerful neighbours – the uncolonized virgin land of the Chaco became more and more for each of them a desired field of expansion.

So far as Paraguay was concerned, the edge of the Chaco lay across the River Paraguay facing her capital city, and had from the earliest days of the Conquistadores been regarded as a legitimate field for adventure, conquest and exploitation. It had entered into the national saga as the land of heroic exploits. Later, stable Paraguayan colonies were established on the edge of the Chaco. In the mid-nineteenth century, large agricultural settlements were founded on the Chaco side of the river near Asuncion. Further north, the tannin industry began to develop, and narrow-gauge railways penetrated deep into the interior to bring the tannin-bearing 'red ironwood' trees to the river-bank for processing. Meanwhile, in the central Chaco, communities of Mennonites of Canadian and Russian origin formed settlements under the aegis of the Paraguayan Government.

The Bolivians, for their part, had done very little to establish themselves in their part of the Chaco. Nevertheless, the region became of enormous importance to Bolivia since its possession would provide her with access to the sea down the River Paraguay. Bolivia had finally emerged from the territorial struggles following independence as the only land-locked Latin-American state. She felt 'imprisoned', and had made ambitious plans for the construction of a port on the River Paraguay some two to three hundred miles above the Paraguayan capital.

From 1879 onwards numerous attempts were made by the two countries to reach some kind of negotiated settlement, but the proposed treaties never gained the necessary ratification from both governments. On each side claims to the whole area were intensified; and as the activities of the rival states were increased, they each began to establish a network of forts and military outposts. Clashes were inevitable. A minor incident in 1928 soon subsided, but in June 1932 opposing patrols came into conflict again and it became clear that this time both sides were prepared for war. They had for some years been stock-piling arms, mainly imported from Britain and the United States, and were prepared to establish their claims by force. This is the major fact which distinguishes the Chaco war from the other territorial disputes we have been considering, and which of course made it singularly intractable as material for any experiment in international peace-keeping.

At the commencement of hostilities, both sides sent protest notes to the Secretary General of the League of Nations, but neither submitted the dispute to inquiry by the League Council – as both were technically bound to do by the Covenant. Instead, the dispute was taken up in Washington by a body known as the 'Neutral Commission' of representatives of various Latin-American states under a US chairman. The Commission produced various compromise plans which were rejected by the contestants. In December the Neutral Commission passed on the problem to a committee of neighbouring states (Argentina, Brazil, Chile and Peru). This committee produced further compromise plans which were also rejected – by Bolivia primarily – and so the neighbours too eventually gave up the unequal task, and the baby was passed on to the League of Nations in May 1933.

Bolivia's intransigence was clearly due to the fact that her armed forces were advancing. She had taken into her employ a German

Commander-in-Chief called General Kundt. Under his leadership a spruced-up Bolivian army had penetrated far into the Chaco, and in his dispatches the General made it clear that he considered complete victory to be well within his grasp. In the circumstances Bolivia had little to gain from a negotiated peace.

The League Council's first move was to press for a Commission to be sent to the Chaco to organize an effective armistice, and if possible to reach some agreement on arbitration of the territorial question. Paraguay agreed fairly readily to a cease-fire followed by arbitration. Bolivia, however, would not accept any arrangement which involved losing what she had gained by military action. The arbitration, she argued, must only apply to that part of the Chaco which was not at the time occupied by Bolivia – and until this was agreed Bolivia would not agree to a cease-fire, since this would strengthen the position of the enemy, who was operating nearer home. In other words, Bolivia would lose the military initiative. The Bolivian arguments made perfect military sense, and presumably emanated directly from the General in the field. It became clear later that the General was at the time preparing a major offensive.

In spite of the discouraging signs the League pushed ahead with plans for the sending of a Commission – even though the two sides could not agree about what it should do when it got there. Then an odd thing happened: Bolivia and Paraguay asked simultaneously for the League Commission to be delayed while the 'Four Neighbours' had another try at reconciliation.

The only likely interpretation of this move was that both sides for some reason wanted to delay negotiations; and the only likely reason for wanting such delay was to clear a space for more fighting. This would mean that Paraguay must be taking a more optimistic view of the military position, so that both sides now thought they held the trump cards. Sure enough, during the four months' delay which the contestants' joint manœuvre imposed on League action, the Bolivians launched their offensive and failed. Argentina closed its frontier and cut off an important Bolivian supply-route, and the brilliant Paraguayan General Estigarribia began to press hard on the over-extended Bolivian forces.

The neighbours of Paraguay and Bolivia had had enough. They declined to get their fingers burnt any more in the Chaco dispute. So after four months' delay the dispute was passed back to the League, and the Commission arrived in December, at a time when the Paraguayan forces were rapidly advancing. The Commission spent some time in the Paraguayan capital, then moved to the Bolivian capital. There, in La Paz, a telegram was received from Paraguay, proposing an immediate armistice and asking for a meeting to be arranged by the Commission so that both sides could discuss terms of peace.

Bolivia, now on the defensive, was ready to agree. The Commission called a meeting in Montevideo, and the Pan-American Conference which had its centre there gave the League full support. The stage seemed set for an apparent victory of international peace-keeping to match that in Leticia (*see below*).

Unfortunately, the contestants had not yet reached their point of stalemate. Paraguay would consider no terms which did not involve a proper system of security for the Chaco, prior to any further efforts to solve the territorial problem; and, by a 'proper system of security', Paraguay meant an occupation of the whole of the Chaco by Paraguayan troops, and a complete withdrawal of the Bolivians. Clearly, for the Paraguayans, the armistice move had been an attempt to crystallize the situation while Paraguay held the advantage – it had been simply a move in the war. For Bolivia, it had been an attempt to reach a compromise when she was in danger of defeat. Paraguay was warned repeatedly that the military pendulum would swing back again – that Paraguay's over-extended forces would soon become vulnerable, just as Bolivia's had been. In the flush of victory, however, she was not prepared to accept such arguments. The prospects of agreement were nil.

The Chaco Commission reported back to the League Council its failure to reach an agreed settlement between the contestants. The Council asked the Commission nevertheless to continue with its work and draw up a report, containing its recommendations for a final settlement.

The Report of the Chaco Commission is a valuable lesson in techniques of reconciliation, though it had no immediate effect. On the security issue, the Commission proposed a division of the Chaco into Paraguayan and Bolivian police-zones, and a reduction in forces, so that security should be maintained and the claims of neither side should be compromised.

Secondly, the Commission sought to take the heat out of the dispute by proposing that each side should agree to renounce claims to the regions which the other side considered most vital. This meant that two regions would be excluded from any arbitration; the Hayes Zone, the Paraguayan-settled area opposite Concepcion, which had been awarded to Paraguay by President Hayes of the United States under a previous arbitration, and the region north of Bahia Negra, which gave Bolivia access to the River Paraguay, and which had been allocated to Bolivia in a treaty concluded between Bolivia and Brazil.

For the settlement of the remainder of the territorial question, the Commission proposed legal arbitration, carried out by the Permanent Court of International Justice. At the same time it proposed a post-war economic conference of the American States, in which the economic issues underlying the territorial problem – especially the problem of oil – should be fully dealt with.

The proposed treaty could not be bettered as a compromise solution; but compromise was not yet desired, and there was no question of both sides accepting the Report. Since the procedure being followed was not that of Article 15, compulsory settlement was not envisaged at this stage.

The Commission did, however, draw attention once more to a very important factor underlying the Chaco war – and that was the escalation of trade in aeroplanes, armoured cars, flame projectors, and automatic weapons, which immeasurably increased the savagery of the war. There is little doubt that the rapid and unpredictable flow of modern weapons into both countries was largely responsible for the unnatural prolongation of the war, and the inability to reach a state of equilibrium. In this respect, the Chaco holds an important lesson for the 1960s.

The Commission did therefore recommend a universal arms embargo on both the belligerents. The suggestion was followed up vigorously by the Council. An urgent appeal was issued to all arms-supplying states. Public opinion had been considerably roused in the United States by the publicity given to the armaments traffic, and this helped to secure American agreement, and by August 1934 the embargo was virtually complete.

The war dragged on. In the summer of 1934 Bolivia brought the dispute formally before the League under Article 15, thus opening the way for the ponderous operation of the whole enforcement machinery. At the same time Bolivia requested that the Assembly should deal with the matter instead of the Council. All the stages were gone through. There was a final abortive attempt to find an agreed solution. Then an elaborate treaty was drawn up, safeguarding the positions of both sides, and this treaty was accepted by the Assembly as its final recommendation for a settlement. Bolivia accepted: Paraguay rejected. Paraguay thus constituted herself an aggressor in League terms if she continued to make war on Bolivia, liable to all the sanctions of Article 16. The only realistic suggestion, however, for applying pressure to Paraguay was that the arms embargo should be lifted in favour of Bolivia. This was proposed by the Assembly Committee, and Paraguay announced its withdrawal from the League.

Meanwhile, the resolution of conflict was gradually worked out in military terms. The Chaco Commission had predicted that the Paraguayan advance would be halted something over two hundred kilometres from the River Paraguay, and that both sides would become immobilized in fortified positions. The prediction was accurate. The final stalemate was reached, and in June 1935, when neither side felt that further military progress was possible, the neighbouring countries intervened to arrange a truce and initiate a peace conference at Buenos Aires.

nationality occupied the river-port of Leticia, and subsequently the whole territory of the Trapeze, setting up fortified positions both on the Amazon in the south and on the Putumayo in the north. Colombian officials fled from Leticia to neighbouring Colombian territory.

The first reaction of the Peruvian government was to disavow the action of its subjects – and it was in fact clear that the invasion had not been carried out on the authority of the Lima government. The Colombian representative in Lima was assured that the Peruvian government would assist the Colombian government to restore order in Leticia, in accordance with the provisions of the Boundary Treaty. For a time it seemed as if the dispute might be settled by negotiation, and Colombia prepared a police expedition, consisting of two small gunboats and about a hundred police, to restore their control over the small village of Leticia.

When the police expedition was approaching Leticia, the dispute suddenly assumed a much more serious character. The Peruvian commander at Iquitos warned the expedition that any reoccupation of Leticia would be opposed by force of arms; and he was immediately supported in this attitude by the central government in Lima. It was at this stage that the long-smouldering dispute suddenly became, through the intermediacy of the League of Nations, a matter for world-wide concern.

The League Council sent telegrams to both sides reminding them of their duties under the Covenant, and they both sent lengthy statements of their cases to the Council. Peru asked the Council to order the suspension of all measures of force. A Committee of Three – Ireland, Spain and Guatemala – was appointed to look into the dispute.

There were two aspects to the Peruvian volte-face. First of all the situation had changed. It is one thing to 'disavow' the actions of subjects – quite another to refuse to defend them when they are under attack. Peru could argue that Colombia had resorted too hastily to violent means of restoring her control, and had thus forced a polarization of attitudes.

On the other hand, it was clear that the government in Lima had reassessed the whole meaning of the Leticia coup; it came to see it as an expression of popular sentiment, and as a means of opening negotiations to modify the 1922 Treaty. Legally, Peru could not but admit the validity of the Colombian claim; morally, however, she pressed hard for a reconsideration of the future of the ceded territory.

The Colombian expedition halted for a while, while Brazil made an unsuccessful attempt to mediate between the two parties, and Brazil's abortive initiative delayed League action for some time. But on 26 January 1933, representatives of the disputing states set forward their cases at length before the League Council, and, at the beginning of February, Brazil withdrew from the picture leaving the field clear for League initiative.

The Peruvian representative, in a masterpiece of double statement, made his ambiguous position as clear as any ambiguity can be. He accepted the Boundary Treaty as a fact, but wanted to call it into question; he dissociated himself from the original coup, but supported those who had carried it out: 'Peru is not the aggressor. The events at Leticia, the expulsion – without bloodshed – of the Colombian authorities, took it by surprise. A group of Peruvians, urged by an excess of patriotism and giving violent expression to public opinion in the country, which condemned the Salomon–Lozano Treaty, seized a Peruvian town founded by the Peruvians more than a century ago, of which Colombia took possession only two years ago in 1930.'

The Colombian case, however, was crystal-clear, and unambiguous. She took her stand on the Treaty which had been signed and ratified, and insisted on the immediate restoration of Colombian sovereignty – though agreeing after such restoration to discuss any other outstanding disputes with Peru in a spirit of conciliation. She could not allow 'an act of force carried out by persons who can then be treated as filibusters to create a situation open to exploitation by a neighbouring government'.

The Council's attitude was quite predictable. It affirmed that

Colombia had the right to take police-measures to restore her authority, and called upon Peru not to interfere with the exercise of this right.

Peru's attitude, however, remained unchanged, and the conflict began to escalate. The Colombian ships moved towards Leticia, were attacked by Peruvian bombers, and withdrew. The Colombians bombarded and retook Tarapaca. War preparations were made on both sides.

The Colombian representative requested the League Council to take up the dispute formally under Article 15 of the Covenant. This the Council did, and the various stages of the procedure were carried through with very little delay. First, a final effort was made to solve the dispute with the consent of the parties. This final effort consisted of a proposal, submitted by the Committee of Three to the Council on 1 March, that the Trapeze should be taken over by a League Commission, commanding Colombian troops; that during the year negotiations should proceed between Peru and Colombia, and if no other agreement had been reached by then the territory should revert to Colombia. Colombia accepted the proposal, but Peru rejected it – arguing in particular that the proposed 'international force' would not be international at all, but Colombian.

The next step was for the Council to issue a report containing its final recommendations. This was done on 13 March; the recommendations, which were preceded by a careful analysis of the whole history of the dispute, were clear and concise: there should be a complete evacuation by the Peruvian forces of the whole territory of Leticia, and a complete withdrawal of support from Peruvians who had occupied the area; and, when this was done, negotiations should be begun between the two parties without delay.

Once more, Colombia voted for the report, and Peru against; but under Article 15 the votes of the parties to the dispute were not to be counted. The report was therefore adopted. If Peru now continued to oppose by force Colombia's efforts to retake Leticia, she would be automatically branded as an international aggressor, and liable to all the sanctions laid down in Article 16 of the Covenant – severance of trade and financial relations with all League members, and whatever military action should be recommended by the Council. An Advisory Committee of Council Members was appointed to implement the report.

Yet still the conflict escalated.

Colombian ships on the River Putumayo were fired on from the Peruvian bank and bombed from the air. The only way in which the Colombian forces could prevent this was by invading Peruvian territory and capturing the fortress of Guepi, on the Peruvian bank of the river, which they did after a sharp struggle. The capture of Guepi, which gave the Peruvians a 'legitimate' complaint against the Colombian 'invaders', was in fact one of the seeds of the future settlement, since it made possible a kind of bargaining arrangement in which each side had to renounce its wrongful gains.

The next serious phase in the escalation of hostilities was the dispatch of a small Peruvian fleet, consisting of a cruiser and three submarines, through the Panama Canal, with orders to sail through the Caribbean and up the Amazon to join the Peruvian forces at Iquitos.

This was a crucial test for the League's peace-keeping machinery. Peru was clearly branded as the villain of the piece. She was engaged in warfare against a member-state, and all League members were solemnly pledged to enforce against Peru all manner of sanctions. The very least that could be expected was that the Peruvian fleet would not be allowed to refuel and take on supplies in League members' ports – and the Dutch port of Curaçao and the British port of Trinidad lay directly en route. The Advisory Committee, at an emergency meeting, called on all member-states to refrain from giving any assistance to the enemy flotilla.

Yet when the Peruvians arrived at Curaçao, they were given sufficient fuel, water and other supplies to proceed to Trinidad. In

Trinidad, the British Governor was in a dilemma because he had received no special instructions from London. He knew of the Leticia dispute, but there was no precedent for refusing supplies, and the Peruvian fleet left Port of Spain fully equipped for its voyage up the Amazon.

The complete failure of two of the League's more committed and efficient members to carry out even a minor 'blocking action' of this kind was an indication of the remoteness of any serious international enforcement action at this stage in the League's history. Even though Peru was militarily a weak and backward nation, the organization and the will to act against her were totally lacking. The condemnation of Peru seemed a sterile and pointless exercise, since no consequences followed from it.

It looked as if Colombia and Peru would subside into a prolonged warfare as fruitless and costly as that in the Chaco. An apparently chance coincidence of events, however, prevented this.

On 30 April 1933, Sanchez Perro, the President of Peru, was assassinated. The new president immediately let it be known that a new policy of conciliation was to be pursued, and direct discussions were initiated between Colombia and Peru.

The result of this was that within a few days the Council's recommendations of 18 March were accepted by both sides, and agreement was reached also on the way in which these recommendations were to be put into effect.

The League Commission was to be dispatched to Leticia without delay, and should take charge of the territory in the name of the Government of Colombia. Simultaneously, Peruvian troops should withdraw from Leticia – and, of course, Colombian troops would withdraw from Peruvian territory. The Commission should then call on military forces 'of its own selection' (to satisfy the Peruvians, they were not defined as 'Colombian') to maintain order in the territory. The Commission should remain no more than one year while negotiations proceeded between the two states, and Colombia was to bear the cost of the administration.

All this was carried out. The League Commission arrived within a month to hoist the League flag over Leticia, and to administer for a year the little township – during which time it was responsible for building three schools, a hospital, and carrying out other public works. It examined a hundred and thirty-eight claims for goods lost and damaged in the hostilities, and made liberal compensation. Throughout the year of its administration there was only one minor disturbance of public order, which was easily resolved by returning certain Peruvian troublemakers to their homes in Loreto.

While tensions in the territory were lessened by this stable and manifestly just administration, negotiations went on between Colombia and Peru at Rio de Janeiro in order to reach a treaty agreement.

It soon became clear that one substantial underlying cause of friction which had to be tackled was the need of both countries to have free access to the Amazon and Putumayo in order to develop their respective trading interests. It was clearly in the interests of both countries to secure agreement on this matter, and rapid progress was made at Rio. It was concluded that a free-trade area should be established between the two countries in the Upper Amazon, that each country should treat the national flag of the other as if it were its own, that neither should use forced or sweated labour, and that there should be a common external tariff. A three-member commission, appointed by Colombia, Peru and Brazil, should supervise the agreements.

At the same time, there was agreement on the demilitarization of the frontier, to be supervised by a technical commission appointed jointly. With all these issues settled, there was no further obstacle to agreement on the frontier problem. Peru agreed formally to restore the territory of Leticia to Colombia, and to reaffirm the original Boundary Treaty of 1922, the validity of which had never been radically questioned by either side.

On 25 May 1934, the governments of Peru and Colombia informed the Secretary General of the League of Nations that they had finally concluded a 'Protocol of Peace, Friendship and Co-operation', which put an end to the dispute between them. And on 19 June the territory of Leticia was solemnly handed over by the Commission to a delegate of the Colombian government, and the Commission was dissolved.

For almost the last time in its history the League was able to score up a qualified success, and to enjoy high prestige in Latin America. It had at least demonstrated that, where the will to peace was present on both sides, the machinery of the neutral commission could be an invaluable aid in separating combatants and assisting towards a negotiated settlement.

CONCLUSIONS

A general survey of the frontier disputes we have analysed may lead to a general conclusion concerning the role of the League of Nations in international peace-making.

In no case except that of Leticia is it possible to say that the final outcome of the dispute was radically different because of the presence of the League. In each case, rather, the dispute was resolved basically by the interplay of power between the disputants. Vilna went to its occupiers; the Chaco was divided according to the relative power of Bolivia and Paraguay; the Mosul was held by Britain because Turkey was not powerful enough to dislodge her; the Aalands remained in the hands of their occupiers. Albania was only saved because Britain suddenly intervened. Even in the case of Leticia, where the League actually mediated an exchange of territory from Peru to Colombia, the crucial event seems to have been a change of power-structure, a coup d'état within Peru itself.

All this is true. Yet the assumption of cynicism is false, and derives largely from a false antithesis of might and right. The two terms are not so easily separable.

To say that these disputes were resolved in accordance with power structures is not to say that they were resolved contrary to justice. The power situation was to some extent based on rights, and gave rise to rights.

If Zeligowsky captured Vilna easily in a wave of patriotic zeal, it was partly because Vilna was more Polish than Lithuanian, and because it was surrounded by Polish territory. If Paraguay was able finally to muster greater force in support of her claim to the Chaco, this was not unconnected with the fact that she had colonized the region with much greater vigour than Bolivia. If Albania survived at all in 1918 to claim the support of the League, it was partly because of the sheer vigour of her self-assertion as a coherent entity in spite of the very confused situation, and it was through this assertion as much as through legal argumentation that she proved her right to exist.

This does not mean, however, that the League acted as a mere spectator, rubber-stamping the status quo. On occasions League action and debate functioned as a catalyst to direct the exercise of power and to modify the course of events.

Although a change of government in Peru was the crucial event which enabled the Peruvians to change position over Leticia, there is no doubt that the expression through the League of an embryonic world public-opinion on the matter, and the open conflict between Peru and the League Council, must have influenced the new government to change direction. It was easy then to include a volte-face on Leticia as part of the general rejection of the previous dictatorship. Similarly, although Lloyd George may have decided in Britain's own interests suddenly to throw in all his weight behind Albania, he would certainly have been strengthened in his moral resolve in this matter by the idealism of national independence which had been focussed on the Albanian affair through the League, thus arousing world-wide concern.

Even where no difference in the actual course of events can be ascribed to the existence of the League, it is not without importance that issues were debated in terms of international justice, that nations were obliged to state their cases in an international forum and to use principles which would find universal acceptance. The Aalands remained with Finland; but their attribution to Finland had much more *meaning* than it could have had if the dispute had not been the subject of international negotiation and arbitration; and the debate over the principles involved, which is still open, may yet influence the course of history in ways we cannot foresee.

What we find in the League initiatives are not so much dramatic interventions which change the status quo, as a focus where pressures can find equilibrium, where neutral opinion can be brought to bear on remote but potentially dangerous disputes, where patterns of justice can begin to emerge from the interplay of politics. At the same time, administrative techniques were developed – notably the Commissions of Enquiry in the Mosul and in the Aaland Islands, and the Administrative Commission in Leticia – which were invaluable aids to international conciliation.

In these respects League experience retains its validity today.

BIBLIOGRAPHY

(1) The primary source-materials for this chapter are the official publications of the League of Nations. Numerous documents relate to the disputes considered, but by far the most important are:

The Question of the Frontier between Turkey and Iraq: 16 July 1925, Report to the Council by the Commission instituted by the Council Resolution of 30 September 1924. C 400 M 147 1925 VII.

The Dispute between Bolivia and Paraguay: Report of the Chaco Commission, 11 May 1934. C 154 M 64 1934 VII.

Documents concerning the Dispute between Poland and Lithuania: Supplement No. 4 to the Official Journal, 4 December 1920.

Albania: Final Report of the Commission of Inquiry, 6 April 1923, Extract No. 14 from the Official Journal. C 259 1923 VII.

The Dispute between Colombia and Peru: 16 March 1933, Colombia's Appeal under Article 15 of the Covenant (Draft Report of the Council). C 194 M 91 1933 VII.

The Aaland Islands Question: (*a*) Report of the Committee of Jurists, October 1920 (Special Supplement No. 3 to the Official Journal); (*b*) Report of the Committee of Rapporteurs, 16 April 1921. Council Document B 7 21/68/106.

(2) In addition, the following background books are of some value:

Wainhouse, D. A., *International Peace Observation*, Baltimore 1966.

Walters, F. P., *A History of the League of Nations*, London: OUP for RIAA, 1952.

Zimmern, A., *The League of Nations and the Rule of Law*, London 1939.

3 THE UNITED NATIONS AND FRONTIER DISPUTES

Alan James

The UN's attempts to resolve frontier disputes may be divided into two broad categories. The first consists of those measures which are immediately related to a settlement, in that they have to do with its negotiation or execution. An impartial fact-finding mission, for example, may be set up to lay the groundwork for an agreement, or a mediator may make direct efforts to obtain one. Alternatively, UN administration of a disputed area, on a long- or short-term basis, may be a valuable ingredient in a settlement, as may its supervision of the withdrawal of foreign troops across a disturbed border.

Such patching-up operations contrast with activities of a second, prophylactic type, which simply try to put a halt to provocative or threatening behaviour. This may be done by calling for restraint or by the dispatch of a mission to the frontier in question, to observe, tranquillize, or obstruct the parties. If successful, a move of this kind may also be sufficient to take the dispute off the danger list. More often, however, the issue with which a preventive operation is called upon to deal will be of a surface character only; further and different treatment will be necessary to eliminate the cause of tension. Thus prophylaxis will generally be seen as the first step in a two-stage process; as a prerequisite for patching-up. That can be attempted once the temperature has been lowered, and it is by no means uncommon for a prophylactic mission to be continued beyond the crisis which brought it into being, so that the work of conciliation will not be jeopardized.

It happens, however, that in respect of frontier, as of other, disputes the UN has achieved greater note as a prophylactic than as a patching-up agency.[1] For, whereas it has made a significant contribution towards keeping violence in check in a number of dangerous areas, its endeavours to settle these, and other, problems have been markedly less successful. The two outstanding examples of this are the UN's activities regarding the Arab–Israel conflict in the Middle East and that between India and Pakistan over Kashmir. Throughout the twenty-year history of each of these disputes the UN has been trying to maintain calm along the demarcation lines between the parties. In both cases its attempts have been interrupted by war. But it can plausibly be argued that the two situations would have been markedly more turbulent in the absence of representatives of the UN. The Organization's conciliatory efforts, on the other hand, despite the periodic spur which has been supplied by the outbreak of hostilities, have made no advance in either area.

This imbalance has attracted critical attention. Some have suggested that it reflects certain technical shortcomings in the UN itself – in the methods it has used, the skill with which it has employed them, or in its understanding of international disputes. On this view, what is needed is greater efficiency in the pursuit of pacific settlement. It may be doubted, however, whether this is an adequate appreciation. Talent and techniques doubtless have a part to play, and it may be that their absence would be fatal for the ameliorative enterprise. But their presence does not guarantee its success. They may be necessary but they are not sufficient, nor, perhaps, even crucial conditions for the ending of border problems. Of much greater importance is the attitude of the parties towards the question of a settlement and the suggestion that the UN should help in securing it.

If both disputants are anxious to bring their quarrel to an end, they may well be glad to utilize the UN for this purpose, and may even be encouraged to move in a conciliatory direction by the

Organization's offer of its services. However, a readiness to settle is not necessarily accompanied by a welcome for the idea of third-party assistance. And where an amicable outcome seems remote – whether on account of an uncompromising attitude on each side or the dominance of the state in favour of change – the suggestion that the UN should become involved may receive particularly short shrift. It is the case that the force of such objections may be lessened by the exact nature of the role which is envisaged for the UN. A plan for an international investigation with a view to the public formulation of terms which are thought to be fair and just, for example, will probably meet much more hostility than the proposal that the UN should merely try to bring the parties to an agreement. But that is just another way of saying that the willingness of states to let the UN intervene in their affairs is in inverse proportion to the degree of embarrassment which they think they could suffer at its hands.

Hence the UN's ability to play a significant role in the settlement of border disputes will often turn on whether it is able to induce the parties to agree to its participation as an intermediary, to accept the solution it has proposed, or, with its help, to make serious efforts to obtain a settlement. However, the pressure which would usually be needed to secure these results is not at all easy to arrange, and may be quite unobtainable if the obdurate state is one of the Great Powers – a situation which reflects the facts of international life rather than the UN's constitutional structure or membership pattern. Third parties may sometimes be ready to demand a cessation of hostilities, a straightforward, negative act which has no necessary bearing on the eventual outcome. Such a move may incur the displeasure of one and possibly both disputants, but not, probably, their lasting enmity. Support for a settlement, on the other hand, implies, at one point or another, a commitment to specific and formal terms. Diplomatically speaking, this is a much more hazardous course. The relatively permanent alienation of at least one of the parties cannot be ruled out, and there may well be substantial difficulties over the enforcement of the approved plan, even though the states concerned are not of the first rank.

In any event, therefore, the UN would probably have found that patching-up often presents considerable problems. And as things have turned out, the obstacles in its way have been greatly increased by the character of international relations since the end of the Second World War. For the mutual hostility and distrust of the Powers has usually prevented the UN from organizing effective pressure in favour of pacific settlement. This has been so not just with regard to disputes within the spheres of influence which have been developed by each of the two super-powers but also vis-à-vis the less powerful states of the third world, exclusiveness in the first case and competitiveness in the second having drastically limited the UN's role. Thus the Security Council has not had a chance to play the part which was envisaged for it by the UN Charter: that of the international society's powerful board of directors.

Another, independent, factor which has had a similar effect has been the growth and popularity of previously unorthodox ideas regarding the right relationship between big and small states. The large number of states which have emerged from colonial tutelage during the last quarter of a century have been very touchy about anything which appears to infringe their new-found independence and freedom. Hence the suggestion that their behaviour should be critically scrutinized, or, even more, that another's claim to some of their national soil is a suitable question for impartial investigation or adjudication, has been particularly unpopular. In itself, this is nothing new, except for the size of the potentially resentful constituency. Additionally, however, the smaller powers have expressed their views in terms of a theory of international relations, asserting, with a confidence and vigour which has grown with their number, the democratic character of the international enterprise. Specifically, they have interpreted this to mean that they have a right not to be ordered around by their larger fellows. This, too, on its own, would have little impact on events. But the catalytic element in the situation has been the response of the Great Powers, who, to a large extent, appear to have accepted the validity of the small powers' claims. In theory, that is. Practice has not always followed the same lines. But this development in the international society's standards of propriety has by no means been without importance, and may be expected to outlive the Cold War.

A further element which has influenced the UN's capacity for playing a significant role in the settlement of frontier disputes has been the growth of scepticism regarding the idea of impartiality. This has close links with the ideological conflict of the post-1945 world, but is also related to the speedy emergence of states which are critical of the old order and have grievances regarding it. Contemporary trends in sociological and philosophical analysis have doubtless contributed to the same trend. Thus the theory that an impartial approach, combined with thoroughness, will disclose all aspects of a problem has not always been well received in the fifties and sixties. And the belief that a group of good and true men, after examining a conflict, can arrive at a solution which is obviously just has been even less popular.

As a result of these factors, the UN has been unable to make much use of the patching-up device which served the League of Nations so well in its early years in respect of frontier disputes – that of disinterested examination of the facts. In the trust territories of Togoland and the Cameroons, where its responsibilities gave it a special position, the UN satisfied itself as to the future of these areas by various investigatory measures.[2] A mission of inquiry was also sent to Eritrea, the disposition of which came to the UN under the Italian Peace Treaty of 1947. In these ways the UN was hoping that the public implementation of the principle of self-determination in the fairest possible manner would avert any disputes as to where the frontier should run, and to all intents and purposes the desired end seems to have been achieved. However, it is vastly more difficult for UN investigators to obtain an invitation to the metropolitan or colonial territory of a sovereign state – where border questions may also give rise to greater passion.

Kashmir is a case in point. In 1947 this predominantly Muslim area acceded to India on the understanding that its ultimate future would be decided by its people. Within a short time it had been divided, de facto, between Pakistan and India, and the circumstances which produced this result also led to the matter being taken to the UN. From the very beginning the UN has worked on the assumption that the dispute should be settled by means of a free plebiscite, but all its endeavours to arrange one have been unsuccessful. None of the Great Powers have opposed the idea, but, equally, none of them have been willing even to contemplate the imposition of the favoured procedure – a course which would present extreme physical difficulties and would be politically disastrous. Thus, it has been left to the parties to take the matter forward, which, here, has been a recipe for stalemate. At first Pakistan was the more difficult of the two, on account of her concern that the plebiscite should indeed be free. Then India began to drag her feet, and lately she has openly disavowed the idea of a plebiscite, asserting that there can be no question regarding the legitimacy of her position in Kashmir.

In these circumstances there is clearly no hope of the UN being able to proceed on the basis of the original plan. Even if, by some chance, it was able to do so, this would be no guarantee of an amicable settlement. For it is not the procedure of investigation which produces an agreement but the disposition of the parties – voluntary or induced – to accept its results. This has been made abundantly clear by two other post-war frontier disputes in which the UN was able to examine the facts, Palestine and Malaysia, for in neither of them did the UN's activities have much real bearing on the outcome.

After the First World War Palestine was administered by Britain under a mandate from the League of Nations. By 1947 the other parts of the former Ottoman Empire which had been treated in this way had reached independence, but in the case of

Palestine the achievement of this goal was obstructed by what seemed an insuperable obstacle – the deep enmity between the indigenous Arabs and the Jews, most of whom had entered the country following Britain's and the League's determination that it should become a national home for the Jewish people. Having failed to bring the two local parties to an agreement, and faced with mounting disorder and terrorism, Britain decided to throw the problem in the UN's lap, making it clear that she was definitely going to leave at an early date. This led to the appointment, in May 1947, of an eleven-member Special Committee on Palestine, whose task was to investigate the situation and find a solution for it. The majority of the Committee recommended that Palestine be partitioned, with Jerusalem coming under an international regime, and in November 1947 the General Assembly adopted this plan. However, although this decision was accepted by the Jewish Agency, it was uncompromisingly rejected by the Arabs. Thus the UN had no chance of arranging a peaceful transfer of power in accordance with its scheme, and, not surprisingly, none of the Powers were prepared to try to impose it. On Britain's withdrawal in May 1948 war broke out, and by the following year the new state of Israel had secured a larger part of Palestine than had been allocated to it by the UN, the bulk of the rest of the country coming under Jordanian control.

In the case of Malaysia, by contrast, the situation developed in accordance with the UN's findings, but this was fortuitous inasmuch as it was clear that those in control never had any intention of departing from their basic plan, whatever the UN's judgment on the matter. The state of Malaya had been created in 1957, and in 1961 it agreed to Britain's proposal that it should be transformed into Malaysia by the addition of some colonies in the immediate area, including North Borneo and Sarawak. At first this produced no problems; then, in January 1963, President Sukarno of Indonesia denounced the idea; but in June he withdrew his objections on condition that the UN Secretary General was able to ascertain that the scheme had the support of the people.

This concession was immediately put in jeopardy by an announcement that the new state would come into being on 31 August, but saved by Malaya's willingness to postpone the date. Britain was not happy about this, nor with the thought of the UN sending inspectors to her colonies, but she reluctantly fell into line and in the latter part of August the inspection got under way, being conducted on U Thant's own authority by a small team from the UN Secretariat. However, before it was complete, Britain and Malaya announced that the new state of Malaysia, including North Borneo and Sarawak, would in any event be established on 16 September. This gratuitous insult to Indonesia and the UN made the latter's findings (which confirmed public support for Malaysia) of academic interest only, and precipitated the 'confrontation' between Indonesia and Malaysia, which continued until Sukarno's fall from effective power three years later.

The factors which have militated against investigation as a means of settling frontier disputes have also influenced the use of mediation, but not in quite the same way. For inasmuch as a mediator is not usually required to advance his own proposals for a settlement but is chiefly concerned with establishing common ground between the parties, the current suspicion concerning the idea of impartiality is less of an obstruction to such work. Clearly, the mediator must be trusted by all concerned, and finding such a person may not be a simple task on account of the prevailing tendency to identify individual and national prejudices. But it is likely to be much easier for the parties to agree that a particular person can be expected to act fairly in trying to reconcile their positions than to accept that a certain individual or group can be relied upon to make a just appreciation of the merits of their case. Then, too, the fact that mediation will probably not result in the proposal of a scheme which calls for implementation or rejection makes it a more acceptable procedure, in that it threatens less of an encroachment on the parties' independence. But by the same token successful mediation is, if anything, likely to be more demanding so far as the necessity for pressure is concerned.

Acceptance of investigation implies, up to a point, that the outcome of the procedure will also be accepted. No such corollary is attached to mediation – so that if an agreement is to result there must often be an imperative call for it from interested and powerful third parties or, more effectively, telling support for the solution to which the mediatory effort points. All of which goes far towards explaining why the UN has sometimes engaged in mediation but has not achieved notable success in this field.[3]

Besides being active in the pre-settlement period, the UN may also have a part to play in the implementation of agreements regarding border problems, by, for example, controlling a disputed area for a time or supervising the withdrawal of troops. In these circumstances there should be no serious difficulties on the score of impartiality, as all that is required of the UN is a manifest disposition to help in the fair execution of already agreed terms. It should not be too hard for the Organization to offer and give satisfaction in this respect. This might seem to imply a relatively insignificant task for the UN, but such a deduction would be incorrect. The smooth implementation of a settlement is an important enough matter, and could turn on the assistance of an uninvolved third party. And, beyond this, it could be that obtaining an agreement in the first place is dependent on the possibility of the UN playing a post-agreement role.

The most ambitious opportunity of this kind which is open to the UN is for it to act as the permanent international government of a contested region. Especially if the area in question has an established identity of its own, this is, theoretically, an excellent way of solving a tricky dispute, and plans towards this end were approved by the UN in 1947 in respect of both Trieste and Jerusalem. However, neither came to fruition, the latter because the local situation prevented it, and the former on account of the rivalry of the Great Powers. This serves to illustrate that even if the parties are agreeable to such schemes – which can by no means be relied upon – their operation depends on the potential governors (i.e. the relevant UN members) being broadly agreed on their desirability.

In the somewhat analogous case of the Saar, for example, which was administered by the League of Nations for fifteen years after the First World War, the major League Powers were prepared to co-operate in the execution of the Organization's responsibilities. In respect of Trieste, however, the competition for influence in the territory prevented the Security Council from agreeing on who was to fill the office of governor. Subsequently, the defection of Yugoslavia from the Communist bloc in 1948 induced the Soviet Union to make concessions to get the arrangement under way. But the same event, together with the heightening of the Cold War, contributed towards a marked loss of Western interest in the idea of international government, and a growing appreciation of the advantages of splitting the territory between the two local claimants, Italy and Yugoslavia, a course which was eventually followed in 1954.

An alternative governmental arrangement which can sometimes assist in the resolution of frontier disputes consists of the transfer of the area concerned from one party to the other through international hands. This, in effect, is what happened in respect of the district of Leticia, which, beginning in June 1933, was administered by the League of Nations for a year as a means of handing it back from Peru to Colombia. Likewise in 1962–63, West New Guinea was ruled by the UN for a period of seven months, the territory being passed to the UN by the Netherlands and then, in accordance with the agreement which brought this thirteen-year-old dispute to an end, transferred to Indonesia. The chief merit of such a procedure is that it permits the departing state to go without a complete loss of face, inasmuch as the immediate surrender is to an international body and not to the enemy. This also has the advantage of allowing a smoother transfer of power than that which might occur if the matter was left to the rival claimants.

Similar considerations may influence the use of another device which the UN may employ in an attempt to ensure the uneventful winding-up of a frontier dispute: international supervision of the withdrawal of foreign troops, or of a border which is to be closed to illegal traffic. In the former case a UN supervisory role may have an important bearing on the orderliness of the operation, and if a unilateral departure is being made the face-saving properties of a UN presence may be greatly valued. An arrangement of this nature may also be welcomed in both kinds of case on account of the promise which it holds out that the solution which has been agreed upon is likely to be implemented. For if a frontier has been violated, openly or covertly, the offended party may not have much faith in the other's offer to withdraw its troops or stop its underhand intervention. If, however, the latter is also willing to submit to international inspection, his verbal and written assurances are likely to be given greater credence, which may not just increase the viability of an agreement but may be a prerequisite for it. The international element can make up for what could be a crucial lack of good faith.

There have been three instances of the UN operating in this manner. The first arose out of the abortive three-power assault on Egypt in 1956, which resulted in the dispatch of the UN Emergency Force (Unef) to Egypt once world-wide pressure (and particularly that of the United States) had secured a cease-fire. The Force has chiefly attracted attention for its prophylactic activities on the Egypt–Israel border,[4] but at first its task was to supervise the withdrawal of the invaders – standing between them and the Egyptian forces and receiving vacated territory for transfer to the lawful sovereign. In this way Unef lubricated the process of withdrawal and also enabled Britain and France to pretend that the UN was assuming the necessary functions which, in the absence of an international initiative, they had felt bound to begin. The second situation which led to the UN's involvement in a post-settlement, supervisory capacity arose out of foreign intervention in civil war in the Yemen, large numbers of troops from the United Arab Republic (as Egypt was now officially called) supporting the new republican government and neighbouring Saudi Arabia assisting the deposed royalists in various ways. By an agreement reached in 1963 the two outsiders promised to disengage, and plans were made for the process to be observed by the UN, rather more than a hundred Yugoslav troops (transferred from Unef) and a Canadian air unit forming the supervisory body. Thirdly, in 1965, following the three-week war between India and Pakistan, which arose out of the Kashmir situation but soon encompassed all of their borders in the west, it was agreed that the UN should supervise the withdrawal of troops. To implement this the observation group already in Kashmir was doubled in size to about ninety, and a new group was set up consisting of a hundred and eighteen observers drawn from the armed forces of ten countries. To a large extent this activity reflected a rare show of Great Power unity and determination in favour of the liquidation of the conflict.

It is significant, however, that in none of these cases was the withdrawal operation entirely straightforward. Britain and France made some difficulties about leaving Egypt, and Israel many more, so much so that she was induced to vacate two areas of particular importance to her – the Gaza strip and Sharm-el-Sheikh (which commands the entrance to the Gulf of Aqaba) – only after very considerable American pressure. Then, the UN group which was sent to India in 1965 found that for several months it was engaged in trying to maintain the cease-fire rather than supervise a mutual withdrawal, and it was not until the Soviet Union took a hand at Tashkent early in 1966 (expressing an attitude which was shared by the United States) that the restoration of the status quo ante got under way. And in respect of the third case, the Yemen, so little progress was made towards implementing the disengagement agreement – the UAR being the chief defaulter – that the UN supervisory group was drastically reduced in size towards the end of 1963 and wholly withdrawn during the following year. Clearly, the fact of a formal settlement is not enough, and even its international supervision is no guarantee that it will be executed. For this the parties must continue to be interested in a settlement, either on account of their own desires or because of the enthusiasm of others who are both concerned and influential. If such states have had a big role in obtaining the agreement in the first place there is also some hope that they will put their weight behind its execution. In this connection it is worth noting that there was much less international concern about the Yemen situation than about the Suez crisis and the India–Pakistan war, which perhaps helps to explain why the Yemen settlement foundered. Another factor here, however, was that the UAR was a state which the Powers were particularly anxious not to offend.

The second type of mission which the UN has established in relation to frontier disputes attempts to provide a basis for a settlement by curbing provocation or violence. This indirect, prophylactic approach towards the resolution of conflict has often elicited more co-operation from the parties than that which concerns itself with the immediate conclusion of a substantive agreement. For whereas the latter may well require the renunciation of part or all of a state's case, the effort to keep belligerent posturing or behaviour in check still allows those concerned to look forward to their later triumph. Also, both by reason of its urgency and because it does not call for a decision on the merits of the issue, a prophylactic move is much more likely to win the support, at least in principle, of uninvolved third parties than an attempt to get disputants to accept terms of settlement which independent investigators or mediators deem appropriate. Hence it is not surprising that the UN has frequently been able to act with greater preventive than conciliatory effect.

However, it is not to be assumed that quarrelling states always take kindly to prophylactic proposals. One or both of them may be intent on making trouble, or may lack what others, from their vantage point above the fray, regard as a proper respect for the opinion of the UN. In these circumstances the Organization's capacity to act prophylactically will probably depend on strong and concerted action by some if not all of its chief members.

Should one or more of them be resolutely opposed to a UN preventive move, it is unlikely, for much more than constitutional reasons, that the Organization will be able to act effectively.

The hope is, of course, and it is very evident in the UN Charter, that the clear readiness of the major powers to use force to repel aggression will usually be a sufficient deterrent to those who might be tempted to misbehave. Thus security will be maintained by the threat rather than the actuality of a collective resort to arms. The classic instance is the frontier skirmish between Greece and Bulgaria in 1925, when a peremptory telegram from the French Chairman of the League Council, subsequently backed by the Council itself, called for an immediate cessation of fighting and the withdrawal of troops. There have been two or three post-1945 analogies: the Security Council's resolution of 15 July 1948 'order[ing]' a Palestinian cease-fire within three days at a time to be determined by the UN's Mediator; that of 20 September 1965 during the India–Pakistan war, when the Council 'demand[ed]' a cease-fire and went on to specify the day and time at which it was to come into force; and a similar resolution of 7 June 1967 addressed to the contestants in the Arab–Israel war. In less extreme circumstances the Council, in April 1956, asked the Secretary General to visit the Middle East in an attempt to exert a cooling influence on a rapidly deteriorating situation. And in November 1967 the Council approved the Secretary General's dispatch of a high-ranking aide to the eastern Mediterranean in an endeavour to avert the war which seemed likely on account of an inter-communal crisis in Cyprus.[5]

However, these cases amply demonstrate that the effectiveness of such activities is closely related to the extent to which they are likely to be supported by telling action. In 1967 Turkey was persuaded to back down over Cyprus, but this was much more the result of the independent efforts of an American envoy than of the UN's. The Secretary General's travels in 1956 resulted in written undertakings to observe the cease-fire provisions of the 1949 armistice agreements, but serious incidents soon began to recur, aided by the fact that the Great Powers were unwilling to take a strong line on the need for Middle Eastern peace. Two of them, indeed, were before long plotting to break it themselves. They all presented a united front eleven years later in the six days war, the resolution of 7 June 1967 being passed unanimously. But they were not in control of the situation, and although cease-fires were reached between all the parties within a matter of days, this was much more a reflection of Israel's victories than of the authority of the Powers. Two years earlier, in the India–Pakistan war, the resolution of 20 September, in which all the Powers concurred, had the desired effect. But here, too, account has to be taken of the fact that by this time, with three weeks of largely inconclusive war behind them, the parties were probably in any case ready to bring their conflict to a halt. The Security Council's resolution of 15 July 1948 remains the most notable of the UN's démarches. It only just obtained the required number of votes, but, as Britain, France, and the United States all voted for it with some enthusiasm and the Soviet Union did no more than abstain, it called for serious consideration, and was heeded by the warring contestants. It may be, however, that both the parties and the interested outsiders soon realized that there was little the latter were both able and willing to do about the Palestine situation, for the truce was infringed a number of times during the next six months, and on none of these occasions did the Council display its earlier determination. Undoubtedly, the UN has never matched the League's efficiency in the Greece–Bulgaria incident. Here, with the Locarno Treaty only a week behind them, the Powers were in just the right mood to assert themselves in the cause of European tranquillity, the more so as it would have been relatively easy for them to bring pressure on either party. And, for their part, the disputants were in no position to act defiantly.

Even at the best of times, however, it cannot be assumed that the Powers are as prepared as they were in 1925 to go to some trouble to enforce their will. And times are not always the best, in which event the Powers may not possess a common will. Certainly, this has only rarely been the position since 1945. As a result, those border disputes which could be interpreted as reflections of the Cold War have usually been dealt with outside the UN, by means of alliances and bilateral associations. Others have been discussed within the Organization, but the overall suspicion and distrust among the Powers has been a major obstacle in the way of anything approaching the resolute prophylactic action which is envisaged by the Charter.

Nevertheless, although the UN has not been able to threaten or use force in order to contain border quarrels, it has engaged in a variety of lesser preventive operations. For its members have generally been favourably disposed towards the idea that the Organization should assist in the discouragement of violent change – provided this can be done non-violently. And the states concerned have sometimes been prepared to agree to the UN's involvement in their dispute, perhaps out of strength, but usually also in the light of the consideration that the stopping of a war does not necessarily injure their bargaining position on the basic issue. Moreover, opportunities for this kind of UN activity have been increased by virtue of the fact that, unlike patching-up, it is sometimes enough to have the co-operation of one party only. This is not much use if the other is clearly spoiling for a fight, for the UN is no more prepared to take a forceful line in that kind of situation than it is willing to impose itself upon a 'host' country. But in less critical situations, and provided that at least one party will have a UN presence on its soil (and only for as long as both those factors hold good), the UN may well be able to make some contribution towards the lessening of tension.

One device which it has used towards this end has been that of observation. The procedure here is to dispatch a team of investigators to a disturbed border in the hope that the promise and actuality of its report will cause those who are making trouble to restrain themselves. Two major instances of this are the UN groups which were active in Greece in the late 1940s and that which was sent to the Lebanon in 1958. In the first case the problem arose out of the attempts by Greece's three Communist neighbours to subvert her shaky right-wing government by helping its guerrilla opponents. First, the Security Council sent a Commission of Investigation, and then, in October 1947, the General Assembly established an eleven-member Special Committee on the Balkans, which was not disbanded until 1951. By that time the danger had largely subsided, and much of the credit for this was commonly attributed to the vigilance of the UN Committee. Likewise in respect of the Lebanon, the threat to that country's political independence which was perceived to emanate from the Syrian province of the UAR evaporated not long after the arrival of the UN Group, which had been built up to about six hundred men by the time of its withdrawal at the end of the year. This result, too, was often claimed to reflect the efficacy of the UN operation.

However, it is very doubtful whether the UN had anything like a major influence on either situation. In the case of the Balkans, the defection of Yugoslavia from the Communist bloc in 1948 together with the growing strength of the American-aided Greek Government were much more significant factors. And in respect of the Lebanon there is some doubt as to the existence of a serious threat from the UAR. The UN Observation Group certainly failed to find it – to the extreme annoyance of its host. But quite apart from this, considerable weight must be attached to two factors. First, to the determination of the United States not to allow the Lebanese Government to be toppled by dissident elements within or beyond the country, a determination which was manifested by the dispatch of a 14,000 strong American force to the Lebanon following the left-wing revolution in Iraq. And, secondly, to the early and peaceful settlement of the internal political crisis which was intimately linked with the charge of UAR intervention.

It does not necessarily follow, however, that these procedures should be regarded as of little importance. For it may be doubted whether those who favour the dispatch of such missions do so in the expectation that they will have much of a direct effect on the local situation. Probably they are more often regarded as chiefly significant for propaganda purposes – and in this respect the Balkans Committee certainly gave good value. Thus the UN will usually send observers to a frontier dispute only if it is anticipated that they will file a report which will be approved by the majority of members. Unpopular or isolated states are unlikely, therefore, to get this kind of help. In 1954, for example, the United States quickly squashed the idea that Guatemala's border should be watched by the UN. And in 1961 Portugal's readiness to have disinterested observers examine the frontier between Goa and India met with no response. In short, the device is generally a means of assisting a country whose ideology or behaviour finds favour with the UN.

The second prophylactic arrangement which the UN has resorted to in respect of frontier disputes, by contrast with the one just considered, requires the co-operation of all the parties. It is an extension of the first, in that it employs observers and hopes that their presence and reports may have some deterrent effect. But it goes much further, its essential and distinguishing aspect being its reliance on contacts with the military forces of both sides to produce a dampening effect whenever the frontier situation threatens to get out of hand. It endeavours to do this by assisting in the settlement of incidents and working for a cease-fire whenever shooting breaks out. In the event of its efforts being unsuccessful it may be able to appeal to the political authorities. But its basic task is to try to keep the temperature down at the frontier: it is a low-level but important anti-escalation device.

It might seem that this is an eminently desirable arrangement whenever hostile forces confront each other. But it is unlikely that the parties will show much enthusiasm for it, even if neither of them want war, for no state likes being supervised by foreign officers. This is especially true where, as here, their activities relate to matters which bear closely on national security. Perhaps, therefore, it is no coincidence that the UN's two operations of this kind arose out of disputes which were already before its political organs: Palestine and Kashmir.

In Palestine the UN's sedative operation has been conducted by its Truce Supervision Organization (Untso). This body, which had no formal beginning, arose out of the arrangements made by the UN Mediator to watch over the truces which are called for by the Security Council in May and July 1948. Then, in the Armistice Agreements of 1949 provision was made for supervision on a continuing basis by the UN, and thus, although the office of Mediator was wound up in August 1949, the supervisory framework which he had established lived on. At first no more than three dozen officers, drawn from three countries, were employed to check on the honouring of the armistice, but Untso was soon expanded in size and source, having been increased fourfold in both respects by 1967. The intervening years clearly revealed that Untso was no obstacle to a calculated war, Israel's Sinai campaign of 1956 and the six day war of 1967 being impeded not at all by the presence of military observers from the UN. This period also underlined the fact that Untso's operations were dependent on the co-operation of the parties, for from 1956 Israel refused to have anything to do with its personnel on her Egyptian border and she insists that all the other supervisory arrangements were destroyed by the 1967 war. But until 1956 on the Egyptian front and 1967 on the three other Arab–Israel borders, Untso's role, albeit subsidiary, was most valuable. For in this highly charged context both sides would often have found some difficulty in making the first cooling move once firing had broken out, as it very commonly did. On such occasions, however, Untso was able to appeal for and arrange a local cease-fire, and so brought many dangerous bouts of shooting to an early halt.

Untso continues to act in this way in respect of two of the three new demarcation lines between Israel and her Arab neighbours, despite Israel's denunciation of the 1949 armistices. For its observers were allowed to establish themselves on the Syrian cease-fire line immediately following the 1967 war, and within a month or so Israel and the UAR agreed that Untso personnel should be posted along the Suez Canal, the new de facto frontier. As before, Untso will be unable to have any influence on governmental plans regarding war and peace[6] but it will continue to exercise as great a sedative influence as the overall political situation allows.

The history of the UN's Military Observer Group in India and Pakistan (Unmogip) along the cease-fire line in Kashmir parallels that of Untso very closely. It arose out of a call for military advice sent out by the UN Commission which was appointed in 1948 to investigate and mediate. But no sooner had some advice arrived in the shape of a Belgian general than he and his staff were required to report on the observance of the cease-fire which came into force on 1 January 1949. Two years later references were being made to the Military Observer Group as a separate entity, and it was clear that its activities in respect of Kashmir were very similar to those being performed by Untso on the Arab–Israel borders. Unmogip's initial strength was in the region of thirty officers, but it soon doubled in size and has remained constant at about that figure, its personnel being drawn from a variety of states who meet with both India's and Pakistan's approval. It was unable to prevent the 1965 war, but at other times has been able to assist the parties to implement their relatively pacific dispositions, its task being greatly eased, as compared with Untso's, by the co-operation it has received from the armed forces on both sides of the cease-fire line. Like Untso, Unmogip seems unlikely to experience an early withdrawal on account of the settlement of the dispute which brought it into being.

The third and final way in which the UN may help to keep a tense border quiet is by establishing a sizeable group between the lines of the two sides, the object being to keep the hostile armies out of each others sights and to prevent infiltration. There is no question here, in the present situation, either of the UN demanding to be let in, or of it being prepared to defend the threatened frontier by force of arms. Its admission depends on at least one of the parties agreeing to its presence – this being a device which can work even though it is established on only one side of the frontier. And the major condition for the success of such an operation is a desire on both sides for a quiet border. If one of them is set on war, or significant troublemaking, there is no future for a UN interpository force. But if the situation is not as bad as that, the UN can make an important contribution towards helping the parties to live in peace.

An example of this is the UN Emergency Force which was established in Egypt following the Suez crisis of 1956. After the invading forces had left, Unef took up a position on the Egyptian side of that country's border with Israel, with a small outpost at Sharm-el-Sheikh, at the entrance to the Gulf of Aqaba. At the outset Unef comprised about 6,000 men drawn from ten countries. Three of the contributors soon withdrew their contingents, and the size of the Force was gradually reduced to about 3,400. However, this had no apparent effect on its efficiency, and for ten years the Egypt–Israel border was exceedingly quiet, this being in marked contrast to the previous seven years. It was, indeed, increasingly provocative infringements by Egyptian commando units which had led to Israel's attack in 1956. Unef's primary task was to prevent the repetition of such incidents, and also, therefore, to remove the danger that one or more of them might precipitate a full-scale war. It did this with great success, but the true nature of its contribution was vividly illustrated in May 1967 when, on the UAR's demand, it was withdrawn. The host country had decided to move its troops right up to the frontier and to occupy Sharm-el-Sheikh, and within a matter of weeks war had broken out. So stated, it might appear that had the UN resisted the UAR's demand war might have been averted. But this argument ignores two crucial points. The first is that, whatever the legal position, Unef's presence, in practical terms, depended on the co-operation of the UAR. And secondly, even if Unef had somehow remained, this would not have prevented the UAR from effectively taking over the areas in which it was determined to deploy its troops – and that, not Unef's absence or presence, was the crucial factor in the chain of events which led to war. Unef was able to contribute to peace only for as long as the parties were disposed to act peacefully.

A basically similar role is being played by the UN Force in Cyprus (Unficyp), which since 1964 has been manning the internal frontier between Greek and Turkish Cypriots. Its contribution is more significant than that which would usually be made by a force deployed along an international frontier, for the nature of the situation gives much more latitude to unofficial troublemakers than does a recognized border between two states. Thus the withdrawal of Unficyp would very likely, in the situation which has existed over the last five years, lead to a resumption of civil war on the island even if the leaders of both Greeks and Turks were pacifically inclined. But if one or both sides were eager for a fight, there would be little which Unficyp could do to prevent it. For its part in keeping the peace is dependent on the mutual restraint of all concerned, and particularly of the Cyprus Government, as the more powerful group within the island, and of Turkey, as the stronger of the rival international backers of the two Cypriot communities.

There are those who criticize the UN for its alleged willingness to countenance some of its lengthening prophylactic successes, their assertion being that refractory states ought not to be helped to keep their disputes going ad infinitum. However, the associated idea that in the absence of a UN holding operation the parties would, as it were, be forced to a peaceful settlement seems very questionable. And the belief of some that in that case it would be better to let the disputants fight it out, with a view to producing a realistic and lasting solution, is also one on which some doubt may legitimately be entertained. In any event, it must be noted that the latter approach is unlikely to find much support in the UN. States may not be willing to make many sacrifices in the abstract cause of peace. But equally the prevailing sentiment is against the settlement of disputes by force of arms. For as long as this situation holds, and provided that the parties, for whatever reasons, are pacifically inclined, the likelihood is that the UN will from time to time continue to be used in attempts to contain as well as to settle frontier disputes. Its role may be essentially subordinate, but that is not to say that it is therefore unimportant.

TEXT REFERENCES

1. Frontier disputes are often assumed to fall into two groups: those which are 'local', in that they arise out of skirmishes between adjoining forces, and those which are territorial, meaning that they relate to one party's claim to part of the area controlled by the other. The latter are generally much the more serious, except where local disputes take place in the context of an already hostile relationship. However, there is a third group of frontier issues, which may be termed ideological. They are those cases where a frontier is threatened or infringed not out of local military zeal or in an attempt at territorial rectification but with a view to the subversion of the government which lies within. The dispute manifests itself at the border, but it is not the border's legitimacy but that of the ruling group which is in question. Post-1945 examples of this kind are the Balkans (late 1940s) and Yemen (1962–) disputes, and also, possibly, that concerning the Lebanon (1958). Situations of this nature will, in this essay, be regarded as part of the category 'frontier disputes'.

2. For further information on these as on the other cases discussed in this chapter, see the author's *The Politics of Peace-keeping*, London: Chatto and Windus, for the Institute for Strategic Studies, 1969, which also contains a more extended examination of the theoretical issues considered here.

3. As mediation is dealt with separately in Chapter 5, the UN's use of this technique is not considered further here.

4. See below, pp. 106–7.

5. Although the Cyprus dispute concerns an internal frontier, it has strong international connections: see below, p. 107.

6. Except, perhaps, marginally: it may be that by helping the parties to implement a pacific disposition the UN may also assist in the strengthening of that disposition.

4 REGIONAL ORGANIZATIONS AND FRONTIER DISPUTES

Peter Lyon

This is an age of many new international political boundaries, and of many new regional organizations.[1] The coincidence is not entirely accidental. Both processes are products of a world where rapid and widespread decolonization has taken place. New states, new sovereign entities, have arisen as successors to the overseas empires of West European powers; and what were once colonial frontiers or boundaries have become international boundaries. New states immediately take up a place in the contemporary international political system. But their viability as states, in terms of their political cohesiveness, their state-wide system of order, administration and law, social, educational and other welfare services, is often more nominal than actual, more proclaimed than practised. Even the precise extent of their territories may be unclear or disputed. Nevertheless, newly independent states are at least as eager as older states to enjoy membership in some international inter-governmental organizations and this often includes membership in one or more of a regionalist character.

In order to explore a little further in this chapter what, if any, are the possible roles in boundary disputes of regional organizations it is necessary to clarify some central terms; some because they are terms of art, others in order to avoid the most glaring ambiguities of popular usage.

Regionalism in international politics involves some kind of formalized alignment and of association between adjacent states.

The existence of a regional organization is prima facie evidence of a disposition to co-operate between the members. What actual form each association takes, how extensive its geographical scope, how specific or general its functions, will vary considerably depending on who the participants are, the ostensible issues initially prompting their regionalist association and serving to keep them in association or to drive them apart. Whether, and in what manner, the members actually do co-operate in any very significant manner varies considerably, of course, depending on time, circumstances and issues. Inter-governmental regionalism presupposes independent states; but the fact of independence does not of itself propel regionalist co-operation. One has only to contrast the experience of South Asia, where very little regional co-operation exists, with, say, Central America, to appreciate this rather obvious point.

The growth of regional organizations is a subsidiary and partly a parallel feature of the growth of international organization generally, and is thus something which, though it has precedents in Europe and Latin America in the late-nineteenth century, has experienced a considerable efflorescence globally mostly since 1945 and in Africa only substantially since 1960. In general it should be remembered that when a frontier dispute flares up one or both of the disputants may be members of the same regional organization(s) or of different ones or not members of any. Thus the relevance or irrelevance of regional organizations to any particular boundary dispute obviously can only be at all adequately seen in relation to the particular facts of the particular dispute.

The old legitimacy of territorial form and control exercised by European colonial powers in their respective overseas domains often originated in coercion and conquest, and continued by prescription, wont and usage. In the immediate aftermath of decolonization, and largely irrespective of whether that decolonization proceeded by means of eviction or by a smooth transfer of power and authority, the new dispensation in most cases becomes the guardian and champion of a territory whose extent and configuration is that bequeathed by the former colonial ruler. Usually this territorial shaping originally resulted from the more or less arbitrary actions and the prevailing caprices of circumstance during the colonial power's ascendancy. Nevertheless, while the old colonial territorial forms tend (with remarkably few exceptions) to be the basis for the territorial shapes of the newly independent states, the leaders of most new states insist that their territories are, or must be, newly legitimatized. This new legitimacy is bestowed by appropriate acts of international recognition and respect, accorded through diplomatic channels and by means of international approval expressible through international organizations or appropriate regionalist bodies. Of course regionalism can serve many other, and not always compatible, purposes. For example, a regionalist organization may: assert a sense of common identity; seek to promote mutually profitable common enterprises; provide participants with allies; or provide opportunities whereby to prevent or inhibit fellow-members from consorting with one's actual or potential enemies.

The paradoxical consequence of proliferating regional organizations is, on the one hand, that, because such organizations are founded and premised on the existing territorial configuration of sovereignties, they serve to perpetuate and legitimatize the existing territorial political status quo; and yet, on the other hand, to the extent that they promote trans-boundary contacts, new combinations and co-operative endeavours, they reduce the actual and potential significance and explosiveness of boundaries as fundamental lines of political and other forms of discontinuity. In short, regional organizations may simultaneously help to perpetuate particular boundaries and yet render them less significant. To date the first function probably has been more successful than the second.

There is a fundamental distinction which should be noted as between frontiers and boundaries: a frontier means a zone, and thus has breadth as well as depth, whereas a boundary signifies a line. Precision concerning the distinction between frontiers and boundaries only began to characterize the writing and mapping of experts towards the end of the nineteenth century, and often not before the twentieth century. The names of Lord Curzon and Sir Thomas Holdich,[2] of Durand and McMahon, must feature prominently in any history and explanation of this process – all, of course, drew on considerable experience in India. Empires in the past usually preferred frontiers to boundaries as surrounds for all or part of the peripheries of their territorial jurisdictions. Frontier zones were thus regarded as buffers, or insulation belts, perhaps as neutral zones, but more likely as areas of suzerainty. In the present-day international political system (principally comprising nation-states) boundaries, lines of political delimitation and demarcation, are the prevailing fashion and are sanctioned by current notions of political legitimacy internationally as well as encouraged by modern communications and techniques of map-making. Frontiers seem obsolete, while boundaries are standard form. Boundaries mark the furthest territorial extent of a nation-state. So although even today while popular usage is very loose and inexact concerning the difference between frontiers and boundaries, in this chapter the distinction is regarded as fundamental. After all, territoriality[3] is a necessary if not in itself a sufficient requirement for independent statehood.

Another, and more technical matter (alluded to in passing in the previous paragraph) is of some importance in an understanding of the systematics of boundary-making: the process whereby a frontier zone becomes narrowed down to a boundary-line, and this requires recognition of the difference between delimitation and demarcation.[4] The delimitation of an international boundary is a diplomatic procedure, the business of statesmen, who decide on the principles to be applied in determining the line of demarcation. To define a boundary in words in a treaty is delimitation. Demarcation is done by surveying the actual terrain itself and erecting marking posts or pillars.

A boundary-marking process has four main stages:

(*a*) agreement between the respective governments in principle to settle the matter of their common boundary
(*b*) the delimitation of the boundary in a treaty
(*c*) demarcation of the boundary on the ground
(*d*) administration of the boundary

It is not necessary that all stages must be in strict consecutive order; but all four stages are nevertheless necessary in order to maintain a thoroughgoing and practical boundary policy. As we shall see, work done with the help of a regional organization may on occasions assist an expert and smooth process of boundary-making.

It is not axiomatic that regional organizations are relevant only to new and/or small states and their boundary problems. But in practice, in the contemporary world, regional organization, if at all relevant to the settlement of boundary problems, tends to operate only with regard to new and/or small states.

It is easy to forget the fact that it is only within the last one hundred years, and often only within the last ten or twenty years that the originally European notions of delimited and demarcated linear boundaries, up to which a centrally organized political system exercises general administrative and jurisdictional control, has begun to shape political activities and alignments throughout much of Asia and most of Africa. What were for the most part once rather remote frontier regions, zones of overlapping authority, regions where local peoples often wandered at will, nowadays become defined and defended, by diplomacy and sometimes by force, as national linear boundaries, the outermost borderlines of newly independent nation-states. The most balkanized former empires are those which bequeath the most numerous and actual or potentially most recurrent border disputes. It is thus not surprising that it is in Latin America (and especially in Central America) since the early-nineteenth century, and in Africa since the Second World War (and especially since 1960) that the most numerous, if not the most dangerous, border disputes have arisen, and where in fact the role of regional organizations seems most relevant today.

These general trends and their most important exceptions can only be sketched lightly in this short chapter which nevertheless attempts in principle at least to be world-wide in scope, dealing first with the Eurasian world-island and its rimlands, and then with Latin America and then Africa, before attempting some general conclusions.

Regionalism, as defined here, is principally, though not exclusively, the affair of governments; and even more emphatically international boundaries are principally, but not exclusively, the concern of governments. Regionalism should thus be seen mainly as an instrument of national policy, seeking more to strengthen than to supersede the independent statehood of the members who collectively associate together in a joint regional enterprise.

The history of boundaries in most long-settled areas (and thus especially in Europe) is a story of increasing definition and precision, and also of perennial adjustment to the changing facts of political geography. The former process is completed when frontiers are reduced to a line, to a linear boundary; the latter is never finally completed. It is a curious fact that the most long-lasting and intractable boundary disputes are often over rather remote and inhospitable terrain, such as the Argentina–Chile Andean frontier, or the China–India frontier in the Aksai Chin.

It is possible to interpret a great deal of the Great Power rivalries and of international politics generally since the Second World War (and even before) as competition and tension along a vast broken frontier zone of 'the world-island of Eurasia'. Territorial rivalries in eastern and central Europe, in the North African littoral, between Israel and her neighbours, in the Arab lands generally and especially for the small Arabian Gulf states, in South and Southeast Asia – in each of these regions actual or potential boundary conflicts fit into a very large and very complex pattern of Great Power tension, and entwine with other explosive issues of prestige, status, security, local and regionalist rivalries and competition for control of resources or the allegiance of peoples. These are what the American political geographer Nicholas Spykman, modifying Mackinder's geopolitical theories in 1944,[5] suggestively called 'the rimlands' of the world-island of Eurasia – and in so doing Spykman gave a remarkably prescient anticipation of the actual preoccupations of subsequent American 'containment' policy, though not of Soviet and Chinese actions and reactions.

It is not possible in this short chapter to discuss in any detail the territorial rivalries and the relevance or irrelevance of regional action in all these 'rimlands', but it is desirable to make some general observations, remembering in this context that regionalism is sometimes used as a euphemism for military alliances (as with NATO, SEATO, CENTO or the Warsaw Pact, which all certainly have their non-military embellishments, and can claim a legitimacy compatible with Chapter VIII of the UN Charter); or else it is a generic title for one or several modes of organized co-operation between adjacent countries which have adopted functionalist arguments for co-operation in the absence of a disposition to combine together for military purposes (witness the contemporary examples of ASEAN and ASPAC).[6]

What is the role of the regional organizations in Europe and around Eurasia?

Around or across the periphery of Eurasia runs an international frontier zone, a broken series of international lines. Contemporaneously this is most marked by partition lines which, according to many passionate patriots, are reminders and scars of the political surgery that 'vivisected' their nation. Thus we can today trace this international fault line from the borders of Ulster with Eire in the north-west, through the Oder-Neisse line, through Cyprus, to and around Israel, to Kashmir, divided Vietnam and partitioned Korea. Merely to describe these partitioned states as constituting boundary problems is to demean their complexity, their many dimensions and their ever-present explosiveness. Each case presents, in some aspect at least, highly intractable boundary problems. What were at first only intended as provisional lines of administrative convenience, which in their origins usually only represent very recent and arbitrarily arrived at lines of demarcation, nevertheless become hardened, entrenched, fortified, as practice confirms again the truth of that sardonic French saying that nothing endures as long as the provisional. When we add, as we must, to the list of the major boundary problems of Eurasia the Sino-Soviet and the Sino-Indian disputes then it is abundantly clear that Eurasia is where the greatest and most internationally threatening boundary disputes still suppurate.

Western Europe is nowadays the portion of the globe which has the most intensive and the most sophisticated experience of regional organization. It is also the area where boundary disputes are either now obsolescent (though it took centuries of bloody strife to reduce them to this condition) or relatively quiescent. Even the continuing Austro-Italian dispute over the territory known either as the South Tirol or as the Alto Adige has never seemed likely to erupt into war. The other great West European centres of local turbulence involving boundaries – such as Ulster and Belgium and formerly the Saar – are not principally boundary disputes; and neither these matters nor the immensely important issue of whether Germany is to continue to be divided, seem likely to be solved or even significantly ameliorated by utilizing regionalist agencies – such as NATO, or EEC, or OECD, or any one or combination of the now many European regionalist organizations. It is not that technically it is impossible to conceive of settlements making use of such agencies; it is that the successful employment of such agencies is very unlikely – for political reasons.

In the late 1960s there were several signs that irredentism was reviving in Eastern Europe. Bulgaria, Albania, Hungary, Poland, Rumania, Germany – all have claims of one kind or another which, if satisfied, would change very considerably the map of Europe as refashioned in 1919 and revised in 1944–45. One thing that the Soviet hegemony in Eastern Europe has done since 1945 has been to hold in check the often ancient rivalries of neighbouring states and peoples. The Warsaw Pact[7] and Comecon[8] are essentially instruments of that Soviet hegemony. If, and as, the Soviet hegemony loosens, these irredentist claims very probably will be reasserted and will throw enormous strains on the ability of the Soviet Union to maintain and sustain the Warsaw Pact and Comecon as regional expressions of her ascendancy, or, to employ fashionable Soviet idioms, they will become imperilled as 'consistently democratic international organizations'.

One very significant difference between Russian and Chinese policy today is that Russia is territorially a status quo power, whereas China (with her insistent demands to 'recover' Taiwan, to 'rectify' unequal treaties, and with her extensive and sometimes unclear acts of cartographic revisionism) most certainly is not. Thus Soviet leaders and publicists were in the 1960s inclined to give conditional approval to some existing regional organizations for their attempts to effect boundary settlements.[9] In marked contrast Chinese publicists either ignored or expressed profound contempt for almost all regional associations (occasional Chinese statements about the Arab League constituting one minor exception), and quite often regarded would-be territorial revisionist governments (such as the Somali Republic, the Yemen, Albania, Pakistan) as friendly associates, though there were always other reasons as well, of course, for such wholly bilateral diplomatic cordialities.

In the Arab world regional organizations have had very little success. All the states of the North African littoral had by the late 1960s become members of the Organization for African Unity (O A U) as well as of the Arab League. But (with the single minor exception of Kuwait, 1961–63) the Arab League[10] notoriously had failed to act at all decisively with regard to boundary disputes affecting its members, and most notably of all, in its various clashes with Israel. Indeed, on three major occasions (in 1948–49, in 1956, and in June 1967) Israel has either temporarily or permanently expanded its territory at the expense of its neighbours, and each of these episodes precipitated major crises within the Arab League.

The Persian (or Arabian) Gulf area[11] is a region par excellence of micro-states, and one where the impending military withdrawal of British power will finally end her former paramountcy after more than a century. The British military disengagement raises questions of acute concern to the local rulers and peoples as to their future security and welfare: whether they could best be insured by means of arrangements with other big outside powers and/or by local agreements with other local powers, perhaps in some overall Persian Gulf regional association. Strong particularist interests and rivalries seem likely to stand in the way of any substantial locally led regionalism.

The Arabian Gulf states comprise eleven countries of which Bahrain, Qatar and the seven Trucial Sheikhdoms have been commonly known as the British Protected States because hitherto they have all had special treaty relations with the United Kingdom; Kuwait since 1961 has been an independent state and a member of the Arab League, and in 1963 she joined the United Nations; and finally there is the Sultanate of Muscat and Oman, an independent state, but not a member of the United Nations. The rate of political, military and economic change in this area since the Second World War has become very great. Consequently, the range of international, political, military, economic and legal problems which arise in relation to this area is considerable and territorial questions feature prominently among these. Boundary disputes mostly have arisen in this area only since the late 1920s and early 1930s when major oil companies first began to operate, and it is actual or potential oil resources which have invested local border disputes with explosive potential.

In this area, too, regional organization (with the one minor but significant exception of Kuwait 1961–63) hitherto has been either non-existent or virtually powerless to prevent boundary disputes erupting and threatening to issue in armed clashes: whether one instances Iran's claim to sovereignty over Bahrain (an aspect of more general Iran–Iraq disagreements about their common boundary), the British–Saudi controversy over the sovereignty of Buraimi, and the Iraqi claim to sovereignty over Kuwait. Only in the third of these cases was a regional organization at all relevant. It is necessary to explain this by reference to Kuwait.

Kuwait is in the enviable position of having the largest per capita income (approximately US $3000 p.a. since independence) of any Middle East country; this is derived from oil revenue (oil was first discovered in 1938 but no significant Kuwaiti production took place until after 1945). Kuwait is located in the north-eastern corner of the Arabian Peninsula, and bounded on the north and west by Iraq and on the south by Saudi Arabia. The state's main problem immediately following its independence in 1961 was Iraq's claim to the Sheikhdom, enunciated by Iraq's Prime Minister, Qasim, following the announcement of Kuwait's independence in June. Fearing an imminent Iraqi military occupation, the ruler of Kuwait requested British military assistance, which was swiftly obtained. Kuwait presented its case before the United Nations, even though a Soviet veto blocked her attempts to join in July 1961 (she eventually became a member in May 1963). The British forces were eventually withdrawn and replaced by troops from certain of the Arab League countries, which in turn were withdrawn at Kuwait's request in January 1963. Common membership of the Arab League had thus facilitated a face-saving reduction of tension; but internal changes within Iraq were more decisive. Pressures from Iraq for annexation of Kuwait were reduced rapidly with the overthrow of the Qasim regime in February 1963, and the new Iraqi government signed an agreement in October 1963 recognizing Kuwait's independence.

The international politics of South Asia are affected in all their aspects by the tensions in Indo–Pakistan relations, which have effectively prevented any regional organization from being launched. However, there have been a number of bilateral boundary settlements and adjustments between India and Pakistan. But Pakistan's[12] membership of multilateral military alliances, begun in the mid-1950s, brought her no direct and uninhibited support for her frontier policies from her formal allies.

Regionalism is increasingly engaging the attention of political leaders in most Southeast Asian countries.[13] Each government is in different ways, and inevitably with different perspectives and sets of priorities, investigating the opportunities for advancing its individual interests by means of regionalist enterprises; but regional organization still remains rather weak and embryonic in Southeast Asia and there are many actual or potential irredentist disputes (especially between Thailand, Vietnam, Indonesia and their respective neighbours). The Philippine claim to a substantial portion of Sabah (before 1963 it was known as British North Borneo) should be called a frontier rather than a boundary claim, for not only does the Philippine government thereby putatively extend what it now regards as the 'national' territory (at the expense of Malaysian 'national' territory) but it is notable that the Philippine government (somewhat like Pakistan's claim to Kashmir) hitherto has been reluctant precisely to define the southern extent of her claim, not least perhaps because this might bring her into conflict with Indonesia. The former association of Southeast Asian states (ASA), and the present association of Southeast Asian nations (ASEAN) have been enfeebled by Philippine persistence with this claim, though some officials said to the present writer in the summer of 1968 that surely this was precisely the issue to test the mettle and demonstrate the utility of regional organization in this area.

Regional intervention has thus not played a major role in any of these areas. Land boundaries are intrinsically and principally bilateral matters, the cardinal concern of two contiguous countries, however much other countries may be interested. This is the simple but major reason why bilateral dealings are usually preferred to regional organizations when contending powers are seeking a settlement concerning their common land boundary or boundaries. Recognition of this obvious but important fact immediately suggests why active and sustained regional interventions in boundary disputes have been relatively few, and also why indubitably successful regionalist interventions have been, and are likely to remain, even rarer. For the late 1960s, and conceivably throughout the 1970s and after, and throughout most of the world at large the comments of one of the most careful and informed of American scholars in this field seem germane:

> Regionalism runs the risk of becoming the latest international fad as more statesmen seek to escape from isolation, respond to the instant brotherhood of regional summit meetings, and deal with the serious political and economic weaknesses of their states. Increasingly, editorial writers and government officials concerned with American foreign policy (and we might add not only those concerned with US foreign policy) seem eager to jump on the bandwagon. New groupings constantly appear – most of them ephemeral. Many existing groupings fail to live up to expectations held by their supporters. There is a danger that over-advocacy of regionalism may lead to a reaction against it. . . .[14]

Let us now look at those areas where regional organization has had rather greater success. The origins of regional organization in South America can be traced back to the early-nineteenth century when most of the states first won their independence from Spain.[15] As weak countries, relatively powerless to deal adequately with what they saw as potentially predatory European powers, some of the leaders of these newly independent countries sought to associate together for their mutual advantage. As early as 1826, Simón Bolívar called a conference of Spanish-American republics at Panama where a treaty of confederation was drafted which envisaged mutual guarantees, the establishment of a representative assembly, and procedures for the settlement of their disputes by peaceful means. But particularism and political chaos following disruptive wars of independence, and rival claims to territories, prevented these efforts from being put into practice. In the nineteenth century these newly independent states of South America engaged in six full-scale declared wars in most of which some elements of contest for territory were present, and in many smaller frontier skirmishes; the legacies of these clashes were not in most cases superficial and short-lived. Fragmentation of the former Spanish imperium proceeded furthest in Central America, with many boundary disputes as one of its legacies.

In 1889 the United States convened in Washington a first international conference of American states. This set in motion a series of conferences which, despite several changes of nomenclature and organization, has continued ever since. At the conclusion of this conference, in April 1890, the embryo of a permanent international regionalist agency, an inter-American system, was launched which eventually developed into the present Organization of American States (OAS). Right from the start there were efforts to develop inter-American peace and security procedures to deal with territorial as well as other contentious issues. The history of these efforts since 1890 can be briefly traced and characterized in terms of three phases.

The first phase in the development of inter-American peace and security procedures, from 1890 to 1936, was characterized by efforts to devise juridical procedures for the peaceful settlement of inter-American disputes, including boundary disputes. Indeed, it was during this first hundred years or so following the eviction of Spanish and Portuguese power that almost all the major boundary disputes which subsequently have tested regional power-relations and organizations first became manifest.

From the earliest days of independence the Roman law principle of *uti possidetis, ita possideatis*, 'as you possess, so you may possess', was invoked with regard to boundary questions in former Spanish America (Brazil and its extensive land boundaries with contiguous neighbours constituting something of a significant exception). The new states of former Spanish America adopted, for convenience, as the basis for their boundaries, the administrative divisions drawn by the former metropolitan colonial power, Spain, taking as their standard the territorial boundary configuration which prevailed at the date when the movements for independence broke out. These convenient 'critical dates' were generally taken to be 1810 for South America and 1821 for Central America. It was widely hoped that the *uti possidetis* doctrine would remove, or at least severely reduce, boundary disputes between the new states of Spanish-speaking America.[16] Though it certainly did not entirely prevent boundary disputes from erupting at all it is at least arguable that enunciation of the principle, and diplomatic efforts mustered on its behalf, did make South American boundary disputes in principle more amenable to settlement than would have been the case had there not been some general existing territorial basis and broad divisions which found rough general acceptance. Regional organization as it has developed in the Americas since the 1890s has in fact given a powerful general, though mostly implicit, endorsement to *uti possidetis*.

But for a variety of reasons (concerning prestige, trade and transit routes, pasturage and access to and control over known or potential mineral resources) successor-states have often disagreed as to the exact limits of vice-royalties, captaincies-general, audiencias, presidencias or provincias. These were the administrative areas of the Spanish colonial rulers, and were originally merely administrative divisions lacking all political significance. Since such boundaries were mostly based on crude maps and inadequate surveys, or merely followed arbitrary lines across uninhabited, uncharted and unexplored territory, there was thus ample scope for dispute. Because regional organization was still rudimentary or untried it was of no great relevance to boundary disputes in this first phase in the development of the inter-American system. War, direct bilateral dealings or arbitration procedures were the means most employed for seeking particular boundary settlements, though generalized pronouncements in favour of respecting the territorial integrity of independent states and observing peaceful settlement of disputes were commonplace.

From very early in the nineteenth century, the United States, by such unilateral declarations as the 'No-Transfer principle' and the Monroe Doctrine, expressed opposition to further European colonization or transference of territory within the Americas; and increasingly it became evident, as the 1890 inaugurating conference of the inter-American system underlined, that the United States undoubtedly was to be the principal power in any general regional arrangements for the Americas. As the material power of the United States grew, the always latent and sometimes active Latin American fears of their 'colossus of the north' acted as an inhibiting effect on their enthusiasm for regionalist ventures. Indeed, some of the larger powers – Argentina, Mexico, Chile, most notably – saw their membership of the League of Nations as a way of reducing the exclusive pressures of the United States within western hemispheral politics, and as affording them greater flexibility and freedom of manœuvre internationally. In the twentieth century the regionalist politics of the Americas always have to be seen also as an aspect of the general phenomenon of international organization and politics.

The second phase of the development of the inter-American system was from 1936 to 1948, that is from the Inter-American Conference for the Maintenance of Peace at Buenos Aires in 1936 until the conclusion of two treaties in the immediate post-Second World War period, which gave the main general organizational lineaments of the present-day inter-American system: the Inter-American Treaty of Reciprocal Assistance (Treaty of Rio de Janeiro), 1947, and the Charter of the Organization of American States, 1948. This period was dominated successively by the shadow, the onset and then the aftermath, of the Second World War, by the onset of the so-called Cold War, with the United States and the Soviet Union as principals, and by the undoubted emergence of the United States from its hemispheral shell to become a world power. Emphasis shifted within the inter-American system from juridical formulas to more practical matters of consultation and the use of collective measures; but, with the notable exception of the Ecuador–Peru dispute,[17] boundary disputes generally were in abeyance in these years.

In this phase, all American states were aware of the increasing involvement of outside powers in the affairs of their hemisphere:

first from Germany; and then, or so it was said by Americans in 1947, from the Soviet Union. The second 'threat' was regarded not only as that of a great extra-hemispheral power acting, or at least prepared to act, in a traditional 'power-political' way, but also as that emanating from the headquarters of a world revolutionary movement, the international communist conspiracy, as it was often described in the Americas of the 1940s – and sometimes, for some people, even later. Besides these novel challenges the entrenched and continuing rivalries of local powers over boundaries and territories seemed, in many senses, distracting – except of course to the principal disputants themselves (and in this phase this meant only the dispute which erupted into war in the early 1940s between Ecuador and Peru,[18] and which the inter-American system eventually helped to quieten).

The third phase of the inter-American system, from 1947–48 up until the present day, has been generally characterized by increasing consultation and attempts at institutionalized regional co-operation between American states, both generally throughout the Americas and more locally, as for example in various Caribbean and Central American regionalist activities.[19] Increasing efforts and examples of regional organization in the Americas is, of course, one aspect of the general proliferation of inter-governmental and other forms of international association, and it should be remembered that in the twentieth century the inter-American system has never been wholly and sharply separated from other developments in international organization. But however useful specialized groupings may be for promoting functionalist co-operation in the Americas, it is in the general arrangements, where the inter-American system is at its most comprehensive, that its relevance for achieving boundary settlements principally has been sought and occasionally achieved.

At the Bogotá conference of 1948, concurrently with the founding Charter of the OAS, the American Treaty of Pacific Settlement, known as the Pact of Bogotá, was drafted. Its primary purpose was to knit together and replace earlier treaties with one consolidated instrument of pacific settlement. The treaty specified the procedures to be followed, beginning with good offices and proceeding by means of mediation, investigation and conciliation, and judicial settlement to compulsory arbitration. Parties were and are permitted to select any one of these procedures in the first instance; but if that procedure fails, they are required to go as far as necessary towards a final arbitration. However, the requirement of compulsory arbitration if other procedures fail has had the effect of severely restricting resort to these procedures. In the late 1960s less than half of the member states of the OAS had ratified the Pact of Bogotá; the United States and most of the larger Latin American states – except Mexico – had not ratified.

Indeed, all the ancient and familiar irredentist and other territorial disputes which became evident in the first half of the nineteenth century, as well as a few which emerged later, still exist (e.g. those concerning the boundaries between Ecuador and Peru, between Bolivia and Chile, Guyana and Venezuela, Costa Rica and Panama, Honduras and Nicaragua) and are actively or potentially (though this is, of course, a practical distinction of some importance) contentious. Even at worst boundary disputes in the Americas nowadays seem not to erupt into open war, but mostly to simmer in the limbo regions of sub-liminal warfare.

There are a sufficient number of examples[20] to demonstrate that inter-American machinery can occasionally be useful in dealing with boundary disputes among Latin American states.

An Inter-American Commission of Inquiry and Conciliation mediated successfully over a dispute between Haiti and the Dominican Republic in 1937, arising out of an incident on their common border in which a number of Haitian labourers were murdered by Dominican soldiers. The proposed solution provided for an indemnity to be paid by the Dominican government in compensation. This was accepted by both parties, though the indemnity was never finally paid in full.

The OAS itself mediated over disputes between Costa Rica and Nicaragua which occurred in 1948 and 1955. In 1948 Costa

Rica accused the Nicaraguan government of supporting an invasion of Costa Rican territory from within its borders. The Organization set up an 'Information and Study Committee' which travelled to the two countries, interviewed a number of people and returned to Washington. The Organization passed a resolution, placing some of the blame on both governments, and calling on them to cease hostile acts against the other, and to observe the principle of non-intervention. A Commission of 'military experts' was sent to ensure compliance with the resolution. Finally the Council persuaded the two countries to sign a Pact of Amity, pledging themselves not to interfere in the internal affairs of the other. In 1955, however, hostilities broke out again on the border and Costa Rica brought a similar complaint, this time calling for military support from the Organization. Again an investigating committee was set up and a committee of military experts established. These confirmed that military attacks were taking place. The Council then set up a system of observers and aerial surveillance on the frontier and established a demilitarized zone. An air corridor was patrolled for a time by OAS planes. Eventually, in January of the following year, a further agreement was signed between the two countries, and this time proved successful.

A more genuine frontier dispute (as opposed to a political quarrel leading to border incidents) was the conflict between Honduras and Nicaragua in 1957. This concerned a piece of territory which had been awarded to Honduras in 1906, but which had not been ceded by Nicaragua. In 1957 Honduras began to take steps to administer part of this area which was still occupied by Nicaraguan forces. Nicaragua strengthened its forces and Honduras took the question to the OAS. The Council appointed a Committee of Investigation. With the help of a committee of military advisers this sought to obtain a cease-fire and drew up a plan for mutual withdrawal, without prejudice to the question of sovereignty, which was finally accepted by both parties. A separate ad hoc Committee then sought to mediate on the underlying dispute and finally succeeded in obtaining a mutual agreement to submit the dispute to the International Court of Justice. Later, in 1960, after the Court had made its award, the services of the Inter-American Peace Committee were used to supervise the withdrawal of Nicaragua from the territory concerned and the necessary movement of population.

Thus, OAS sometimes has effectively drawn on regional legal and diplomatic traditions and has developed procedures consonant with the Latin American political and cultural mores prevailing in the inter-governmental relations of these countries. At least since 1919 the possibility of resort to and reliance on a regional agency or agencies has existed in Latin America alongside the alternatives of bilateral dealings or recourse to the more generalized facilities of the League of Nations or the United Nations. The Act of Washington of 18 December 1964 paved the way for new members to join the OAS. Trinidad and Tobago gained membership in February 1967 as the twenty-second member, and the first new member since 1948. Barbados became the twenty-third member in November 1967 and Jamaica was in the process of joining in mid-1969. With the prospect of several more new members for the OAS from the ranks of the newly independent small Caribbean islands, with their mostly English language speaking leaders, or from the few recent or remaining colonies of the Caribbean rimlands; with the prospect that is of Guyana, Surinam, British Honduras (and the more remote prospect of Canada) becoming future members of the OAS, it may be that these political, legal and cultural mores will change – as some people hope or fear. Each of these three Central (or near Central) American countries mentioned above have active or latent boundary disputes with their neighbours, and are already active or prospective participants in some local regional organizations.

Experience suggests that the capacity of the OAS is severely limited in disputes involving non-American states (as in the case of the Argentinian claim to the Falkland Islands, or with regard to the future of Surinam or British Honduras). Clearly it is difficult (though recent examples from Asia and Africa – most notably

Mauritania and Malaysia – show it is not impossible) to decolonize when some of the powers contiguous to the colony do not want that colony to remain territorially intact and to become an independent state, but wish rather to satisfy their own irredentist ambitions at the contiguous colony's expense.

The future, just as the past and present, ability of the OAS to participate actively in the settlement of boundary disputes depends principally, though never exclusively, on the policy of the United States and on the consent of the contentious parties. Only the United States can mobilize the necessary power to deal with serious conflicts (and the record suggests that the United States has seldom deemed South American border disputes so serious as to necessitate her own unilateral direct armed intervention – at least not since the Mexican War – nor does this seem likely to change); and sometimes only the OAS can provide the requisite multilateral framework to provide emollients.

The newly independent countries of Africa have launched a considerable number of regional schemes in the few years which have elapsed so far since most of them gained their independence. And African regionalist co-operation to date has been more than exclusively politico-diplomatic. There were, by early 1969, almost a score of organizations seeking to further the economic development of the continent. The United Nations Economic Commission for Africa, founded in 1960, is the oldest and most general of these bodies; but the African Development Bank is pioneering in the field of financial development assistance, and various river and lake basin groups (such as the riparian countries along the Senegal River and around Lake Chad) are experimenting in co-operation on specific common developmental problems. And there are many other functional co-operative ventures. The very fact that almost all these developments have taken place within the last decade should caution against confident conclusions regarding the significance of regionalism in Africa. Furthermore, it should be remembered that the few attempts at mediatory activities which so far have been attempted through the aegis of the OAU to deal with boundary disputes[21] have depended much more on the skills of the personalities concerned, and also on the impalpable chemistry of inter-personal contacts between a few outstanding leaders, than upon the frail and mostly untried formal machinery provided by any extant regional organization.

A vociferous aversion to the international boundaries drawn by the colonial powers, and perhaps their complete rejection, was a recurrent theme of anti-colonial nationalism in Africa and of pan-Africanism before the 1960s. But with the rapid emergence of many former colonies into independent statehood the hitherto widespread denunciation of these 'colonialist' borders has swiftly given way to their almost unanimous acceptance by the governments of the new African states.

At the All-African Peoples' Conference in Accra in 1958 a declaration was widely approved which denounced 'artificial frontiers drawn by imperialist powers to divide the people of Africa, particularly those which cut across the ethnic groups and divide people of the same stock' and called for 'the abolition or adjustment of such frontiers at an early date'. But subsequently by far the majority of actual African leaders have not endorsed these views (which were probably considerably influenced by the contemporary boundary issue between Togo and the Cameroons). For very soon after the 1958 declaration a number of potentially explosive boundary disputes (for example, those between Ghana and Upper Volta[22] and especially those concerning Somalia and Morocco) emerged, or re-emerged. It was in the light of these developments that in 1964 the Organization of African Unity (OAU) strongly repudiated the earlier attitude: an overwhelming majority of member states meeting in Cairo at an Assembly for heads of states and governments of OAU, pledged themselves 'to respect the boundaries existing on their achievement of national independence' – the objections and reservations of Somalia and Morocco notwithstanding. It may well prove in the long run that this general acceptance of inherited boundaries, similar in some respects to the doctrine of *uti possidetis* adopted by the former Spanish-American colonies, is the most sensible policy for African states to adopt. No doubt the intention of the resolution of July 1964 was to stabilize the status quo not only of the existing borders but also of peoples within states and thus to deny in effect the right of minorities or of provinces (such as Katanga 1960–63 or Biafra 1965–) to secede.

There is already a considerable literature concerning the Somalis' basically ethnic and pastoral irredentism, and about Morocco's claim to re-establish a territorial sway equivalent to what was supposedly held by the present Alaouite dynasty when it was first founded in the seventeenth century. Here it is only necessary to comment briefly about the role of the OAU in relation to these two cases. It is in general still true, as Saadia Touval wrote in 1967, that nearly all of the peace-making and mediating activities in the Somali and Moroccan disputes have been performed by individual statesmen, independent of the OAU. In both cases Touval's conclusions are apt, and are worth summarizing.

With regard to the Somali dispute, Touval argues that the role played by the OAU has been limited. It probably contributed to a successful cease-fire and disengagement of the Ethiopian and Somali armies in 1964. But subsequently the OAU has not been called upon to renew any peace-keeping efforts, nor does this seem very likely with regard to any of Somalia's territorial disputes with its neighbours.

In the dispute between Algeria and Morocco the OAU Council of Ministers was persuaded to establish an ad hoc commission to consider the dispute, as was explicitly requested by a number of African leaders who had signed a communiqué to this effect at Bamako in 1963. But subsequently the commission was unable to accomplish its mandate; and the OAU then and ever since has appeared reluctant to take positions which might arouse the resentment of either party. Early in 1969 Morocco and Algeria signed a 'Treaty of solidarity, good neighbourliness and co-operation' by which they agreed to deal in future with their mutual problems wholly on a bilateral basis, which meant that the OAU's ad hoc committee was now de facto without any purpose.

Since the adoption of the July 1964 OAU resolution no other crises have arisen over territorial questions in Africa which have been directly dealt with by the OAU. None of the territorial disputes with which the OAU so far has been concerned have been finally resolved; but they have been contained, and the OAU can claim some modest credit for this.

It is evident, then, that interest in the political boundaries of Africa has been greatly intensified recently because of the rapidity of political change throughout the continent. But recent experience also appears to suggest that international boundaries are unlikely to be radically altered in the foreseeable future. Every boundary is a unique political feature, a unique divide, which has to be seen in its individual cultural, social and economic, indeed in its overall environmental, setting. It is true that today the 'suitability' of many African international boundaries is being questioned, and, in some areas and for particular reasons, some modification of existing international boundaries would seem to be desirable – if agreement can be reached between the states concerned. Undoubtedly, however, in contemporary Africa, as elsewhere, the most powerful prevailing arguments and forces generally support the retention of existing boundaries. Looked at in a long perspective we know that ideas about boundaries change. Will the future modification of African international boundaries turn mainly on status or functional changes rather than on the physical relocation of boundary lines? And will regional organization be able to play a significant regulatory role with regard to Africa's boundary questions in the future? If past and present indications are any guide to the future then regional associations will continue to be at least minor constraints upon African governments prosecuting border disputes, for they constitute a part of the international environment which has to be taken into account.

It can be seen from this outline survey, which has been illustrative rather than exhaustive in scope, how various and elastic are the solutions which have been devised and adopted, even in the rather few cases where regional organizations actively have tried to forestall, or to settle, or at least to ameliorate, boundary disputes.

With the emergence into independence of many new states the number of actual and potential boundary disputes has risen. The decline in numbers and importance of prolonged struggles for independence against West European overseas colonial rule has been succeeded by an upsurge of post-colonial internal disorder and of many actual or incipient boundary disputes. Because there are now so many regional associations in existence it is natural and inevitable that they should sometimes be thought of as possible instruments for settling boundary disputes. But, as we have seen, outside Latin America and contemporary Africa this seldom happens.

None of the regional groupings of the contemporary world can be expected to intervene at all in a dispute between major powers when the disputants regard the matter in dispute as central to their national interests. It is most unlikely that there will ever be a regional grouping which will intervene successfully in the India–Pakistan dispute over Kashmir, still less in Sino–Soviet border disputes. Even when smaller states are the disputants active regional intervention may be rare.

The general legitimating function of regional organizations is in fact more fundamental than any specific acts of settlement which they can occasionally perform. The general endorsement of existing boundaries by a regional organization must be regarded as more than a merely ritualistic incantation, even though such endorsement does not, and cannot, of course, of itself provide absolute guarantees for any existing territorial status quo. Nevertheless, the OAU has provided a considerable political and moral presumption in favour of maintaining the general territorial arrangements prevailing at the time when decolonization takes place, and has thus thrown the burden of making and justifying change on the shoulders of the few would-be revisionists. The Pan-American Union (and now the OAS) probably has had a similar salutary inhibiting effect on would-be revisionists.

A boundary regarded by neighbouring states as equitable is, in itself, the best boundary. This is a tautology, but it is a practical truth which is too often overlooked by ingenious and familiar, but not fundamental, assertions and arguments about 'natural' and 'artificial' boundaries – especially when we remember that any proposal for boundary revision is always in some sense an expansionist claim.

The stability of a boundary depends only to a small degree positively on physical, or economic, or even strategic conditions. Stability is primarily a function of relations between the collectivities which it separates. When there is agreement concerning legitimacy there is no conflict. Regional organizations can assist in the spread and acceptance of common notions of territorial legitimacy. It is the preventive rather than the remedial diplomacy of regional organization which is most potent in relation to boundary questions.

Whenever a boundary dispute breaks out between two members of a regional organization, all the members of that organization are faced with a choice – to think in terms of an amelioration and possible solution, or to ignore the challenge. Since many more boundary conflicts are conceivable and likely to occur – especially in Africa – this choice is, in general terms, no evanescent one.

Obviously, joint action of any kind by a regional organization has to be conditional on the free consent of the disputants, and any measures undertaken in the name of the organization have to be acceptable to both disputants, except in the very unlikely contingency that a collective decision be taken to coerce one party.

It is seldom possible to make confident estimates of the precise degree of influence upon state behaviour exerted by the recommendations of regional organizations or by regional actions. But there is enough evidence to suggest that the seal of approval and the stigma of disapproval are not taken lightly, especially by newly independent states. There is considerable room for disagreement and uncertainty concerning the merits and demerits of regional intervention in a boundary dispute. Any particular intervention may be for better or for worse, whether evaluated in terms of its effect upon the interests of a particular state or upon the prospects for a stable settlement. Regional organization can prove highly relevant or very irrelevant to a particular boundary dispute; but, except perhaps in Africa, regional organizations are not much employed nowadays in reaching specific boundary settlements.

Regional associations are obviously not proof against boundary disputes, but it can at least be said that as long as a regional organization continues actively to function, this is significant indication that it is unlikely that a boundary dispute between members will erupt into a serious international dispute. However, if and when a boundary dispute does break out between members, then it is more likely that the organization will suffer than prove capable of ending or calming the dispute.

Fruitful regional intervention in boundary questions could be helped in future by promoting common cartographic and surveying methods, standardizing maps, and making the appropriate regional organization a repository of technical information and advice. But it must be recognized that, valuable as these relatively technical measures can occasionally be, the principal causes of conflict over boundary matters are often much more than technical, and are thus not to be dispensed with only by technical remedies.

Regional boundary commissions could serve either to facilitate the avoidance of conflict over boundaries, or to help perhaps to put the finishing touches to boundary agreements; they are unlikely to function effectively in the midst of a boundary dispute. The setting up of regional boundary commissions as advisers and/or as repositories of information, maps and survey teams could be helpful, especially where regional organization is already in existence or the idea of further regional co-operation is popular.

These regional boundary commissions could, or ideally should, exercise wide powers covering the delimitation and demarcation, the supervision, control and maintenance of established boundaries as well as the settlement of minor border incidents. More serious boundary disputes undoubtedly will remain primarily the jealous preserves of the governments concerned. But permanent regional boundary commissions, especially when associated with other regional enterprises of a functionalist character, might prove more acceptable and useful than any merely ad hoc bodies.

The past and prospective record of regional organizations with regard to boundary questions has not been entirely negligible. But neither has it been profuse or profound.

TEXT REFERENCES AND BIBLIOGRAPHY

This short essay about a very large and complex subject, which has hitherto only been written about in a very peripheral or particularist way, has gleaned many of its ideas and facts from a very wide and scattered number of materials. Hence the rather extensive list of references given here, with some occasional attempts to indicate their character and worth. It will be clear even from these selected references that there is a considerable literature about frontiers and about regional organizations considered separately, but very little which is concerned with their mutual interaction. The article by Saadia Touval, cited below, is thus a rare and welcome exception. I have concentrated on general trends and hypotheses in this essay, but more detailed case-work and comparisons need to be done

1. According to The Geographer of the Department of State in the US Government there were, in August 1968, 278 international boundaries or other jurisdictional lines separating differing sovereignties – this figure included cease-fire and armistice lines. According to the same authority about 43 international boundaries were then in active dispute; and he calculated that if every country had a channel of communication in common with every other country there would be 17,590 such channels. This figure was based on the assumption that there are 134 independent countries, and this excluded regimes which the US does not recognize (North Korea, North Vietnam, Communist China, East Germany, and Mongolia). No less than 64 of these 134 countries had gained their independence within the previous twenty-five years. See US Department of State, *Foreign Policy Briefs*, vol. 18 (4), August 1968. According to one American scholar, bringing together the research of others: 'The number of international regional arrangements is increasing. Of twenty-three regional

groupings . . . only one – the inter-American system – existed before World War II. By a recent account 92 countries are members of one or more of the nine regional organizations with mutual security commitments.' See Nye, Joseph S. Jr, *International Regionalism. Readings*, Boston 1968, p. v.

Regionalism should be seen as an aspect of the growth of international organization generally. In numerical terms this can be traced in the *Yearbook of International Organizations*, published by the Union of International Associations, Brussels, but which does not appear annually. The first yearbook appeared in 1909–10 and then listed 213 international organizations; five editions and forty-seven years later the figure was over 1000. Five editions later, separated this time only by ten years, there were over 2000.

The most crisp and cogent discussion of regionalism in relation to the League of Nations and United Nations systems is in Claude, Inis L. Jr, *Swords Into Plowshares*, 2nd ed., New York 1959. For texts of some of the main regional organizations see Lawson, Ruth C., *International Regional Organizations: Constitutional Foundations*, New York 1962.

One seminal article which, though it is not directly related to the theme of this essay has important methodological and practical suggestions and findings relevant to regionalism and boundary problems, is Alger, Chadwick F. and Brams, Steven J., 'Patterns of Representation in National Capitals and Intergovernmental Organizations. A Research Note' in *World Politics*, vol. 19 (4), July 1967, pp. 646–63, which concludes that organizational ties provide most states with far greater access to the outside world than do diplomatic ties. While only one-eighth of all states have diplomatic representatives in more than half the world capitals, seven-eighths of all states have organizational affiliations with more than half of all other nations. The authors also show that there are more regionally oriented inter-governmental organizations in Western Europe and Scandinavia than in all other regions taken together.

2. Curzon of Kedleston, *Frontiers*, The Romanes Lecture 1907, Oxford 1907; Holdich, Sir T. H., 'Political Boundaries' in *Scottish Geographical Magazine*, vol. 32, 1916, pp. 497–510, and *Political Frontiers and Boundary-Making*, London 1916; McMahon, Sir A. H., 'International Boundaries' in *The Journal of the Royal Society of Arts*, vol. 84, 1935.

3. See Herz, John H., 'Rise and Demise of the Territorial State' in *World Politics*, vol. 9 (2), July 1957, pp. 473–93. This is an original and provocative article with many suggestive insights; but it elides some significant differences in the meaning of crucial terms in the argument, such as territoriality, impermeability, indefensibility, as if they were synonyms – which they are not.

4. See Curzon, op. cit., p. 21 fn. and fn. 16 below.

5. See Spkyman, Nicholas, *The Geography of the Peace*, New York 1944, and 'Frontiers, Security and International Organization' in *Geographical Review*, vol. 32, 1942. Halford J. Mackinder's geopolitical theories were expressed most fully in his *Democratic Ideals and Reality*, London 1919.

See also Hall, H. Duncan, 'Zones of the International Frontier' in *Geographical Review*, vol. 38, 1948, pp. 615–25.

6. See Lyon, Peter, *War and Peace in South-east Asia*, London: OUP for RIIA, 1969, pp. 154–60.

7. See *The Warsaw Pact, Its Role in Soviet Bloc Affairs*, US Senate, Sub-Cttee on National Security and International Operations, 89th Congress, 2nd session, US Govt Printing Office, 1966, and Mackintosh, Malcolm, *The Evolution of the Warsaw Pact*, London: The Institute for Strategic Studies, Adelphi Paper No. 58, June 1969.

8. See Kaser, Michael, *Comecon: Integration Problems of the Planned Economies*, London: OUP for RIIA, 1965.

9. See, e.g., Molodtsov, Stepan, *Peace to Frontiers*, Moscow 1965. OAU initiatives with regard to the Algeria–Morocco and Ethiopia–Somalia boundary conflicts are commended, inter alia (see pp. 29–30).

10. Macdonald, R. W., *The League of Arab States*, New Jersey 1965.

11. Albaharna, Husain M., *The Legal Status of the Arabian Gulf States*, Manchester 1968; Kelley, J. B., *East Arabian Frontiers*, London 1955.

12. See a London University Ph.D. thesis recently completed by Razvi, S. M. M., *Frontier Problems in Pakistan's Foreign Policy* (London Ph.D. 1969); and Lamb, Alastair, *Asian Frontiers: Studies in a Continuing Problem*, London 1968.

13. Gordon, Bernard K., *The Dimensions of Conflict in South-east Asia*, New Jersey 1966, and Lyon, Peter, *War and Peace in South-east Asia*, ibid., especially ch. 5.

14. Nye, Joseph S. Jr, *International Regionalism*, ibid., p. v.

15. On Latin America generally see: Ireland, G., *Boundaries, Possessions and Conflicts in South America*, Cambridge, Mass. 1938, and *Boundaries, Possessions and Conflicts in Central and North America and the Caribbean*, Cambridge, Mass. 1941; Marchant, Alexander, *Boundaries of the Latin-American Republics 1493–1943: An Annotated List of Documents*, Dept of State, Office of the Geographer, Washington DC 1944; Clissold, Stephen and Hennessy, Alistair, 'Territorial Disputes' in *Latin America and the Caribbean. A Handbook*, edited by Veliz, Claudio, London 1967, pp. 403–13; Wainhouse, David W. and associates, 'Cases Under Inter-American Organizations and Procedures' in *International Peace Observation. A History and Forecast*, Baltimore 1966, pp. 86–215; Fenwick, Charles G., *The Organization of American States, the inter-American regional system*, Washington 1963; Connell-Smith, Gordon, *The Inter-American System*, London: OUP for RIIA, 1966.

16. See Boggs, S. W., *International Boundaries*, New York 1940, pp. 79–80; and Cukwurah, A. O., *The Settlement of Boundary Disputes in International Law*, Manchester 1967, pp. 112–15. For a contrasting view of the value of the principle of *uti possidetis*, see Prescott, J. R. V., *The Geography of Frontiers and Boundaries*, London 1965, pp. 116–17: 'The legal basis of claims in South America is usually the principle of *uti possidetis* . . . [which] has probably worsened the territorial conflicts. There are at least two interpretations of the principle, and states tend to advance whichever suits them best.' Some states regard the limits as those in force at the time independence was gained; while other states regard the limits as those which were observed for practical admini-

stration by the colonial authorities. Venezuela as the heir of the former Captaincy-General has employed both interpretations at different times.

17. See Clissold and Hennessy, op. cit., p. 405.

18. See ibid., p. 405, and Wood, Bryce, *The United States and Latin American Wars 1932–42*, New York 1966.

19. See Nye, J. S. Jr, 'Central American Regional Integration' in *International Conciliation*, No. 562, March 1967, and Gregg, Robert W., *International Organization in the Western Hemisphere*, Syracuse 1968, and Denham, Robert E., 'The Role of the U S as an External Actor in the Integration of Latin America' in the *Journal of Common Market Studies*, vol. 7, No. 3, March 1969.

20. Notably those mentioned briefly in Luard, Evan, *Conflict and Peace in the Modern International System*, Boston 1968, ch. 4 'Frontiers'. Some familiarity with the inter-American peace-keeping machinery is necessary, and may be gleaned from Fenwick and from Connell-Smith (ibid. above). The nine treaties of the inter-American system providing for direct negotiation, good offices, mediation, investigation, conciliation and arbitration are primarily bilateral in character although they may be multilateral in form. These are to be distinguished from the Rio Defence Treaty, the O A S Charter and the Inter-American Peace Committee, which are essentially collective.

On the Leticia dispute 1932–35, see Connell-Smith, p. 84 and Wainhouse, pp. 64–68; Bryce-Wood, pp. 169–251. On the Chaco dispute, see Wainhouse, pp. 94–102 and Mecham, John Lloyd, *The United States and Inter-American Security 1889–1960*, Austin, Texas 1961. On the Haiti–Dominican Republic dispute, see Wainhouse, p. 167. On the Honduras–Nicaragua dispute, see Wainhouse, pp. 135–41 and O A S Inter-American Peace Committee Report to the Council of the O A S on the termination of the Honduras–Nicaragua Mixed Commission, Washington P A U 1963, 43 pp. (O E A/Serl. III/66.9) 16 July 1963.

The so-called Football War between El Salvador and Honduras, in July 1969, though it involved troops from the former country crossing into the territory of the latter at a variety of points along their 850-mile common border (which has never been legally defined) and the intervention of the O A S to supervise a cease-fire and troop withdrawal, was not the result of a boundary dispute – see the excellent dispatches of the Latin American correspondent of *The Christian Science Monitor*, James Nelson Goodsell, during July 1969 and especially on 23 July 1969.

21. On Africa generally, the best single treatment, which I have relied on heavily here, is Touval, Saadia, 'The Organization of African Unity and African Borders' in *International Organization*, vol. 21 (1), 1967, pp. 102–27. See Herstlet, Edward, *Map of Africa by Treaty*, 3 vols, London 1896, for texts of boundary delimitation treaties during the age of the so-called scramble for Africa.

Kapil, Ravi L., 'On the Conflict Potential of Inherited Boundaries in Africa' in *World Politics*, vol. 18 (4), July 1966, pp. 656–73, is a scholarly article, wide-ranging in scope, based particularly on research in the Somali Republic (and more optimistic in its conclusions than Touval), which argues that 'there is a low conflict potential in contemporary African boundaries and that earlier predictions of instability are not likely to be borne out'. See also Legum, Colin, *Pan Africanism: A Short Political Guide*, London 1962, which includes the text of the then much publicized rejection of borders contained in the resolution on 'Frontiers, Boundaries and Federations' of the All African Peoples' Conference which met in Accra in 1958 (ibid., pp. 229–32). For the text of the resolution which stressed that 'the borders of African states on the day of their independence constitute a tangible reality', and which secured the overwhelming but not unanimous support of the African Heads of State and Government at the Cairo Summit Conference in July 1964, see OAU Document AHG/Res. 16 (1); see also Touval, Saadia, ibid. above, pp. 122–25.

Some other useful references are: Wild, Patricia Berko, 'The Organization of African Unity and the Algerian-Moroccan Border Conflict: A Study of New Machinery for Peacekeeping and for the Peaceful Settlement of Disputes Among African States' in *International Organization*, vol. 20 (1), 1966, pp. 18–36; Wallerstein, Immanuel, 'The Early Years of the OAU: The Search for Organizational Pre-eminence' in *International Organization*, vol. 20 (4), Autumn 1966, pp. 774–87; Austin, Dennis and Nagel, Ronald, 'The Organization of African Unity' in *The World Today*, vol. 22 (12), December 1966, pp. 520–28; Ashford, Douglas E., 'The Irredentist Appeal in Morocco and Mauretania' in *Western Political Quarterly*, vol. 15, December 1962, pp. 614–51; Reyner, Anthony M., 'Morocco's International Boundaries' in *Journal of Modern African Studies*, vol. 1, September 1963, pp. 313–26; Marian, Mesfim Wolde, 'The Background of the Ethiopian–Somalian Boundary Dispute' in *Journal of Modern African Studies*, vol. 2, July 1964, pp. 189–219; Nye, Joseph S., *Pan-Africanism and East African Integration*, Cambridge, Mass. 1965; Zartman, I. William, 'The Politics of Boundaries in North and West Africa' in *Journal of Modern African Studies*, vol. 3, August 1965, pp. 155–73.

22. Touval, op. cit., shows that the OAU's only direct role in the Ghana–Upper Volta dispute, which came before the OAU Council of Ministers in Cairo in 1964, was to make the recommendation of a procedure for working towards a settlement – by suggesting direct negotiations. But its very discussion of the Upper Volta complaint helped to bring about the Ghanaian withdrawal. The dispute was not about historical rights, ethnic nationalism or self-determination. It was essentially about technical questions concerning the interpretation of documents and maps by which the boundary had been earlier defined. The border dispute between Dahomey and Niger which erupted in November 1963 was never brought before the OAU but was dealt with by the Union Africaine et Malgache (UAM) and by the Entente Council, an example of action by another type of regional organization.

5 MEDIATION

Naomi Schwiesow

Among the ways that disagreements over boundaries may be ameliorated, direct negotiation between the states involved is often the best. But disagreements that admit of this kind of settlement are for that very reason not likely to present crises in international relations. It is precisely when direct negotiation between two states breaks down, or cannot be initiated, that a boundary question risks leading to an armed confrontation. To forestall war, or to accomplish a cessation of hostilities that have already begun, the good offices or mediation of a third state or states is often the most immediately effective means.

This is so because states whose claims against each other are so serious that they cannot discuss them unaided, much less agree between themselves, are not likely to be willing, as a first step, to submit the disputed issue to more formal procedures of settlement such as arbitration (which binds them in advance to accept a decision made by others); or adjudication (which, in considering a question primarily from the legal point of view, cannot always encompass the often more fundamental political grounds of a conflict). Regional organizations may be unable to deal with boundary conflicts that have reached a critical juncture, where passions are intense, because they have not the authority or power to lead the disputants to compromise, or because they fear to take sides and thereby risk inner schism.

The United Nations has sometimes performed several kinds of role in boundary disputes. In particular, the Secretary General, or his representatives, have mediated some of these issues (for example between Cambodia and Thailand). But the United Nations is frequently unable to serve with much success in frontier conflicts, partly because it is a collection of diverse groups that realign from issue to issue according to separate interests, and partly because it has advocated principles or policies that would disadvantage one or the other claimant. States may therefore hesitate to submit their disputes to such a judge, or to accept or act on the demands it makes.

Although, then, a variety of other forms of negotiations may sometimes be employed, mediation by third states is often the most helpful way to deal with border disagreements. A mediating state offers not only its good offices but also specific suggestions of possible forms of settlement for a conflict. Disputing states who request or consent to mediation are not bound to accept the proffered solution, as they are when they submit to arbitration; for this reason mediation proceedings may be accepted more readily than arbitration. In bringing the disputing states to agreement on a particular solution mediators have not the same legal force that supports arbitrators. But, since mediators, to be successful, are compelled to discover politically acceptable solutions, the effects of their intervention may well be more lasting than the decisions of arbitrators.

Mediation is a process that lends itself well, because of its flexibility, to the complicated and diverse nature of border questions. The proceedings may be formal or informal. They may preserve whatever degree of secrecy is convenient, allowing sensitivities and inhibitions to be treated in the most judicious manner. And they may offer the states that are involved the opportunity to interpret the negotiations, for public opinion at home or abroad, in a way that may save face where otherwise it would be lost. Mediation can of course be provided by more than one state, simultaneously or consecutively, in a single crisis. It may offer a series of proposals around which the disputants can bargain. It can persist in spite of setbacks and be renewed if a tentative compromise collapses. Mediators may offer inducements of their own in return for concessions on a border issue by the disputants.

When it is conducted by an interested country, especially a large power, mediation may be an effort to settle a frontier dispute between two other states in a way preferred by, or at least satisfactory to, the mediator without its active military intervention, or to prevent the intervention of other states or organizations when this might have a less desirable outcome. A weak state may request mediation by a third party in order to strengthen its position in a dispute; a strong state may seek mediation as a means of legitimizing part or all of its claims or gains against a weaker state. But where the disparity of power between conflicting states is great, the stronger state may believe that it can win its claim by overwhelming pressure on the weaker state, and may find little reason to agree to mediation.

Usually a mediator must be a strong or influential state, at least with respect to the disputing parties. He must have sufficient authority so that his proposals will carry weight. He must seem fully impartial, perhaps by appealing to each disputant on different grounds, in order to be acceptable to both. At the same time, the mediator may need some special knowledge of or involvement in the question at issue in order to be effective. For this reason, states that have been imperial powers are often successful mediators in disputes involving their former colonies.

During the early period of the Cold War, it was probably more difficult than at other times to find a state that could satisfy all of these requirements for mediation, since the principal and even the secondary powers were so closely bound to the two major political blocs, whose contest seemed to intrude in every corner of the globe, that they could not seem impartially disposed in even a small and remote dispute. However, where two states were in dispute in an area that was clearly within one of the major blocs, the dominant power in that bloc might have served as mediator. Today, when divisions have arisen within the major Cold War alliances, and since some parts of the world have receded from the arena of active confrontation between the super-powers, the impartiality of the Great Powers and the suitability of middle-range powers as mediators in some disputes may well become enhanced.

It may be useful to consider some recent cases of mediation to examine their effectiveness. In the eastern part of the Arabian Peninsula, south of the Persian Gulf, disagreement persists about the border between Saudi Arabia on the one hand and the Abu Dhabi Sheikhdom and Muscat and Oman Sultanate on the other. The disputed area extends from the base of the Qatar peninsula in the west to the Buraimi Oasis in the east, along the western and southern frontier of Abu Dhabi, and then southwards of Buraimi along the western edge of Oman. The Buraimi Oasis lies on the frontier between Abu Dhabi and Oman.

During the nineteenth century there were occasional invasions and temporary occupations of Buraimi by Najdi tribesmen from the west, but the last of these intrusions ended in 1869 and control of the group of settlements at Buraimi was after that time shared by Abu Dhabi and the Sultanate of Muscat and Oman. In 1914, by a convention with Britain, the Ottoman government, which controlled Najdi territory, accepted as the eastern boundary of Najd a line running directly south from a point on the Persian Gulf just west of Qatar. When Ibn Saud succeeded to Ottoman sovereignty in Najd and Hasa in 1922, this line was understood to be binding on him as successor in law also to Ottoman treaty obligations concerning the border. At that time Ibn Saud did not object to the boundary. But in 1935 the Saudi government proclaimed a new border reaching much further eastward than the 1914 line, although it remained far west of Buraimi and south of the Liwa Oasis, a major group of settlements south-west of Buraimi. Britain, acting for the Sultan of Muscat and Oman at his request, and for the Trucial Sheikhdoms under treaty relations first established in the nineteenth century, made a counter-proposal following the general pattern of the Saudi claim but lying somewhat to the south and west of it. No agreement was attained with respect to these borders.

It was most likely the post-war renewal of the search for oil along the Persian Gulf coast and in Oman that led to a new and vastly expanded Saudi claim in 1949 to territory along the coast east of Qatar and in the Abu Dhabi hinterland to a point implying the inclusion of Buraimi. Apart from the prospect of oil reserves in the area of the oasis, Buraimi offered a landward entrance to Oman, and served as a centre of trade and transportation. Saudi Arabia's extended claims in this region were supported, and probably to some extent provoked, by Aramco, the American oil company holding a concession in Saudi Arabia. Yet the Saudi demand for rights in the high seas of the Persian Gulf, off the newly-claimed coastal stretches near Qatar, was met with a protest by the American government.

Britain rejected Saudi Arabia's 1949 claim and protested against the violation of Abu Dhabi territory by Aramco surveyors and Saudi agents; but in reply it received only counter-protests and enlarged demands from Saudi Arabia. No basis for discussion of the difficulties could be agreed on. At last, Britain, though it asserted that Saudi Arabia bore the burden of proof for its claim, offered, under certain conditions, to take part in a joint commission to investigate the political allegiances of tribes in the disputed area, and to submit the question to arbitration if the commission's findings did not lead to a solution. Saudi Arabia agreed, for the most part, to these proposals in September 1950. However, it was not until the following April that agreement was reached that the commission should begin investigations in the autumn of 1951. During these long delays, despite meetings of Saudi and British representatives in London in August 1951 and in Dammam in January and February 1952 (meetings that reconfirmed the original agreement that the parties should abstain from almost all activity in the disputed area while the commission's investigation was pending), there is strong evidence that Saudi agents went to great lengths to sway the tribal leaders in the area in a way that would directly influence the outcome of the commission's inquiry.

The efforts apparently made by Saudi Arabia to substantiate its claims were mainly attempts to collect zakat, or certain taxes or tribute, and to obtain declarations of allegiance from tribal leaders. But in this part of Arabia political authority may be said to have been traditionally a matter of authority over persons, that is, over tribes, which are to some degree nomadic, rather than over strictly delimited territorial areas. Moreover, political allegiance was often given not so much to a ruler, as the head of a continuing and legitimate government over territory or tribe, but rather to whoever was powerful enough to demand it successfully. And it was often not clearly distinguishable from allegiance to religious authority. So, among the tribes in the Saudi–Abu Dhabi frontier, it was not obvious what were the determining signs of political allegiance, especially when by nature it shifted according to the political fortunes of those who aspired to command it. Nor was it obvious how determining the allegiance of the tribes would in any clear way indicate a definite territorial border between the two states.

What brought to a crisis the persistent disagreement over Saudi Arabia's eastern border was finally that country's dispatch of a political envoy with forty retainers across mutually recognized Abu Dhabi territory to Buraimi, where they settled in direct violation of the accords earlier reached with Britain. During several weeks of charges and counter-charges that produced no useful result, the Sultan of Muscat sent reinforcements to some Buraimi chiefs at their request and gathered more than eight thousand men to defend the oasis against the Saudi intrusion. The British Political Resident in the Persian Gulf had also sent troops from the Trucial Oman Levies to one of the villages in Buraimi. In turn, the Saudis strengthened their original contingent in Buraimi. There was acute danger that a widespread tribal war would ensue from attempts by the Sultan of Muscat and Oman to repulse the Saudis from Buraimi. On the brink of this imminent military clash, the American ambassador to Saudi Arabia intervened. Perhaps encouraged by American oil company representatives in Saudi Arabia, he persuaded Britain to ask the Sultan of Muscat to refrain from an attack on Buraimi: this request was successful. He also made specific proposals that were included in the Standstill Agreement accepted by Britain and Saudi Arabia on 26 October 1952. This agreement provided essentially that both sides should remain in their positions in Buraimi, that replacements and supplies might be brought in but no reinforcements, that there should be no provocative moves and no activities that might influence a later border decision, and that direct negotiations should be resumed. Direct military conflict was thus for the moment forestalled by American mediation at this point.

Negotiations during 1953 and 1954, when the United States maintained a generally neutral position, established a mutual withdrawal of forces, except for policing activities, and an agreement on terms for arbitration of the dispute. The arbitration tribunal that met in Geneva in September 1955 was, however, short-lived, for the British member soon resigned, complaining of Saudi duplicity. Britain was then accused by Saudi Arabia of sabotaging the proceedings out of fear that the decision would be unfavourable. In any event, the Sultan of Muscat and the Sheikh of Abu Dhabi entered and held the Buraimi Oasis in the autumn of 1955 to prevent further Saudi incursions in the wake of the fruitless arbitration proceedings. Britain then declared a boundary very close to its 1935 offer. Saudi Arabia at first threatened to take the dispute to the United Nations Security Council. But by the end of January 1956 it was willing to try to renew friendly relations with Britain, which was also in a somewhat more conciliatory mood. Both attitudes were perhaps supported at least indirectly by the United States after the meeting between Eisenhower and Eden at that time, for the United States may have desired British concessions at Buraimi in return for Saudi support against the danger of communist subversion in the Middle East.

But in November 1956 Saudi Arabia broke off diplomatic relations with Britain over the Suez dispute. Occasional talks between Britain and Saudi Arabia since that time, partly under the aegis of the United Nations Secretary General, have made little progress, although diplomatic relations between the two countries were resumed in January 1963. At present, amid Abu Dhabi's plans for federating with six other Persian Gulf sheikhdoms and Bahrain and Qatar, Saudi Arabia is not pressing its Buraimi claims, though neither is it disavowing them.

The instance of American mediation that took place in this dispute in 1952 succeeded in averting the immediate threat of military conflict that occasioned it. Also, the agreement it effected, in renewing direct discussions between Britain and Saudi Arabia, doubtless significantly promoted the eventual achievement of an agreement to arbitration. But the outcome of these efforts was unhappily far from wholly beneficial. The breakdown in arbitration proceedings made further attempts at mediation or arbitration unacceptable and deepened the mutual distrust of the two states. It also resulted in the forcible re-establishment of Abu Dhabi and Muscat in Buraimi, at a cost perhaps greater than what would have been incurred by carrying out their determination to expel the Saudi enclave from the oasis in 1952. Another difficulty produced by averting the use of force at this stage was that the Sultan of Muscat and Oman, having acquiesced in American-British pressures to refrain from driving the Saudis out of Buraimi, found his authority over the sometimes rebellious Omani tribes seriously undermined. Partly because of his weakened position, the Sultan was unable to contain Omani resistance. When widespread uprisings occurred in 1957, he needed British assistance to restore order.

Granted that these occasions of conflict could not have been foreseen with certainty at the time when mediation was conducted, the question remains whether diplomatic intervention here succeeded, even as a limited endeavour to prevent more warfare than was otherwise likely to occur. It is conceivable that attempts to avoid an impending military clash, even if in the immediate event successful, may sometimes exacerbate rather than soothe a border conflict taken as a whole and together with its connected circumstances. As for the contribution of mediation towards some resolution of the substantive issues involved in the dispute, it was apparently nil. One is tempted to regard the imposition of a de facto solution in 1955 by the forcible reoccupation of Buraimi by British-led forces of Abu Dhabi and Muscat and Oman, supported by Britain's subsequent declaration of the border it recognized, as the most substantial movement yet made towards an eventual settlement of the issue, one that may be strengthened by usage over time and that would be consonant with the extent of effective authority of the disputants.

In terms of the general hypotheses introducing this chapter, the mediator in this case had a clear interest in the area where the crisis arose, for American oil companies conducted major operations in Saudi Arabia as well as some activities along the Persian Gulf coast, and the United States was concerned beyond its natural protection of these interests to forestall disruptive events that might encourage communist subversion in Middle Eastern states, which were critically close to Soviet dominions. The United States was also a far greater power than either of the disputants, and was therefore in a strong position to exert effective pressures on both. Britain's alliance with and dependence on the United States made her acquiescence in American mediation to some degree natural. Moreover, if Britain seriously wished to avoid the military encounter that threatened to occur over Buraimi, it was doubtless helpful to her, in asking for concessions from Abu Dhabi and Muscat, to be able to present herself as pressed by the United States, so that she would not seem, to the Sheikh and the Sultan, too willing to bow to Saudi pressures. On the other hand, American mediation must have appealed to Saudi Arabia, partly because of Saudi ties with the American oil companies, which had actually aided the Saudi government in arguing its territorial claims, and partly because the substance of American efforts could not but appear favourable to Saudi Arabia's position. Despite these circumstances favouring mediation, however, American intervention in 1952 did little more than temporarily restore a measure of order. It seems possible that, if the United States had pressed its efforts at mediation further, it could have achieved some progress towards a more substantial resolution of the issues. But in the circumstances, especially since direct talks between Saudi Arabia and Britain were agreed upon, this did not seem to be a compelling task.

A second case of mediation by a third country in a border dispute that remains unresolved is the continuing American search for a modus vivendi between British Honduras, or Belize, and Guatemala, which claims the entire territory of its opponent. This conflict originates principally in differing interpretations of the meaning and effects of a treaty concerning British Honduras that was negotiated between Guatemala and Britain in 1859, although other questions are also involved. The history of the dispute is therefore mostly legal and diplomatic.

By the Treaty of Madrid of 1670, Britain gained title to its de facto possessions in the West Indies and the Americas, but whether this claim included British Honduras was not agreed upon by Britain and Spain. During the seventeenth and eighteenth centuries British activities in the area around Belize were sometimes disputed by Spain. The Treaty of Paris of 1763 and the Treaty of London of 1786 forbade British fortifications in Belize but permitted British operations (mainly woodcutting) in a limited area. Sovereignty was, however, reserved to Spain. Despite these agreements British activities continued to expand, and in 1798 Spain attempted an attack on Belize town. British Honduras repulsed the attack, but Britain could not be said to gain rights thereby, since the peace treaties of 1802 and 1804 re-established the status quo ante 1796. After protesting in 1813 and 1816 against Britain's continued expansion and fortification in Belize, Spain ceased to exercise her rights in the area and in practice Britain acted as the sovereign authority there, reaching as far as the present extent of British Honduras during the period of the Central American Federation from 1823 to 1838. There is no sign that the Spanish administrative territories of Guatemala or Yucatan exercised any powers in the area of British expansion in the early nineteenth century.

However, Guatemala claims that Spain's sovereignty over the area of British Honduras continued until Guatemala's independence in 1821 as the Federal Republic of Central America, and that it then inherited all the sovereign rights of Spain in the former entity of Guatemala. It further claims that Britain refused to recognize the Central American Federation because the new republic would not give up its sovereignty over British Honduras. Britain, on the other hand, argues that the populations of Central America, in acquiring independence, gained control only of the areas over which they actually had effective authority, but that by 1821 effective control of Belize was in Britain's hands. It also maintains that it never considered its sovereignty over Belize open to question, as a right that could be granted by the federation in return for recognition, and that it withheld recognition for lack of signs that the new state could maintain itself stably or fulfil obligations it might undertake. But British sovereignty was not explicitly claimed at this time. In 1835 and 1836 Britain did ask Spain to resign any rights of sovereignty that it felt it still had in British Honduras, and Spain suggested that there would be no difficulty in doing so but did not make a formal reply.

The Treaty of 1859 was undertaken between Britain and Guatemala to describe the boundaries of British Honduras with Guatemala. It also provided, in Article 7, for the construction jointly by both states of a road from the coast of Belize inland to Guatemala. This has never been done. In the Treaty Guatemala did not explicitly question, and may be said to have acknowledged, British sovereignty in Belize. The Treaty itself seemed to recognize that a Guatemalan border with an area under British sovereignty had existed for some time. But Guatemala argues that the

Treaty was actually, although tacitly, a cession of territory previously Guatemalan to Britain, for which the provision in Article 7 for building a road was compensation rather than a mutual undertaking for the benefit of both states. Guatemala therefore now maintains that the non-fulfilment of Article 7 nullifies the Treaty and that it thereby regains its former right to the territory of Belize. Britain's position is that the Treaty never concerned a question of cession and that the territory was rightfully British before 1859, as indicated by the Treaty itself and for the reasons noted above. Britain also says that the obligation to build a road was a joint one and not a compensation for cession (at most an 'inducement' for Guatemala to give up its questionable claim); therefore the non-fulfilment of the article is a mutual omission, which the two countries may try to repair but which in no case invalidates the whole Treaty. At most it gives Guatemala a right to satisfaction with regard to that particular issue. Moreover, since British sovereignty in Belize did not depend on this Treaty, even its invalidation would not give Guatemala a claim to the area.

There is some evidence from British Foreign Office correspondence at the time of the Treaty that Britain did take it to be, as regards at least part of the Territory of British Honduras, a treaty tacitly ceding possession from Guatemala to Britain. Some official memoranda suggest that the question of cession could not be made explicit in the Treaty because it might have seemed to violate the Clayton–Bulwer Treaty of 1850 between Britain and the United States, which cast some doubt on Britain's rights in Belize.

In any event, immediately after 1859 difficulties arose about the obligations incurred by each state in Article 7 of the Treaty. In 1863 a convention was made to replace the article, providing that Britain should pay £50,000 towards the construction of the road. But this was never ratified, both states being partly responsible for the failure to do so, and in 1867 Britain claimed that it had no further obligations under Article 7. None of the compromises offered by either state since then has been agreed on.

In 1880 Guatemala proposed arbitration of the questions whether Guatemala had not a right to require the fulfilment of Article 7 in some way, and what were the effects of its non-fulfilment. But Britain would not agree to arbitration. After fifty years of near silence on the matter, Britain in 1933 asked that the boundary between Guatemala and Belize be finally demarcated. Guatemala then once more proposed arbitration of their differences, by the President of the United States. Britain held that the Hague Court should be the arbitrator. In 1938 Britain gave the opinion that there was no use in pursuing the question, and Guatemala declared the Treaty of 1859 void. In 1940, however, Britain renewed its proposals for arbitration of legal questions raised by Article 7 of the Treaty. Guatemala insisted that the issue was not merely legal and that its decision must take account of all the circumstances and antecedents concerning its territorial rights. In 1946 Britain again suggested that the International Court determine the validity of the 1859 treaty, but it then rejected Guatemala's demand that an equitable and not only a legal decision must be made about its rights in Belize. Controversy over the grounds on which the dispute might be resolved was thus during this time the principal feature of the disagreement.

Apart from informal discussions with Britain in 1957, Guatemala did not actively pursue its claims against Belize until 1961 when it proposed further conversations. British Honduras protested that it would never agree to become part of Guatemala. But Guatemala's aim seemed to be some sort of federal association between the two countries. At the close of 1961, however, Guatemala's President complained that neither direct talks with Britain nor negotiations within the United Nations could be of any use, and he threatened a diplomatic break with Britain. At the same time he mentioned that the United States had promised to mediate in the dispute (it has been suggested this was in exchange for Guatemalan aid to Cuban rebels). Partly as a result of this speech, talks between Britain and Guatemala were held in Puerto Rico in the spring of 1962, and joint recommendations emerged for improving economic co-operation and political relations between Guatemala and Belize. But in July 1963 Guatemala broke off relations with Britain because internal self-government had been promised to British Honduras for 1964. Despite this break, talks were held between British and Guatemalan representatives in Washington in December 1963, agreeing to refer the questions discussed to the governments of the two states with the aim of settling the dispute and renewing political relations.

After these talks, Britain and Guatemala requested mediation of their dispute by the United States, which appointed a lawyer, Mr Webster, to recommend forms of settlement. His plans for an arrangement between the two countries included independence for British Honduras but co-operation with Guatemala in foreign, military, and trade matters, with some new benefits for Guatemala including a road and port, for Guatemalan products, provided by Belize. When these proposals first appeared in 1966, there was widespread public protest against them in Belize. When they were finally officially published in substantially the same form in the spring of 1968, British Honduras rejected them and Guatemala was unfavourably disposed. To British Honduras, the advantage of such a relationship with Guatemala, which has long been comparatively backward and highly unstable, is hardly obvious. Guatemala would almost certainly reap economic benefits from the arrangement but seems to shrink from abandoning its territorial claims as a price for these gains. Britain also finally turned down the proposals as unacceptable to British Honduras.

In this case mediation was adopted only after a century of failure to resolve the dispute either by direct negotiations or by submitting the disagreement to an arbitral tribunal or the International Court for a judgment. Where differences exist over the nature of a border dispute or over the grounds on which it ought to be decided, agreement to more formal methods of settlement (which often require that the basis of decision or the scope of competence be precisely stipulated beforehand) may be comparatively difficult to attain. But mediation, in seeking a solution acceptable to both parties, may proceed on any grounds that are helpful in reaching a compromise. Since the disputants are free to reject a mediator's proposals, they can more easily accept his intervention even without assurance that the issue will be considered in a way favourable to them.

The United States' predominant role in American affairs and its particular interest in Guatemala since the 1954 intervention (perhaps also arising from the alleged Guatemalan support for anti-Castro activities), made it an obviously suitable mediator in the Guatemala–Belize dispute. What is less clear is, not so much why Guatemala and Britain should request American diplomatic intervention in particular, but, rather, why they initiated the process of mediation at all, when the disagreement had in the main been allowed to ride for so long. But there were some obvious motives. With little doubt, Britain would prefer to be able to arrange its relations with British Honduras, including the colony's independence, without the annoyance of a diplomatic break with Guatemala. To Guatemala, if British Honduras gains independence in spite of her claims, the claims would become more difficult to maintain. Therefore, for both parties the crisis in relations arising from the prospect of imminent independence for Belize could be sufficient motive for the active pursuit of negotiations. However, from Guatemala's point of view, the primary virtue of negotiation, and one possessed particularly by mediation because it is an open-ended process, was as a way to keep the issue alive over a long period of time, thus forestalling inconvenient moves on Britain's part, while allowing Guatemala to use its demands as a unifying issue when internal stresses become especially severe. When border claims are kept open in this way, they usually remain available for bargaining purposes in a variety of situations, both for domestic effects and as foreign policy instruments, because they are always translatable into the threat or even the use of force.

Yet if in this case it is true that mediation was sought by the disputing states without the pressure of imminent armed conflict, and that therefore mediation is concerned not simply with how to avert a momentary threat but rather with how to resolve the fundamental disagreement in a lasting way so that conflicting claims are abandoned, it is also true that in this more intractable task mediation has accomplished little. It is also difficult to nourish hopes for its future success unless, perhaps, British Honduras can be persuaded to grant concessions in return for Guatemalan recognition, and unless, when it is on the verge of independence, Guatemala chooses to consolidate what gains it can make from the issue while the opportunity remains. But other less satisfactory outcomes of American mediation may easily be envisaged as well. At present it is far from clear that these intervening efforts will decide the issues that have been raised. But they have gained in the meantime whatever advantages are to be found in delay.

The Rann of Kutch incident in the border dispute between India and Pakistan offers another instance of mediation by a third-party state, although its resolution was ultimately arbitrated under the auspices of the United Nations.

The Rann of Kutch conflict grew out of the disagreement between India and Pakistan concerning the status of Kashmir, which was not settled when the two states became independent after the Second World War. In 1948, the United Nations Commission for India and Pakistan was formed to attempt to mediate the conflict that quickly arose over Kashmir; the following year, a Military Observer Group was established to oversee the cease-fire line that had been agreed upon by this means. But further efforts by the United Nations to mediate a reasonably stable arrangement between India and Pakistan in Kashmir were not successful, largely because Pakistan refused to withdraw from Azad Kashmir, or to consider its demilitarization, which would deny Pakistan its gains won in battle and expose it to attacks from India, while India refused to weaken its hold on the rest of Kashmir. India demanded that Azad Kashmir be eliminated as a separate entity, as a punishment for and protection against Pakistani attack. On this issue, the United Nations mediator, Mr Frank Graham, who had replaced the Commission in this task, could not obtain an agreement between the disputants. And in 1953 he advised that India and Pakistan engage in bilateral negotiations as the most likely means of reaching some accord.

In 1954 border incidents flared briefly again in Kashmir; but by 1960 India and Pakistan were able to conclude treaties concerning the Indus River water-supply and parts of the boundaries between the two countries. Despite these agreements, Pakistan remained frustrated over its failure to obtain a plebiscite or any other settlement in Kashmir, and over the inaction of the United States in its support. In 1963 Pakistan was able to make an agreement with China in which Pakistan's right to control of some areas in Kashmir was recognized. But, at the same time, Pakistan did not take advantage of India's conflict with China in 1962 to gain headway in Kashmir, and ministers of India and Pakistan met occasionally from December 1962 to May 1963. During 1963 India made various moves intended to assimilate Kashmir's form of government with that of the other Indian states, thereby gradually absorbing Kashmir into the Union. Although conversations between India and Pakistan took place again in October 1964, they accomplished little, and towards the end of that year India renewed its efforts to integrate Kashmir.

Pakistan required some more dramatic means of opposing India's activities. Finding himself in a strengthened position vis-à-vis India, which was for several reasons internally weak at that time, Ayub Khan again approached China as a way of bringing pressure to bear upon India. Incidents along the boundaries between India and Pakistan increased as Pakistan attempted to bring the problem of Kashmir to world notice. The outbreak of hostilities in the Rann of Kutch in the spring of 1965 was most probably provoked by Pakistan for the same reason, to forestall the gradual loss of Kashmir that India's policies threatened to bring about. It may also have been meant by India as a kind of warning to Pakistan over the Kashmir issue, or by either state as a kind of test of war between them.

The Rann area, marshy and of little intrinsic value, separates West Pakistan from the Indian state of Kutch. The proper border between India and Pakistan at this point, as it had been historically viewed, may be said to include the Rann in Indian territory; but in 1947 Pakistan had claimed the northern half of the Rann, arguing that it was an extension of the Arabian Sea and therefore ought to be divided along its mid-line between the two states. Apparently accidental incidents had occurred along the northern border of the Rann in January 1965. In early April, more serious hostilities erupted, each side claiming that the other had invaded past established positions along the border.

At this point a form of mediation proved successful. After about three weeks, British intercessions between India and Pakistan were able to produce an informal break in the fighting. That this was possible depended largely on the two states having early achieved at least the minimum required objectives: India had successfully resisted a serious Pakistani incursion, and Pakistan had drawn attention to its claims against India. Moreover, the impending rains would flood the Rann and might spread a persistent struggle to other areas; and neither India nor Pakistan was ready to accept such a risk. During the pause in hostilities, Britain attempted to mediate a formal cease-fire and an agreement to negotiate the Rann issue. The Indians and Pakistanis did not meet directly with each other during these efforts. The British High Commissioners to the two states were the chief intermediaries, and India and Pakistan also received messages from Prime Minister Wilson during May. The two disputants agreed upon the desirability of a cease-fire and of further negotiations to establish a final settlement. But India maintained that the forces of both sides should return to the positions held in early January 1965, whereas Pakistan demanded that India should withdraw to south of the twenty-fourth parallel before the cease-fire agreement could be made.

It is likely that not only the work of the mediators at hand, but also and especially the mediation of Prime Minister Wilson between Shastri and Ayub Khan at the Commonwealth Prime Ministers' Conference in June 1965, led to a resolution of the Rann incident. The agreements signed on 30 June as a result of Britain's mediation included procedures for troop withdrawals (but without provision for enforcement) as well as provision for a formal cease-fire, for resumption of police patrols, for a meeting of ministers to negotiate a settlement of the border, and for the creation of a tribunal of arbitration, which was to render a decision if the ministers were unable to reach one, and which was to remain established until its decision had been implemented.

However, as India and Pakistan could not themselves arrive at a settlement of the Rann of Kutch question, an arbitral tribunal was appointed as agreed, the United Nations Secretary General choosing Gunnar K. A. Lagergren as chairman. The tribunal met from 15 February 1966 until 14 July 1967 and on 19 February 1968 awarded Pakistan most of its claim in the Rann (though India retained nine-tenths of the territory). According to the tribunal, its decision was based partly on political grounds, that an Indian presence on the northern edge of the Rann close to major cities in Pakistan would be destabilizing or perhaps provocative, but mainly on historical grounds. The arbitral award was accepted by both states the same month, and demarcation of the border began in March 1968.[1]

The instance of mediation in the Rann of Kutch dispute occurred at the moment when such an approach is most likely to succeed: that is, when further open conflict, which was not intended mainly to accomplish territorial gains but rather to serve as a demonstration or a test, had become more or less useless, and when a truce without loss of face was of value to both disputants. Since both were eager for a resolution of the immediate situation, the mediation had a good chance of success. The success of British mediation in producing an agreement to ultimate arbitration of the dispute depended largely on the fact that the dispute was much less substantive than symbolic: that the territory itself was not valuable or materially crucial to either side. In cases where the area at stake in a border dispute is intrinsically valuable to both contestants, and where the substance of the dispute is the possession of territory, one must expect that mediation would be much less likely to achieve an agreement that would lead to successful arbitration, as the Buraimi Oasis dispute shows.

At the beginning it was suggested that former colonial powers could be expected to act as mediators of disputes between their former colonies in some circumstances. Britain's mediation in the Rann of Kutch issue indicates that former colonial states may possess not only sufficient impartiality between their former colonies, but also sufficient prestige in their eyes, to be acceptable mediators. That this is true not only when decolonization has been relatively graceful, but also when it has been disruptive, seems likely in the light of France's present close ties to her former colonies in Africa.

A related and familiar case of mediation of a border war, or a war over disputed territory, occurred at Tashkent in January 1966 when the Soviet Union persuaded India and Pakistan to agree to a cease-fire in their conflict over Kashmir. Without a further review of the history of the Kashmir question, a few elements of this occasion of mediation are instructive in the present context.

The United Nations was not a promising agent or arena of settlement when the war in Kashmir broke out in the summer of 1965. Because the United Nations supported the principle of self-determination, which favoured Pakistan's desire to decide the question of Kashmir's fate by a plebiscite, and because the organization had been the scene of several attempts to condemn Indian action in Kashmir, its efforts to resolve the dispute were unacceptable to India. Division between the super-powers within the United Nations also diminished its effectiveness: the United States participated in the predominantly pro-Pakistan attitude of the United Nations while the Soviet Union generally supported

India's position. United Nations appeals for a cease-fire were at first disregarded by both sides, and the cease-fire that was finally agreed upon in September was repeatedly violated. In the end, the United Nations could do no more than resolve that India and Pakistan should meet with a representative of the Secretary General for more discussions.

As the United Nations seemed unlikely to be able to halt the war in Kashmir, many offers of good offices or other diplomatic aids were made by third-party states. Among them, those made by the smaller African or Asian states were not of much use, for most of these states had in some way prejudiced their relationships with one or the other of the disputants. Moreover, such states could wield little power or influence in trying to bring about a settlement of the conflict.

The United States was in a poor position to mediate the Kashmir dispute. As an ally of Pakistan, it could not readily gain Indian acceptance of any measures it might propose. It had alienated India still more by appearing to share responsibility with Britain and Malaysia for attempts to accuse India in the United Nations. By ending military aid to Pakistan during the war, the United States succeeded in consolidating its ineffectiveness as a mediator. Great Britain, which earlier in the year had successfully mediated the clash in the Rann of Kutch, embittered India during the Kashmir war by a corresponding withdrawal of military aid, so that it too lost the impartial status that an acceptable mediator must approach.

But the Soviet Union, eminently suitable for mediation in the India–Pakistan conflict by virtue of its great strength and influence, and with its special interest arising from its nearness to the two states at war, maintained its acceptability. It befriended India in the United Nations proceedings concerning Kashmir, and maintained its military assistance to that state during the war. But it would not accuse Pakistan, either, of responsibility for the outbreak of hostilities. And the Soviet position of the early 1960s, generally favouring India over Pakistan, had been modified after

Khrushchev's demise toward a more impartial stance between the two states. Largely for these reasons, the Soviet Union's offer of its good offices and of a meeting-place at Tashkent for negotiations between the disputants gained India's assent in September 1965. Pakistan accepted the Soviet proposal two months later, when the United Nations endeavours to gain a settlement had reached an impasse. The meetings at Tashkent in January 1966 produced agreement to observe a cease-fire, to withdraw forces, and to continue negotiations on substantive matters. Ministerial conferences began in March 1966 between India and Pakistan.

The availability of a suitable and effective mediator was one ground for the Tashkent conference's success in bringing the military conflict between India and Pakistan to a close for a time. Another was the significance of their confrontation to the two states at war. For Pakistan, the usefulness of a military crisis in Kashmir was partly, and perhaps chiefly, as in the Rann of Kutch outbreak, that it drew general attention to the fact of the continuing territorial disagreement, and thus helped to forestall India's gradual assumption of political authority over the disputed area. For India, military measures seemed to be required in response to Pakistani infiltration across the 1949 cease-fire line. For both states, their immediate purposes were fairly satisfied by limited military expeditions, and a further escalation of the conflict proved rather unsuccessful for both. Since they soon reached a general stalemate, the disputants were inclined to accept some diplomatic assistance in bringing the war to a close, so long as an appropriate mediator, and one whose intervention would not cause either party to lose face, could be found.

As in two of the cases of mediation that have been outlined, however, substantive progress in deciding the fundamental question of whether India or Pakistan ought to exercise political authority in Kashmir, or of whether or how the territory should be divided between them, was not achieved. The Tashkent agreements provided for continuing conversations between India and Pakistan on outstanding issues of concern to them, including the

Kashmir dispute, but the disagreement remains unresolved. Mediation may here be said to have furthered some fairly permanent settlement of the dispute only in very indirect ways: by encouraging normal diplomatic relations and discussions, which might otherwise not have been readily resumed even if the fighting in and near Kashmir had died down of itself, and which might in time make some negotiated agreement over Kashmir possible; and by reinforcing the 1949 cease-fire line as the de facto boundary between Pakistan's and India's spheres of more or less effective control in Kashmir. One may consider the issue to be in some sense provisionally resolved by this division as long as major military encounters do not erupt over the cease-fire line. However, the Kashmir dispute does not seem likely to remain politically or propagandistically dormant for long, and the risk that armed conflict will be renewed seems high. It may be argued that if the Kashmir war had continued until some sort of decisive military outcome had been achieved, a more stable, if less formal, resolution of the dispute might have been attained; but it is not at all certain that either side could have won a clear victory, even if mediation had not procured a cease-fire. In any event, the effects of Soviet mediation in this instance must be judged significant only in checking, for a time, overt military conflict between the disputing states, and not in gaining broader ends.

To sketch in so summary a fashion these border or territorial disputes can barely suggest the variety of the questions at issue in each case. It also carries the risk of erring, especially in interpretation or emphasis, for the sake of brevity. Yet, despite its weaknesses, such a review of several cases of mediation indicates that certain conditions are likely to accompany effective attempts to deal with border disagreements by this means in the future. It also illustrates some of the limits of what mediation may be expected to achieve.

In the instances given in this chapter, mediation was accepted by disputing states in several different circumstances. Where war had already broken out, as in Kashmir and the Rann of Kutch, the disputants acceded to proposals for mediation when to prolong hostilities was difficult and not of much value for either side. Mutual exhaustion or stalemate in war might reasonably be expected to favour some negotiation, at least of a truce, on terms acceptable to both parties; in these cases, mediation achieved that. In the Rann of Kutch incident, mediation also brought about agreement to an ultimately successful arbitration of the dispute; but in this case the territorial dispute was not the most significant aspect of the confrontation. Where a military confrontation was apparently not in prospect, in the Belize dispute, mediation lent itself to more or less opposing aims – for some resolution of the issue on the part of Britain, and for delay on the part of Guatemala. Where war was imminent, in the Buraimi Oasis dispute, mediation was acceptable because avoiding hostilities was generally to the advantage of the Saudi position; and because it was probably preferred also by Britain, which acted for the Saudis' opponents diplomatically and could therefore sway them. (Among the cases of mediation considered in this chapter, a distinctive feature of the Buraimi Oasis dispute is that the Trucial Sheikhdoms and Muscat and Oman were diplomatically represented by Britain, which not only acted directly for them but also to some extent controlled their moves according to its own preferences. The impetus of these states was to take military action against Saudi Arabia rather than to accept some negotiated perpetuation of the Saudi presence in Buraimi, and it is doubtful whether they would have acceded to such a settlement without Britain's intercession on the mediator's behalf.) Common to these situations is that the border conflicts or disputes had developed to a point at which negotiation was advantageous to both sides. But when disputing states believe that they may well gain their objectives in a border conflict by military means at some acceptable cost, mediation is not likely to gain their consent.

In the border disputes that have been reviewed, mediation was possible not only because the circumstances of the disputes permitted it, but also because an acceptable mediator offered its services, or was available to the disputants, or was able to impose its preference upon them. The importance of the conjunction of these two elements in accomplishing mediation of a dispute emerges most clearly in the two instances in which war actually broke out. In the case of Kashmir, several states offered to mediate the conflict but were refused. Only when a suitable third-party state or states became available did mediation occur. The attributes of the mediators in the four occasions of mediation were quite in accord with the speculations about them that introduced this chapter, as the separate discussions of each case have suggested at greater length.

Yet, when mediation did occur, the substance of its achievement was mainly limited to forestalling or bringing an end to a war. Negotiations of mediation have included provisions that the disputing states should continue to discuss their disagreements, or that the issues should be submitted to arbitration; but in only one exceptional case among the disputes studied have even these measures led to a final determination of the questions at issue. Apparently, mediation, like other forms of international negotiation, seldom accomplishes a permanent settlement of the matters at stake in a border conflict. Mediation may then reasonably be said to be successful if it wards off hostilities that are imminent, or brings to at least a temporary close hostilities that have begun. Where and when a border dispute is not highly explosive, or is overshadowed by other issues, this may be a satisfactory achievement. But one must expect that mediation will often, perhaps usually, fall short of a fundamental resolution of the political and territorial questions involved in border disputes, partly because it rarely occurs except when such a conflict has been exacerbated nearly to, or beyond, the point of military engagement.

One aspect of these observations about mediation, particularly in the light of the exceptional nature of the Buraimi Oasis dispute, is that such negotiations cannot always be depended upon to prevent border war when a dispute approaches crisis. This judgment is not simply a negative one. For in the Buraimi Oasis case the prevention of a military confrontation at one juncture may have contributed to the scale of the clash that did eventually occur, as the result of a situation that was not in accord with the relations of power between the disputants. In cases where border wars are not forestalled by mediation, as in Kashmir, the disputing states may emerge with relations that are in some respects improved. Small military encounters may be helpful in clarifying the real relations of power and in thereby indicating the shape of an appropriate settlement of particular border questions, a settlement that carries some prospect of enduring.

In the coming years many old border disputes may persist and new ones will arise, especially among the newer states, which are still in the process of establishing effective authority throughout their territories, and which have not yet everywhere confronted the competing authority of neighbours. Border wars, conducted with whatever resources are available, may remain frequent. Among the ways of managing these disputes, or resolving such wars, if not of obtaining ultimate settlements, mediation will probably continue to be one of the most frequently attempted, and one of the most successful. The effectiveness of legal and organizational remedies for such disputes is not likely to increase. But mediation may adapt to, and make use of, changing power-relationships to obtain appropriate political adjustment, or at least relaxation, of critical border disputes.

TEXT REFERENCE

1. For a discussion of the arbitration over the Rann of Kutch (as against the British mediation), see Chapter 6 below, pp. 169, 192–93.

BIBLIOGRAPHY

For an excellent brief discussion of mediation in general, see the article by Darwin, H. G., 'Mediation and Good Offices', in David Davies Memorial

Institute of International Studies, *Report of a Study Group on the Peaceful Settlement of International Disputes*, London: DDMIIS, 1966.

For more complete accounts of the border disputes that have been considered in this chapter, see especially: Kelly, J. B., *Eastern Arabian Frontiers*, New York 1964 and Phillips, Wendell, *Oman, A History*, London 1967; Humphreys, R. A., 'The Anglo-Guatemalan Dispute', in *International Affairs*, vol. 24, 1948, pp. 387–404; Clegern, Wayne M., 'New Light on the Belize Dispute', in *American Journal of International Law*, vol. 52, 1958, pp. 280–97, and *British Honduras*, New York: British Information Services, 1964; Lamb, Alastair, *Crisis in Kashmir: 1947 to 1966*, London 1966 and Brines, Russell, *The Indo-Pakistani Conflict*, London 1968.

6 ARBITRATION

Hazel Fox

Ever since the Jay Treaty in 1794 introduced the machinery of international arbitration as a means of settling disputes outstanding between the United States after independence and the United Kingdom, international arbitration has proved a satisfactory method of settling a limited territorial issue between the parties. The early Anglo-American treaties employed the mixed commission composed of one or two commissioners appointed by each party who together chose a third or fifth by agreement or lots. The members of the arbitration tribunal were, consequently, almost entirely confined to nationals of the two parties. In later arbitrations, the national element of the members of the tribunal was increasingly reduced. First, as in the Puget Sound Agricultural Company Award,[1] a neutral third party was empowered to nominate the third or fifth member of the tribunal, failing agreement between the national members; then, as in the Bulama Island Award, 1870, and the San Juan de la Fuca case,[2] a neutral head of state was nominated as Arbitrator and he increasingly delegated his duty to an individual expert or committee of experts who were able to give a reasoned award. Finally, the form of the collegiate international court, first successfully practised in the Alabama Claims arbitration, 1871–72,[3] received the approval of the Hague Peace Conferences, whereby each party nominates two members of the tribunal (by the Hague Convention of 1907 only one of these might be a national) and the four members thus nominated agree on a fifth as umpire or chairman – failing agreement some third party (in post-Second World War *compromis* the President of the International Court of Justice or the Secretary General of United Nations is sometimes named for this task) nominates the fifth party.

Thus, in the Lac Lanoux arbitration, 1957, between France and Spain, of the three non-national members, France appointed a Swiss, and Spain a Belgian, but as they could not agree on a President, the King of Sweden in accordance with the *compromis* was requested to appoint and did appoint the President of the Arbitration Tribunal. He selected M. Sture Petren.[4] In the uncompleted Buraimi arbitration the three non-national members were a Belgian, Professor Charles de Visscher, a Cuban and a Pakistani. In the recent India–Pakistan Western Boundary case (concerning the Rann of Kutch) a three-man tribunal was employed, none being a national of the parties: India chose a Yugoslav judge, Pakistan an Iranian diplomat, formerly a President of the General Assembly, and failing agreement between the parties on the third member, the Secretary General of United Nations nominated the Swedish Judge Gunnar Lagergren as President.

Whilst the three-man or five-man tribunal in which the neutral members are in the majority has the advantage of securing eminent international jurists or technical experts of two or more nationalities, it lacks the authority and effectiveness which the backing of a modern government can give to the decisions of an arbitration tribunal, a backing which is particularly valuable in a territorial dispute where much expert work in the form of surveying or mapping may be required. In the Argentina–Chile arbitration Queen Victoria (and on her death Edward VII) was the Arbitrator in the proceedings which culminated in the Award of 1902, though the findings were made by a three-man committee headed by Lord Macnaghten: in the 1966 proceedings which were instituted by Chile in pursuance of Article V of the General Treaty of Arbitration of 1902 between Argentina and Chile, Queen Elizabeth II acted as Arbitrator delegating her powers to a three-man tribunal under the chairmanship of Lord McNair. Thus, throughout the Argentina–Chile dispute the United Kingdom was a participant in the sense that they had undertaken to achieve a friendly settlement between the two states and were in a position to utilize their national resources to that end. In the Buraimi arbitration the Arbitrators were reduced to impotent individuals when the proceedings broke down. Even during the continuance of the proceedings, they were totally dependent on the parties for the execution of their powers. Whilst the same was, in theory, true in the Argentina–Chile proceedings since none of the Court of Arbitration's decisions to visit the area, to have it surveyed, etc. could be effected without the consent of the parties, in practice, backed by the administrative machinery of the United Kingdom Government, their wishes could be more effectively executed.

The primary attraction of arbitration as a method for the settlement of boundary disputes has always been the high degree of control over the proceedings which the method permits the states – parties to the dispute in arbitration – to exercise. True, they surrender their independent action by agreeing in advance to accept the award of the arbitrator as binding, and in general (save where exceptional power is granted to decide *ex aequo et bono*[5]) submit the dispute to be judged by the standards of international law and not of national interest. But, in the choice of the person of the arbitrator and in the selection of the terms of reference, and in the detailed provisions relating to the conduct of the proceedings, the parties retain a considerable control over the procedure. By a narrow definition of the areas to be determined, states may prevent a general inquiry into the validity of a frontier line; thus, in the San Juan de la Fuca arbitration the German Emperor was confined to deciding between the Rosario Channel favoured by the United Kingdom and the Haro Channel favoured by the United States of America,[6] and in the Buraimi arbitration the issues were confined to the location of the common frontier between Saudi Arabia and Abu Dhabi and to the determination of 'the sovereignty in the area comprised within a circle whose centre is in Buraimi village and whose circumference passes through the point of junction of latitude 24° 25′ N and longitude 55° 36′ E.'[7]

The definition of the issue is important politically, in that it reflects some approximation of the parties' views, but more so legally, in that it confers jurisdiction upon the arbitrator. Although it is now well established that an arbitrator has inherent jurisdiction to determine the limits of his own jurisdiction,[8] it is equally well established that he may not determine issues which have not been referred to his arbitration. If the *compromis* or special agreement of the parties is ill drawn, the award of the arbitration may equally be ill determined.[9] Or, dissatisfied that either state's contention has been established, the arbitrator may find in favour of a third, as did the King of the Netherlands in the North-East Boundary case between the United States and the United Kingdom in 1831,[10] or attempt to solve the issue by a legal solution other than that favoured by the parties, as did the Queen of Spain when, being invited to determine sovereignty, she considered the question of servitudes in the Aves Island case.[11] Both awards were challenged as nullities on the ground that the Arbitrator had exceeded his jurisdiction and decided beyond the scope of the *compromis*. In the India–Pakistan Western Boundary case, despite the fact that the Arbitration Tribunal decided that it had no power to decide the dispute *ex aequo et bono*, by majority decision it awarded the two deep inlets of the Rann on either side of the Pakistan peninsula of land known as the Nagar Parkar to Pakistan though Pakistan had made out no legal title to them. The President of the Tribunal stated (and the Iranian member, Ambassador Entezam, agreed with him): 'In my opinion it would be inequitable to recognize these inlets as foreign territory. It would be conducive to friction and conflict. The paramount consideration of promoting peace and stability in this region compels the recognition and confirmation that this territory, which is wholly surrounded by Pakistan territory, also be regarded as such.' Similarly the Tribunal awarded a straightened boundary along the outer edges of the Nagar Parkar and up to the Eastern Terminus on the ground that, as a jagged one, 'it was unsuitable and impracticable as an international boundary'.[12] On the publication of the Award, these findings were criticized by Indian lawyers who pointed out that the Tribunal had exceeded its terms to determine the border in the light of the respective claims of India and Pakistan. None-theless, India has confirmed that she will execute the Award in full.

The history of the delimitation of the southern boundary between Argentina and Chile, which received its latest demarcation in an award made by Her Majesty Queen Elizabeth II in 1966,[13] demonstrates the scope of the function which international arbitration can play in the solution of territorial disputes.

In the 1966 proceedings between Argentina and Chile the parties were unable to agree themselves on the terms of reference to the Arbitrator but the Treaty of 1902, under which the United Kingdom was appointed Arbitrator, contained a provision empowering 'in default of agreement either of the parties . . . to invite the intervention of the Arbiter, whose duty it will be to determine the Agreement. . . .'[14] This was done at the invitation of Chile, and the United Kingdom, in consultation with the parties, formulated the issue. This somewhat unusual provision was an early attempt to confer limited compulsory jurisdiction on the Arbitrator once the parties had submitted to his arbitration. By Article 53 of the second Hague Convention for the pacific settlement of international disputes a similar power was conferred on the arbitration tribunal to settle the *compromis* where one of the parties to the arbitration would not agree its terms, but the occasions on which the tribunal might so act were very limited. The International Law Commission in its Model Rules on Arbitral Procedure overcame this difficulty of the refusal of one of the parties to agree a *compromis* or special agreement by an article empowering the arbitration tribunal to dispense with it and to proceed and determine the issue on the application of one of the parties alone after the lapse of three months and provided the dispute was one which was agreed by the parties or had been determined to be arbitrable.[15] The feasibility, however, of such proposals all turns on the prior existence of an arbitration tribunal and, as this too is dependent on the parties' agreement, a state which wishes to prevent an arbitration may obstruct it from the first by refusal to agree an arbitrator.

Such obstruction was not possible in the Argentina–Chile proceedings. In 1896 Argentina and Chile agreed to seek the aid of Bolivia in the settlement of the northern part of their boundary but to submit any difficulties arising further south and covering a distance of approximately 1760 miles to arbitration by the British Government. The United Kingdom was, therefore, nominated Arbiter prior to the crystallization of any dispute and could thereafter be unilaterally seised by either party. Further it could continue to supervise the execution of its award on the ground; in the 1966 proceedings the United Kingdom, with the agreement of the parties, improved on the procedure adopted in 1902, and avoiding the duality of responsibility between Arbitration Tribunal and Demarcation Commission (which in part may have contributed to the error of fact which led to the 1966 proceedings) appointed a three-man Court of Arbitration and empowered it not only to 'decide definitely each point in dispute' as defined in Article I, but also to direct a survey for the purposes of the arbitration, and for the execution of the Award by its demarcation on the ground, the Court of Arbitration 'not to be *functus officio* until it has approved any such demarcation and has notified Her Majesty's Government that in the opinion of the Court of Arbitration the Award has been executed' (Article IX). The parties undertook to give free access to their territory, including the disputed territory, without prejudice to their rights of ownership thereto and to share the costs of the proceedings.

The facts of the Argentina–Chile Award of 1966 are in the main particular to the district and of little general interest. Argentina and Chile, as successors in title to Spain, by a treaty of 1855, recognized the principle of *uti possidetis* in the determination of their common boundary, namely, that each should retain the territories which they possessed in 1810 at the time of their separation from Spain. Such a principle, as the Arbitrator indicated in the Guatemala–Honduras Boundary Award,[16] is practically of small assistance when the border areas of the countries concerned were at the time unexplored and unappropriated by the officials or nationals of either country. Not surprisingly, therefore, further treaties followed, notably the Treaty of 23 July 1881, which stipulated that the boundary should follow the main Cordilleras of the Andes as far as 52° S and that it should, moreover, follow the line of the highest peaks of the mountains passing between the sources of the streams flowing down to either side. This general principle of demarcation made no allowance for the areas where the geographical configuration of the country failed to conform with its requirements. It is a good example of a general rule, like the 49th parallel, which while excellent as a rule of thumb, must inevitably lead to disputes caused by the impossibility of applying it to particular instances. Argentina and Chile signed a Protocol dated 1 May 1893, to the Treaty of 1881, in which they specifically spelt out the implications of the agreement stating that the Argentine Republic should hold in perpetuity all territory to the east of the line of the highest peaks which divide the waters while the Republic of Chile was to hold in perpetuity all territory to the west of that line.

Considerable progress in the joint demarcation of the boundary was made, but four sections were left where the line of the highest peaks and the line of the surface water-parting did not coincide, and these areas formed the subject of the Award of 1902 which awarded the richer land to Argentina but the larger share to Chile. The greater part of the Award was executed by the parties, but in the remote three hundred mile area at the southern tip of the continent several areas remained undemarcated. From time to time the two countries have attempted to arbitrate these disputed areas; in 1960 and again in 1966 Ministers of the two countries sought without success to agree a reference of the dispute concerning the islands in the Beagle Channel off Tierra del Fuego to the International Court of Justice.

In respect of a forty-mile-long district between Boundary Posts 16 and 17 where the interpretation of the 1902 Award proved difficult to apply on the ground, Chile succeeded in initiating the proceedings which terminated in the Award of 1966. This area, some forty miles long, is bounded in the south by Lake General Paz, on the northern shore of which Post 17 had been erected, with the agreement of the two states, by the British Demarcation Commission in 1903 when they had fixed the Award on the ground. Out of Lake General Paz the River Carrenleufú flows eastwards and after completing a wide arc to the north it flows westwards towards the Pacific Ocean where in its lower reaches it is known as the River Palena (and will hereafter be referred to by this name). The Award of 1902 sought to delimit the area between the northern loop of the River Palena and Lake General Paz by reference to two geographical features, a mountain called Cerro de la Virgen to the north of the Lake and a tributary of the River Palena, named the River Encuentro. According to the description in the Award and the map annexed to it, the western branch of this River Encuentro rose on the western slopes of Cerro de la Virgen and flowed northwards till it joined the River Palena. The course of this river was to constitute the boundary and its juncture with the River Palena was to be marked by Post 16.

It was the misnomer of this boundary river in the Award and in the accompanying map and the inaccurate depiction of its course from which the subsequent difficulties of applying the Award on the ground arose.

The Award of 1902 in Article III, after awarding to Argentina the upper basins of the rivers above the fixed boundary points which it had made and to Chile the lower basins below those points, continued: 'From the fixed point on the River Palena, the boundary shall follow the River Encuentro to the peak called Virgen, and thence to the line which we have fixed crossing Lake

General Paz and thence by line. . . .' This description was amplified in the accompanying Report: 'Crossing the Palena at this point, opposite the junction of the River Encuentro, it shall then follow the Encuentro along the course of its western branch to its source on the western slopes of Cerro Virgen. Ascending to that peak, it shall then follow the local water-parting southwards to the northern shore of Lago General Paz at a point where the Lake narrows, in longitude 71° 41′ 30″ W.'

The problem was unfortunately complicated by the action of the British Demarcation Commission in 1903 when they marked Post 16 on the ground. Had they never done so, future difficulties might have been avoided since, as later became known after more thorough surveys of the district, the River Salto, another tributary of the River Palena joining it further west, broadly corresponded in its course with that attributed to the Encuentro in the Award and, in particular, a western branch had its source on the slopes of the Cerro de la Virgen. The misnomer might thus have been rectified by the agreement of the parties as they might have accepted that the Arbitration Tribunal had intended to select the River Salto but had misnamed it the River Encuentro.

Unfortunately, however, the British Demarcation Commission did not place Post 16 opposite the juncture of the River Salto with the Palena. In the company of Argentine and Chilean representatives they surveyed the River Palena in 1903; they first placed Post 16 opposite the junction of a tributary (the Cajón) further up the River Palena but later, realizing this was a mistake, they moved the post to opposite a lower tributary (which thereupon became known as the Encuentro and in subsequent maps was so described). The Argentine representative initially contended that Post 16 should be moved to further down the River Palena, but having explored without finding a lower tributary he eventually agreed with the Chilean representative and the British Demarcation Commission that Post 16 had been placed in the correct position.

As it was, the original misnomer of the River Salto in the Award

h-map illustrating the United Kingdom's Arbitration, in 1966, of a
n of the Argentina-Chile frontier.

was additionally complicated by the agreed placing of Post 16 at the junction of a tributary which, it had also been agreed, ought properly to be named the Encuentro referred to in the Award. The Award of 1966 summarizes the position:

> . . . it must be borne in mind that the river which became the Encuentro as the result of the 1903 demarcation is not the river which the Arbitrator had in contemplation when he pronounced the Award; that it is not the river shown on the Award Map; that the river now known as the Encuentro, although it appears to be shown on the Award Map, is not named thereon; and that the course of that river, though in parts inaccurately depicted on that Map, is shown as having two channels. Nevertheless, there is no doubt that, as a result of what happened in 1903, the river opposite Boundary Post 16 is the Encuentro and has to be understood as such for the purpose of interpreting and fulfilling the Award (p. 80).

In the light of these discrepancies Argentina and Chile both agreed that a geographical error of some sort had been made in 1902–03 but differed on its nature. Chile, who throughout adopted an 'all or nothing' approach (the Award of 1966, p. 71), accepted that Posts 16 and 17 were rightly placed but maintained the wrong depiction of the topography on the Award Map made nonsense of the boundary-line which had been drawn between these points. She accordingly advanced as the proper boundary-line the main eastern channel of the River Encuentro (i.e. the river that from 1903 was named as such) despite the fact that its course went far further east than the boundary-line depicted on the Award Map and its source was not on the slopes of the Cerro de la Virgen. She supported her contention by relying on the subsequent conduct of the parties and Chilean display of state activities and the fact that Argentina had misled her as to the true geographical facts. As regards the difficult point that the River Encuentro did not have its source on the slopes of the Cerro de la Virgen, she sought to identify other geographical features which would comply with that description, namely a line of mountains known as the Cordon de las Virgenes and a more easterly height known since 1955 as Pico Virgen, and generally relied on the Award's acceptance of the principle that the river basins below Post 16 should belong to Chile. If Cerro de la Virgen was accepted, this principle would not be observed and the boundary would sever the basin of the River Salto, leaving part of that basin within Argentine territory.

Argentina, on the other hand, took a more restrictive view. She submitted that the boundary between Posts 16 and 17 was in large part settled, certainly as between Post 16 and the River Encuentro to the point (the Confluence) where it divided into two streams, and as between Post 17 on Lake General Paz and the mountain Cerro de la Virgen. The Court of Arbitration accepted this submission of Argentina. Further, Argentina maintained that from the Confluence, either by the express wording of the Award of 1902 or by its more precise application by a mixed Boundary Commission of 1955, the boundary was settled to the point where the southern channel of the Encuentro had its source. Argentina conceded that the boundary-line between the source of the southern channel of the Encuentro as identified by the Mixed Boundary Commission of 1955[17] and Cerro de la Virgen remained to be determined.

Both parties alleged mistake in the original Award but asserted that the Award remained valid. The Court of Arbitration did not discuss the legal effect of mistake and indicated that the defect in the 1902 Award might more properly be classified as external impossibility resulting in the frustration of the Arbitrator's intention. In any event as the terms of the Compromiso had authorized the Court of Arbitration to interpret and fulfil the 1902 Award its continued legal validity could scarcely be in issue. The 1966 Award has, therefore, nothing to say on the controversial subject when and what type of mistake invalidates an arbitral award.

The legal interest of the Award arises from the interpretation which it placed on the parties' acts in relation to the disputed territory. The proper evaluation of the parties' acts of possession in relation to the disputed territory and their acts in relation one to another must be the crux of every adjudication in a territorial dispute. In disputes relating to sovereignty, acts of discovery and annexation by formal proclamation have been replaced, as information became more accurate and state administration more intensive, by more precise tests of the first comer (Guiana Boundary case, 1904),[18] effective display of state activities and acquisitive prescription (Island of Palmas case, 1928).[19] In areas where display of state activities was minimal, doctrines of contiguity and continuity to an occupied area were employed. More recently a doctrine of historic consolidation has been elaborated to enable a state to lay claim 'to territories not finally organized under a state regime' on the basis of 'proven long use which . . . merely represents a complex of interests and relations which in themselves have the effect of attaching a territory . . . to a given state'.[20]

In boundary disputes, the emphasis shifts from acts of possession to the relation of the parties one to another.[21] Evidence of state activities along a boundary-line becomes relevant not to prove an act of appropriation of a *res nullius* but to establish the party's intention towards its neighbour. From the conduct of the parties, consequently, may be spelt out an agreement relating to the boundary or a representation by one upon which the other party has relied concerning the boundary. This shift in emphasis is reflected in the Award of 1966 which, while treating evidence of state activity in the disputed area with considerable indifference, took up a large number of pages evaluating the evidence concerning the parties' attitudes to the dispute. Thus, the Arbitration Court said of the evidence designed to show effective Chilean administration:

> The evidence consists of material frequently employed for substantiating claims to territorial sovereignty, e.g., registration of land titles; imposition of land tax; registration of settlers with the police; registration of births, marriages and deaths; animal brand registers; imposition of military service; electoral rolls; legal transactions; administrative, police and judicial activity of various kinds; taking of censuses; provision of health and educational facilities and so on.

After referring to similar evidence produced by Argentina in support of her claim, the Court of Arbitration continued:

> But, taken as a whole, the evidence is just what one would expect in any disputed zone. It shows settlers not surprisingly turning to the authorities of both countries in case of need and doing their best to keep on good terms with both sides. The evidence is quite insufficient to establish any abandonment by Argentina of her rights under the 1902 Award or any acquisition by Chile through adverse possession of territory adjacent to those parts of the boundary-line settled in 1902–03 . . . (p. 76).

Having disposed of the Chilean argument that the boundary-line which it sought to advance was supported by acts of state administration, the Court of Arbitration turned to consider the evidence relating to the parties' conduct. In probably one of its most authoritative passages, it was emphatic that the subsequent conduct of the parties had no relevance to the task of interpreting the Award of 1902:

> The Court is of the view that it is proper to apply stricter rules to the interpretation of an Award determined by an Arbitrator than to a treaty which results from negotiation between two or more Parties, where the process of interpretation may involve endeavouring to ascertain the common will of those Parties. In such cases it may be helpful to seek evidence of that common will either in preparatory documents or even in subsequent actions of the Parties. But with regard to the 1902 Award, the Court is satisfied that in order to determine the intention of the Arbitrator it is not necessary to look outside the three documents of which the Award consists, namely the Award itself and the Report and Maps referred to in Article V of the Award. It is not so much a question of the Arbitrator's intention as of that intention being frustrated by an incorrect appreciation of the geography. As for the subsequent conduct of the Parties, including also the conduct of private individuals and local authorities, the Court fails to see how that can throw any light on the Arbitrator's intention (p. 77).

This passage may well reassure those whose task it is to construe local boundaries but, before excluding from their deliberations all evidence other than the text of the Award, they should peruse the reasoning of the Court of Arbitration to its finish. For though, in general terms, they dismiss as irrelevant evidence of the subsequent conduct of the parties, in their detailed study of the meaning of the Award they admit evidence of a very similar nature.

Both parties relied on the subsequent conduct of each other as estopping it from making certain assertions concerning the 1902 Award. Chile submitted that Argentina in a note of 9 December 1913, had represented that the boundary ran along a river further east than that indicated in the Award and had thereby precluded herself from setting up a different boundary-line in the present proceedings. Argentina submitted that Chile in the LLanquihue Map sent to Argentina on 26 December 1913, and in later official Chilean maps up to 1952, had shown the boundary running in a north–south direction along a river named 'Rio Encuentro' through Cerro de la Virgen, and then along the water-parting down to Boundary Post 17 and that this boundary was quite inconsistent with the boundary along the eastern channel of the Encuentro as asserted by Chile in the arbitration proceedings.

In recent years the principle of preclusion or estoppel has received considerable judicial attention. Based on a general principle of consistency which requires a state 'to maintain towards a given factual or legal situation an attitude consistent with that which it was known to have adopted with regard to the same circumstances on previous occasions',[22] it has been applied to debar the United Kingdom from challenging a Norwegian fishery regime tolerated since 1869, though in contradiction with the then generally accepted three-mile limit (Anglo-Norwegian Fisheries case),[23] to prevent Nicaragua from pleading its non-ratification of a treaty and the nullity of an award (Arbitral Award made by the King of Spain on 23 December 1906),[24] and to render a Declaration part of a treaty though contained in separate documents (Ambatielos (jurisdiction) case).[25] In the field of territorial disputes the principle has long been recognized. The Grisbardarna case,

1909, gave expression to the basis of the rule: 'It is a settled proposition that a state of things which actually exists and has existed for a long time should be changed as little as possible.'[26]

The scope of this proposition may be wider than that of estoppel since it may be used as a rebuttable presumption to determine the burden of proof; or as an irrebuttable presumption to exclude evidence contrary to that which a state has represented to exist; or it may be used as a rule of substantive law. The rule of estoppel was at first considered an evidential rule as in the Legal Status of Eastern Greenland case where a statement made by M. Ihlen, the Foreign Minister of Norway, that Norway would not oppose Denmark's claim to Eastern Greenland was held (inter alia) to defeat Norway's attempt to oppose the claim before the Permanent Court of International Justice.[27] The most remarkable application of the doctrine to date is to be found in the Temple of Preah Vihear case[28] in the International Court, and here the summary by the Court of Arbitration in the Argentina–Chile proceedings of 1966 on the scope of the decision is of great interest (particularly in view of Lord McNair's great distinction as an international jurist and former President of the International Court):

> It seems clear that from the decision of the International Court of Justice in the case concerning the Temple of Preah Vihear (Cambodia v. Thailand) Merits, . . . and especially from the learned Separate Opinion of Vice-President Alfaro in that case, that there is in international law a principle, which is moreover a principle of substantive law and not just a technical rule of evidence, according to which 'a State party to an international litigation is bound by its previous acts or attitudes when they are in contradiction with its claims in the litigation' . . . Again to quote from the same Opinion of Vice-President Alfaro: 'Whatever term or terms be employed to designate this principle such as it has been applied in the international sphere, its substance is always the same: inconsistency between claims or allegations put forward by a State, and its previous conduct in connection therewith, is not admissible (*allegans contraria non audiendus est*).' That this principle can operate with decisive effect in international litigation, and especially in a boundary dispute, is clear

from the Temple case itself where one party was held to its acceptance of a map even though the frontier line traced on this map did not correspond with the watershed line provided for in the boundary treaty between the two disputant countries.[29]

It is to be noted that the Court of Arbitration accepted estoppel as a rule of substance confirming the opinion of Professor Johnson (who was Registrar to the Court in the Argentina–Chile proceedings) that 'the principle of preclusion . . . is now seen to be an extremely significant one in international law, clearly a rule of substance and not of procedure . . .' and its effect 'should be to place governments more than ever on their guard, particularly as to the acts and omissions of their officials, not necessarily always officials of the highest rank'.[30]

In the light of this fast-developing rule, governments will find with some relief that the Court of Arbitration in the 1966 proceedings did not take such a strict view of the acts of Argentine and Chilean officials. The Court refused to treat their representations as creating estoppels and from this refusal the limits of the doctrine can begin to be discerned.

The Argentine representation contained in the note of 9 December 1913, referred to the source of the boundary river as being in the vicinity of the Peak Herrero. The Court held this would not preclude Argentina from contending in the proceedings that the source of the Encuentro was elsewhere. In its reasons, it noted that the representation was contained in a single sentence of one note, the object of which was directed to the removal of Post 16 rather than a discussion of river sources; that Argentina herself had no clear appreciation of the facts 'in the still uncertain state of the geographical knowledge of the area prevailing at the time'; and, most important, that Chile neither relied upon nor was misled by the statement (Award, p. 68). As regards later Argentine representations in the diplomatic correspondence of 1952, the Court held the words River Encuentro and California were so vague in meaning that the parties were not *ad idem* as to their significance.

As regards the Chilean representations in official maps of 1913–52 showing the boundary to follow a direction quite inconsistent with that maintained by her in the arbitration proceedings, the Court of Arbitration again accepted that in view of the remoteness of the area and uncertain geographical knowledge, Chilean ignorance was excusable. Chile sought to go further and to maintain that Argentina had misled her by leaving her in ignorance of the error in the Award; consequently any representation made by Chile was made as a result of Argentine misrepresentation of the facts and Argentina was under a legal duty to inform her or the Arbitrator when she became aware of the error. This the Court of Arbitration firmly rejected. Chile was as capable as Argentina of ascertaining the facts concerning their common border; they were available to both and if Chile considered her position aggrieved by the Award (which was final between the parties) it was for her to challenge it. In addition the Court held the Argentine note of 9 December 1913 to put Chile on notice of the error.

It would, therefore, appear that in the Court of Arbitration's view, a representation made by a state could create no binding estoppel if it concerned matters which at the time it was made had not, in the knowledge of both parties, been fully investigated, and which was still largely unsupported by detailed factual information. Further, such estoppel would not be binding unless it misled the other party or the other party could be shown to have relied upon it. Chile certainly had not done so in respect of the Argentine representation as she had authorized the issue of maps showing a boundary running in a quite different direction. Nor could she be said to have relied or been misled by Argentina's non-disclosure of the error since the error was made by the Arbitrator and not by Argentina and any change of position would have resulted from the error and not Argentina's acts. Nor had Chile misled Argentina by her maps since Argentina from her own knowledge knew of the uncertain geographical information available in respect of the area.

Further, it would seem that the 1966 Award supports the conclusion that the parties must be *ad idem* as to the meaning of the representation before one can rely on it against the other. If one state intends it to relate to one matter and the other state relies on it concerning another, there can be no estoppel. Finally, it seems clear that, at the lower official level, a single statement in one diplomatic note will not be sufficient to bind a state for the future.

In the Temple case, the International Court placed little emphasis on Cambodia's reliance on Thailand's acts but stressed rather Thailand's enjoyment of benefit as a result of her acquiescence: 'she has, for fifty years, enjoyed such benefits as the Treaty of 1904 conferred on her, if only the benefit of a stable frontier.... France, and through her, Cambodia, relied on Thailand's acceptance of the map. Since neither side can plead error, it is immaterial whether or not this reliance was based on a belief that the map was correct. It is not now open to Thailand, while continuing to claim and enjoy the benefits of the settlement, to deny that she was a consenting party to it.'[31]

In the Argentina–Chile Award both the parties pleaded error and had in fact alleged it since 1913 onwards. More significant, perhaps, is the fact that the benefit of a stable frontier derived in this case, not from a treaty between the parties where one party might accept with binding effect the other's interpretation of its meaning, but from an Award the true meaning of which might be independently determined by reference to a third party and not by one party's construction relied upon by the other. Certainly, as long as one of the parties was able to request an interpretation of the Award, or to challenge it as a nullity, this distinction would seem to be a valid one. But if, as a result of one party's acquiescence in a boundary award, a long period of time had elapsed, making it impossible to refer back or to challenge the award, there would seem to be little ground to distinguish between enjoyment of a boundary settlement based on a treaty and enjoyment of a boundary settlement based on an arbitral award.

The Court of Arbitration, while refusing to hold the parties estopped by their representations, commented that they, nonetheless, provided valuable evidence in determining geographical and government opinion in the two countries at the time. Consequently, the representations were treated as of evidential value. In the task of assessing evidence, tribunals have in recent years paid some attention to the critical date rule. First referred to by Judge Huber in the Island of Palmas Award,[32] it was seriously relied upon by the United Kingdom in the Minquiers and Ecrehos case to exclude evidence of French sovereignty after the crystallization of the dispute, and the International Court, in discussing the critical date in that case, stated: 'in view of the special circumstances of the case, subsequent acts should also be considered by the Court, unless the measure in question was taken with a view to improving the legal position of the Party concerned. . . .'[33]

There has been some ambiguity in the proper meaning of the term 'critical date'. In one sense, it is largely procedural: 'the critical moment is, normally, not when the dispute was born, but that on which it crystallized into a concrete issue . . . one object of the critical date is to prevent one of the parties from unilaterally improving its position by means of some step taken after the issue has been definitely joined.'[34] This evidentiary notion of the critical date is designed to prevent window-dressing. 'It comes about when the parties define their positions in the dispute so as to make it an object of litigation.'[35]

The Court of Arbitration in the Argentina–Chile case had to deal with argument on these lines and indicated that, used thus, the critical date might be little more than a pleader's device. 'It is agreed by both Parties that by this expression is meant in a general way a date after which the Court should not admit evidence of the activities of the Parties. It is clear, however, that each Party, viewing its own activities as confirmation of an already existing sovereignty and the activities of the other Party merely as an intrusion and an effort to build up a new claim, sees the critical date rather as a means of shutting out evidence of its opponent's activities than of excluding its own' (p. 68).

The Court of Arbitration also recognized that the term might be used in a substantive sense, its function being to mark the closing of the period of a state's consolidation of title or its failure to effectuate such title. 'The critical date doctrine comes into operation when a catalytic event, which, converging as it were with a series of acts constituting a state's inchoate relation to a territory, crystallizes that relation and presents it for a decision whether the acts in question have consolidated the title claimed or have failed.'[36] Thus, in the Argentina–Chile dispute, the establishment of the Argentina–Chile Mixed Boundary Commission in 1941 might be argued as a closing date for 'any attempt to establish sovereignty over a disputed frontier region merely through the exercise of administrative acts'. Alternatively, as Chile alleged, 1945 or 1952 might be so accepted as dates subsequent to which no challenge of Chilean administration of the territory could validly be made. But, as the Court argued, other dates might also be termed critical: 'In so far as the Court is asked to interpret and fulfil the Award of 1902, there is obviously a sense in which the critical date is 1902 itself – or at the latest 1903, the date of the demarcation. Neither Party is free to put forward a claim that flies in the face of the Award. In so far, however, as the Court is also asked in the Compromiso to say to what extent, if any, the course of the boundary between the territories of the Parties in the sector between Boundary Posts 16 and 17 has remained unsettled since the 1902 Award, there is equally obvious a sense in which the critical date is the date of the submission of the dispute to the Arbitrator, i.e. 1964.' The Court accordingly concluded: 'For these reasons the Court has considered the notion of the critical date to be of little value in the present litigation and has examined all the evidence submitted to it, irrespective of the date of the acts to which such evidence relates' (p. 69).

Up to this point the Court of Arbitration had adopted a negative attitude to the aids offered by general international law to the solution of the dispute. It had refused the assistance of *travaux préparatoires* or subsequent conduct of the parties on the ground that it was engaged in the strict interpretation of an Arbitral

Award; it had refused to find against states on the basis of any representation of fact made by them constituting an estoppel; and it had refused to exclude evidence on the ground that it was subsequent to the adoption of a definite attitude by a state or to the crystallization of the dispute.

This negative attitude is, however, deceptive; the Court in fact treated certain acts of the parties as decisive of the issues to be determined but it did so by using them as material in the determination of the specific issues referred to it. Thus, the Court confined itself narrowly to the question referred to it: 'To the extent, if any, that the course of the boundary between the territories of the Parties in the Sector between Boundary Posts 16 and 17 has remained unsettled since the 1902 Award, what, on the proper interpretation and fulfilment of that Award, is the course of the boundary in that Sector?'[37]

This question is dealt with in three parts. First, it found only a small part of the boundary between Posts 16 and 17 remained unsettled; it found the boundary between Post 16 and the Confluence and between the mountain Cerro de la Virgen and Post 17 to be settled and did so by reference to evidence showing the parties' conduct in respect of these boundary-lines and to evidence designed to show effective state administration in the area. Second, the Court determined that the task of interpretation and fulfilment of the award was one for the Arbitrator and not the parties and required the Arbitrator, while avoiding any modification or revision of its terms, to supply any deficiencies therein in a manner consistent as far as possible with the Arbitrator's intention. Here, therefore, momentarily the Court excluded conduct of the parties subsequent to 1902 as irrelevant to fulfilment of the award. The exclusion was temporary. For, in the third stage, in supplying the deficiencies of the 1902 Award, and determining where the boundary should run between the Confluence of the eastern and southern channels of the Encuentro River and the peak Cerro de la Virgen, the Court called in aid two principles, the first of which permitted reference to the parties' conduct:

'The first is the general principle that where an instrument (for example, a treaty or an award) has laid down that a boundary must follow a river, and that river divides into two or more channels, and nothing is specified in that instrument as to which channel the boundary shall follow, the boundary must normally follow the major channel' (p. 80).

The question which is the major channel, the Court of Arbitration stated, is to be determined by reference to both historical and scientific evidence. Once again, in the guise of historical evidence, the Court relied on the parties' conduct – here, it reintroduced the representation of 9 December 1913, which it had refused to accept as creating an estoppel against Argentina. Along with two other statements made by other Argentine officials in 1907 and 1941 it held that this representation *recognized* the eastern channel of the Encuentro to be the major channel. As regards the scientific evidence, the Court preferred the criteria of length, size of drainage area and discharge (where possible in annual volume) in determining which was the major channel. It did not place much stress on tests of lineal continuity or changes in drainage pattern relied on by Argentina nor on arguments concerning age, gradient water level and nature of bedload advanced by Chile.

The second principle which the Court of Arbitration directed itself never to lose sight of, was the Arbitrator's true intention 'to concentrate on the simple, straightforward words in the Award "follow the River Encuentro to the peak called Virgen" '. This it did and found in favour of the eastern channel of the River Encuentro to the point where it deviates from the direction of Cerro de la Virgen, at which point it drew the boundary along the local water-partings until it reached the peak of Cerro de la Virgen.

The Award was accepted with satisfaction by both parties. Argentine representatives maintained that they had received seven-tenths of the area in dispute but Chilean officials stated that they were well satisfied to be awarded the more valuable valleys of the north where Chilean settlers were to be found. Accordingly, although the Award in its reasons states that it is placing no reliance on acts of Chilean administration, it is very possible that in coming to its decision (where a subjective evaluation of the merits of the case undoubtedly plays a part) these acts may have been of some importance.

From the above account it is clear that the process of arbitration resolved no major political issues between the two states. Indeed, the matter which was referred to the United Kingdom for arbitration was only one of several outstanding border disputes which Chile has with her more affluent neighbour, and, in truth, it may be because it was that in which national interests were least engaged (it concerned cowboy country of no great economic value) that its settlement was considered one suitable for the process of arbitration. Even while Argentina and Chile were presenting their cases in this arbitration, a Chilean policeman was killed in 1964 in a border incident in the Lago del Desierto district further south and a Chilean claim to islands in the Beagle Channel off Tierra del Fuego has for many years been a source of irritation to the navies of both countries. Since the outcome of the 1966 proceedings and following a further incident, Chile has attempted to repeat her former action of unilaterally referring the matter to the arbitration of the British Government under the Treaty of 1902. But Argentina to date is opposed to such a solution. These problems undoubtedly prevent the closer economic co-operation between the two countries which Chilean governments have been anxious to achieve – the Chilean oil at Punta Arenas is awaiting its development in supplying the Argentine market.[38]

In the recent dispute between India and Pakistan over the Rann of Kutch, the reference of the matter to arbitration and the acceptance by the two countries of the published award was made possible by the fact that the disputed area had little economic value and was very sparsely populated. Pakistan, indeed, maintained that throughout the hundred and fifty years of British administration, from 1819 when Kutch became a vassal state under British Paramountcy, the exact boundary between the north of Kutch and the neighbouring province of Sind, annexed by the British in 1843, was so unimportant that it had never been defined; consequently the whole of the Rann – a 'marine feature', something akin to a marsh – formed an undetermined broad belt of boundary between Kutch and Sind, and between India and Pakistan, as their successors, after 1947. Pakistan accordingly asked the Arbitration Tribunal to reduce this wide boundary to a widthless line using the principles of the median line and nearness of shores where evidence of effective sovereignty was lacking. India challenged the Pakistan case and relied on a great number of British maps and surveys which showed the boundary between Kutch and Sind as running along the northern edge of the Rann. Accepting these and other acts of the British authorities to be acknowledgements of Kutch sovereignty over the Rann and consequently of India's sovereignty as successor to Kutch, the Chairman of the Tribunal, with whom the Iranian member agreed, said: 'I conclude as follows. In respect of those sectors of the Rann in relation to which no specific evidence in the way of display of Sind authority, or merely trivial or isolated evidence of such a character, supports Pakistan's claim, I pronounce in favour of India. These sectors comprise about ninety per cent of the disputed territory. However, in respect of sectors where a continuous and, for the region, intensive Sind activity, meeting with no effective opposition from the Kutch side, is established, I am of the opinion that Pakistan has made out a better and superior title . . .' (p. 152).

Although the arbitration proceedings over the Rann of Kutch were preceded by large-scale fighting between Indian and Pakistani forces, it is probably true to regard this warfare as symptomatic of conflicting national passions generally between the two countries rather than in relation to the Rann. The long-standing dispute over Kashmir has, by very reason of the fact that it affects so much more fundamentally the vital interests of both countries, resisted all third-party attempts to settle it.

To expect arbitration to solve a major political issue between states is to exaggerate its importance as a procedure of peaceful settlement of international disputes. Apart from the Alabama Claims which resolved the political tension between the United States and the United Kingdom after the American Civil War arising from the active display of British sympathy with the Confederate cause, it is difficult to point to any arbitration which has resolved for states vital interests of the first importance. It can, of course, be said that by the deliberate decision of states to arbitrate, much of the heat is taken from a dispute which might otherwise rank as a political difference of major importance between the two countries; yet, even here, the successful solution of a major problem springs less from the happily-worded award of the arbitrator than from the determination of the two governments concerned (probably from quite extraneous political motives) to remove the issue from the political limelight and to subordinate immediate national interests to an agreed settlement. Dr Julio Philippi, the Chilean Foreign Minister, showed his government to be of that determination when, in referring to a border incident in 1964 in the district under arbitration, he said: 'Naturally we consider it a grave situation as long as our border-patrols continue to be intercepted by Argentine troops in a territory that is in litigation. But I am sure that with a measure of good will our two governments will soon be able to work out a satisfactory solution. What is important for the success of future diplomatic moves is that the dispute should be kept well outside national political passions.'[39]

Nonetheless, while it is dangerous to overrate the capacity of international arbitration to solve major political disputes it is equally unwise to underestimate its value as a supplementary procedure for the demarcation of boundaries between states. Although the frontiers of the United States of America were in the main defined by political negotiation and treaty, as in Louisiana, Texas, Alaska, much useful work was done by Mixed Commissions set up under the Jay Treaty of 1794 and the Treaty of Ghent, 1814, in applying the general boundary-line agreed in the north with the United Kingdom in the Peace Treaty of 1792 to areas where ambiguities of interpretation had arisen, as with the true meaning of the River Sainte Croix, or the sovereignty of islands in the Bay of Fundy.[40] These commissions failed, however, to settle the boundary in districts where major national interests were involved, and the North-East Boundary, a matter which had also proved too intractable for settlement by arbitration by the King of the Netherlands,[41] and the North-West Frontier were only resolved after further negotiation by the Webster-Ashburton Treaty of 1842 and the Oregon Treaty of 1846.[42] The latter neglected to clarify the water boundary off Vancouver Island and this was eventually resolved by an Award made by the Emperor of Germany in 1872.[43] In Central and South America, international arbitration has also played a useful role, particularly in the delimitation of the boundaries of British Guiana,[44] Venezuela[45] and Costa Rica,[46] though again the vast majority of the boundaries were settled by negotiation and treaty.

The interplay of political negotiation, treaty, and arbitration is also to be seen in the gradual refinement of the boundaries drawn by colonial powers in Africa – boundaries which in a Resolution of the Organization of African Unity made in 1965, member states pledged themselves to respect 'as the boundaries existing on their achievement of national independence'.[47] The Anglo-Portuguese political accommodations which culminated in the Anglo-Portuguese Treaty of 1891 defining their spheres of influence in East and Central Africa was subsequently elucidated by two awards, one given in respect of the Manica boundary by a former President of the International Court of Cassation,[48] the other in respect of the limits of the Kingdom of Barotseland by the King of Italy.[49] Elsewhere in Africa a small but useful function was played by international arbitration, the extent of German South-west Africa was defined in a limited respect by the Walfisch Bay Award of 1911,[50] the boundary between South Africa and Portuguese Mozambique clarified by the Delagoa Bay Award.[51]

The conclusion would seem to be that the definition of boundaries is primarily achieved by treaty either as the result of political negotiation between the parties or by international conference such as the Conference of Berlin, 1885, which accorded recognition to the new state of the Congo, and the Peace Treaty settlements made under the supervision of the League of Nations at the end of the First World War. Treaty, from its method of conclusion, encourages the adoption of general principles – the *uti possidetis* rule, the watershed, the *thalweg*, the line of greatest elevation – and necessarily can only define a boundary by reference to the information disclosed in the surveys and cartography of the time. From the generalizations and errors of fact made by treaty makers the large proportion of difficulties relating to the demarcation of the agreed boundary on the ground arise, and it is in the elucidation and settlement of these difficulties that international arbitration serves one of its most useful purposes.

TEXT REFERENCES

1. FO 94/558.
2. Moore, *International Arbitrations*, vol. 5, p. 1909 and p. 1920.
3. Moore, op. cit., vol. 1, p. 653.
4. *UN Rep. of Int. Arbit. Awards*, vol. 12, p. 281.
5. Bulama Island arbitrations, UK and Portugal, (1869): Moore, *International Arbitrations*, vol. 5, p. 1909. Chaco case, Bolivia and Paraguay, (1938): *UN Rep. of Int. Arbit. Awards*, vol. 3, p. 1819.
6. Moore, op. cit., vol. 5, p. 1920.
7. *BFSP*, vol. 161, p. 187.
8. Rio Grande Irrigation and Land Co., (1923): *UN Rep. of Int. Arbit. Awards*, vol. 6, p. 135–36.
9. Costa Rica–Panama Boundary case, (1914): *UN Rep. of Int. Arbit. Awards*, vol. 11, p. 519.
10. Moore, op. cit., vol. 1, p. 119.
11. Lapradelle and Politis, vol. 11, p. 408.
12. The India–Pakistan Western Boundary Case Tribunal, Award, 19 February 1968 (Introduction, Conclusions and three Maps), p. 153.
13. Award of HM Queen Elizabeth II for the arbitration of the controversy between the Argentine Republic and the Republic of Chile concerning parts of the boundary between their territories, 24 November 1966, HMSO Code No. 59–162.

14. *BFSP*, vol. 95, p. 759.
15. A/CN 4/92, April 1955.
16. (1933) *UN Rep. of Int. Arbit. Awards*, vol. 2, p. 1322. In the Rann of Kutch arbitration a similar principle was discussed in determining what areas India and Pakistan had succeeded to on the partition of the British Dominion of India.
17. Argentina asserted the competence of the Mixed Boundary Commission to decide questions of demarcation referred to it; and while this was not in principle challenged, provided the terms of reference of the Mixed Boundary Commission were sufficiently wide to confer such power, and the Boundary Commission had completed its task, at any rate in respect of one sector of the boundary, the Court of Arbitration was not prepared to treat an isolated decision of the Commission as binding on Chile and Argentina, particularly where the obtaining of the approval of the two governments to other aspects of the boundary was under discussion. The identification by the Commission of the source of the Encuentro was therefore held not to be binding on the parties or the Court.
18. United Kingdom and Brazil: *UN Rep. of Int. Arbit. Awards*, vol. 11, p. 11.
19. United States of America and the Netherlands: *UN Rep. of Int. Arbit. Awards*, vol. 2, p. 829.
20. De Visscher, *Théories et Réalités en Droit international public*, 3rd ed., 1960, p. 256.
21. Bastid, S., 'Territorial Problems in the Jurisprudence of the International Court of Justice', *ADIRC*, vol. 3, 1962, p. 360.
22. McGibbon, 'Estoppel in International Law', 7 *ICLQ*, 1958, p. 468, at 512.
23. *ICJ Reports*, 1951, p. 116.
24. *ICJ Reports*, 1960, p. 192.
25. *ICJ Reports*, 1952, p. 27 (Preliminary Objection).
26. *UN Rep. of Int. Arbit. Awards*, vol. 11, p. 147.
27. *PCIJ*, Ser. A/B No. 53 (1933).
28. *ICJ Reports*, 1962, p. 6 (Merits).
29. *ICJ Reports*, 1962, p. 39.
30. 11 *ICLQ*, 1962, p. 1183 at 1203.
31. *ICJ Reports*, 1962, p. 30.
32. *UN Rep. of Int. Arbit. Awards*, vol. 2, p. 831.
33. *ICJ Reports*, 1953, pp. 59–60.
34. Sir Gerald Fitzmaurice in his argument to the International Court the Minquiers and Ecrehos case, Judgment of 17 November 1953, 2 *ICJ Pleadings, Oral Arguments, Documents*, 69 (18.lx.1953).
35. Goldie, 'The Critical Date', 12 *ICLQ*, p. 1266.
36. Ibid., p. 1265.
37. Article 1 of the Compromiso dated 1 April 1965.
38. *New York Times*, March 1960, September 1966.

39. *New York Times*, 2 August 1964.
40. Moore, *International Arbitrations*, vol. 1, p. 1 and p. 45.
41. Ibid., p. 85.
42. *BFSP*, vol. 30, p. 360; vol. 34, p. 14. Twiss, *Oregon Question Examined*, 1846, p. 375.
43. Moore, *International Arbitrations*, vol. 1, p. 196.
44. British Guiana–Brazil Boundary arbitration, (1904): *BFSP*, vol. 99, p. 930. British Guiana Boundary dispute, (1899): *BFSP*, vol. 89, p. 57.
45. Venezuela Boundary arbitration, (1899), supra. Colombia–Venezuela Frontiers arbitration, (1922): *UN Rep. of Int. Arbit. Awards*, vol. 1, p. 223.
46. Costa Rica–Nicaragua Boundary arbitration, (1888): Moore, *International Arbitrations*, vol. 5, p. 5074. Costa Rica–Panama Boundary dispute, (1921): *UN Rep. of Int. Arbit. Awards*, vol. 1, p. 519.
47. OAU Doc. A.H.G./Res. 16 (1).
48. Moore, *International Arbitrations*, vol. 5, p. 4985.
49. (1905), *UN Rep. of Int. Arbit. Awards*, vol. 11, p. 59.
50. Ibid., p. 263.
51. Moore, *International Arbitrations*, vol. 5, p. 4984.

BIBLIOGRAPHY

Cukwurah, A. O., *The Settlement of Territorial Disputes*, Manchester 1967.

David Davies Memorial Institute of International Studies, *Report of a Study Group on the Peaceful Settlement of International Disputes*, London 1966.

De Visscher, C., *Théories et Réalités en Droit international public*. 3rd ed., Paris 1960.

Jenks, C. W., *The Prospects of International Adjudication*, New York 1964.

Moore, J. B., *International Arbitrations*, Washington 1898, vol. 5.

Simpson, J. L. and Fox, Hazel, *International Arbitration*, London 1959.

7 JUDICIAL SETTLEMENT

Henry Darwin

The judicial settlement of international disputes is a recent development of the international order. But a number of international frontier disputes have been reviewed by this method. Even if the material is not abundant, therefore, it merits examination in any general survey of frontier disputes.

Among the methods of settling disputes generally recognized by international practice, judicial settlement and arbitration stand together as methods involving legal procedures and normally applying legal standards as the basis on which to adjudicate. They therefore stand apart from negotiation, mediation and other methods in which the political aspects of the dispute may be allowed to determine the outcome.

Before we turn to the substance of the cases, it may be convenient to deal with certain general aspects of judicial settlement and particularly the International Court of Justice; and, in doing so, to draw some distinctions between such a settlement and arbitration.

Three advantages may be claimed for the International Court of Justice, as for its predecessor, the Permanent Court of International Justice, over arbitration as a method of settling disputes.

First, it provides a ready-made Court and procedure, whereas for an arbitration it is necessary to select the arbitrators and arrange the procedure. Indeed, in the case concerning the Award made by the King of Spain of 23 December 1906 (Honduras and Nicaragua),[1] one of the grounds on which Nicaragua declared an arbitral award by the King of Spain in a frontier dispute to be a nullity was that the complicated procedures for the selection of Arbitrators had not been complied with. But it seems likely that, in those cases of frontier disputes which went to the International Court of Justice by agreement, namely, the Frontier Lands case[2] and the Award of the King of Spain case just mentioned, it would have been possible to agree upon an Arbitrator. In the latter case, the nullity of an Arbitral Award was in issue, and there might seem to be some arguments for hearing such an issue in a larger tribunal than gave the original Award, since the questions arising have some features in common with appeals or at least 'revision', as understood in continental legal practice. But in fact there have been a number of cases where a further arbitration has been held to review for alleged nullity an earlier arbitral award.

The existence of a permanent Court has certainly not destroyed the practice of arbitration. There were a number of arbitrations[3] on boundary disputes during the existence of the Permanent Court of International Justice between 1920 and 1939. Furthermore, since 1946 there have been other significant arbitrations, in particular, the Rann of Kutch arbitration between India and Pakistan[4] and the Buraimi arbitration between Saudi Arabia and the United Kingdom (on behalf of the Ruler of Abu Dhabi and the Sultan of Muscat and Oman),[5] though the outcome of the latter is hardly an advertisement for the procedure.[6] The Rio Encuentro arbitration between Argentina and Chile[7] is perhaps a special case in that it was founded on a Treaty of 28 May 1902, which itself provided an Arbitrator and gave him power to settle the procedure.

In the diplomatic handling of frontier disputes, an offer to take the dispute to the International Court may be a way in which a state, which relies on legal arguments, can place on record its legal case and register its strength as against the case advanced by the other side. Thus in 1955 in the Antarctica case,[8] the United Kingdom filed applications to the International Court against Argentina and Chile complete with evidence and argument to substantiate the claim to those parts of its sector of Antarctica which were also claimed by Argentina and Chile. So also in 1946 the United Kingdom accepted the jurisdiction of the International Court as to the borders of British Honduras on which claims had been made by Guatemala;[9] the latter responded, not by acceptance, but by offering to accept provided that the Court would make its decision *ex aequo et bono*; thus identifying the claim as one unlikely to win on strictly legal arguments but believed to have a better chance on more equitable considerations. But the offer to take the case to court does not necessarily lead to a solution of the question.

Secondly, a court permanently established may be expected to show greater continuity of decisions and thus consolidate the law. Few decisions on frontier disputes have been made by the International Court, so one cannot say whether this is true for this field of its activities. Furthermore, though there have been many arbitrations on territorial questions, it has not generally led to too widely divergent decisions on salient points. On the other hand, the sequence of cases in the International Court may have led the Court to consolidate its doctrines at least on some incidental points, such as 'preclusion',[10] which have figured in a number of its cases.

The third advantage of the International Court of Justice, as of the Permanent Court of International Justice which preceded it, is the provision of an easy and simple procedure in Article 36 (2) of the Statute of the International Court of Justice, the 'Optional Clause', whereby States can accept the jurisdiction of the Court 'as compulsory ipso facto and without special agreement' in all or a certain class of cases.

This is not a facility available only by virtue of the establishment of a court. A general treaty on arbitration can provide for obligatory acceptance of arbitration, and the Rio Encuentro arbitration just mentioned is an example of an arbitration under such a treaty.

Declarations of acceptance of the jurisdiction of the International Court have been put in by forty-three states but only one case of a frontier dispute, namely, the Temple case,[11] has been brought before the Court on this basis. It is significant that, in this case, as in another case closely related to frontier conditions (namely, the Right of Passage case,[11] which concerned Portuguese access to certain enclaves across Indian territory), the respondent sought unsuccessfully by legal argument to deny the jurisdiction of the Court. It can therefore hardly be said that the facility to make declarations has meant that states are in fact willing to accept general judicial settlement of frontier disputes.

This may be in part because of the reservations which many states attach to their acceptances. While none of these expressly exclude territorial disputes, out of forty-three declarations in force at July 1968,[13] twenty-six included limitations that the dispute, or the facts and circumstances relating to the dispute, must have arisen after various relatively recent dates. Certainly the dates chosen in most cases were at a time when the existing frontiers of the state concerned had crystallized in their present position. These reservations could, because of the condition of reciprocity almost invariably incorporated, be invoked also by any state against which any of these twenty-six states made an application. Among the remaining seventeen states whose acceptance is not so qualified by date, there are only three common frontiers. A substantially similar picture obtained in the past.

In the circumstances it is surprising that the compulsory jurisdiction should have ever given rise to a case. But it did when Cambodia, whose declaration was unqualified by date, made an application against Thailand in the Temple case just mentioned. Even then Thailand contested the jurisdiction, though its highly technical objections were unanimously rejected by the Court.[14] Though the case of the Award of the King of Spain could apparently have been brought within the acceptances of both Honduras and Nicaragua, it was in fact brought on the basis of a special agreement, possibly in order to define the question put in a mutually acceptable form.

In the current reserved attitude to compulsory jurisdiction, it seems unlikely that the International Court will be widely used to determine frontier disputes. But equally it seems unlikely that frontier disputes are a field where states will soon be ready to widen their acceptances of compulsory jurisdiction, or even to bring cases by agreement. There are certainly fields of international disputes of less importance than territorial disputes, at least to the national sentiments of mankind. But it will remain a useful facility for those cases where the states concerned are prepared to put at risk their frequently minor territorial interests for the sake of impartial and authoritative settlement of the dispute.

Let us next consider the decisions of the International Court in cases involving disputes concerning frontiers. To complete the picture, the decisions and advisory opinions of the Permanent Court of International Justice in such cases between 1920 and 1939 are also briefly noticed.

In considering these, we have tried to bring forward those aspects of the cases which specifically concern frontier disputes as distinct from other kinds of dispute and other fields of law. But those readers who do not wish to examine the details may wish to pass to the last few paragraphs of the account of each case, which give general observations on it.

No attempt has been made to include in this examination cases involving disputes relating to a frontier, but which do not concern the line of the frontier but rather a frontier arrangement or regime, such as the Rights of Passage case[15] or the case concerning Eastern Carelia,[16] the Free Zones of Upper Savoy and the District of Gex,[17] or maritime frontiers or claims such as the Minquiers and Ecrehos case[18] or the Delimitation of Territorial Waters between Castellorizo and Anatolia.[19] So also competing claims to territory lying far away, such as in the Eastern Greenland case,[20] and not between two adjacent territories, have not been considered, since they are more akin to the many arbitrations about oceanic islands.

I CASES CONSIDERED BY THE PERMANENT COURT OF JUSTICE

The Advisory Opinion regarding the delimitation of the Poland–Czechoslovakia frontier (Question of Jaworzina)[21] arose out of the following circumstances. On 11 July 1920, the Conference of Ambassadors of the Allies determined the frontier as between Poland and Czechoslovakia by laying down the line of the frontier. The Polish government sought to reopen this question and the Council of the League of Nations asked the Court whether and how far the question of delimitation was still open. The Court found[22] it was not still open except in so far as the Delimitation Commission competent for the Area might in the course of its work of physical demarcation propose to the Conference of Ambassadors. The case is of interest for those studying the work of the Supreme Council of the Allies and the Conference of Ambassadors and their procedures. But it does not touch on matters of general interest in connection with judicial procedures on frontier disputes.

The Advisory Opinion regarding the delimitation of the Serbia–Albania frontier at the Monastery of Saint Naoum[23] is somewhat similar since the question put was whether the Conference of Ambassadors had discharged its functions in taking a decision which gave the monastery to Albania. While it is true that this Opinion, unlike that in Jaworzina, does consider topographical questions of the area in the light of relevant historical instruments, the Court found them of no assistance in forming its opinion. It therefore presents no features of general interest.

The Advisory Opinion concerning the interpretation of Article 3, paragraph 2, of the Treaty of Lausanne (Frontier between Turkey and Iraq),[24] in reply to the question put by the Council of the League, advised that the Council had power to indicate in binding fashion the frontier between Iraq and Turkey and that a decision on this point required the unanimity of its members, not taking into account the votes of parties to the dispute.

It will be seen immediately that all these cases in the Permanent

Court of International Justice concern more the competence of decision-making organs than the title to land. To apply the analogy of national law, they are in the field of administrative law rather than land law. The Supreme Council of the Allies, with its subordinate organ the Conference of Ambassadors in Paris, and, to a much lesser extent, the League of Nations, exercised executive functions in the subsequent working out of certain aspects of the great range of questions dealt with in the Treaties of Peace resulting from the Great War of 1914–18; the Permanent Court of Justice, though on an advisory basis only, is here giving guidance as to the legal effect of those decisions.

II THE TEMPLE CASE

The principal decision concerning frontier disputes given by the International Court of Justice is in the case concerning the Temple of Preah Vihear.[25] As this case presents features most characteristic of frontier disputes, in which title to territory must be determined, it merits special study here.

The frontier between Cambodia and Thailand in the area is laid down in Article 1 of the Treaty of 13 February 1904 between France and Siam. This Article, for this section, provides that it follows the watershed between the basins of the Nam Sen and the Mekong on the one hand and the Nam Moun on the other. This watershed lies at the Temple along the ridge of the Dangrek range of mountains.

The Temple is situated at the apex of a triangular spur jutting southwards out from the main line of the Dangrek range of mountains. This range is an escarpment sloping gently towards the northern or Thai side and falling away as steep cliffs to the Cambodian plain on the south. The spur on which the Temple stands follows the character of the escarpment and thus has its highest point at the Temple and falls away to the north.

Article 3 of the 1904 Treaty, however, provides that there shall be a delimitation of the frontiers, to be carried out by Mixed Commissions composed of officers appointed by the two contracting countries. The work was to 'relate to the frontier determined by Articles 1 and 2. . . .'

The Mixed Commission met and by about the end of 1906 considered that it had completed its work. But no meeting of the Commission was held to produce a final record of the line, perhaps because those concerned became involved in a negotiation relating to another section of the frontier.

The only map dating from that time is the one put in evidence by the Cambodian government and in the case called the Annex I Map. This map shows clearly a frontier line running north of the Temple, thus assigning it to the Cambodian side.

It is one of a series of eleven sheets prepared in the autumn of 1907 on the basis of a survey by Capts Kerler and Oum, both in the French service, and printed in Paris. It was at a scale of 1:200,000, so that the 500 metres between the frontier line and the Temple area is represented by only 2·5 mm. on the map. As a document it was in no way incorporated in the records of the Mixed Commission. But there was clear evidence that the Siamese negotiators requested the French to prepare maps. It is also clear that a number of copies of the resulting map were sent to the Siamese authorities who circulated them to diplomatic missions in Bangkok and within their own administration.

After 1907, there were a number of occasions when the Siamese authorities could have raised objections to the map, e.g. in treaty negotiations in 1925 or 1937, although these did not specifically relate to this part of the frontier. Further there were a number of occasions when the Siamese authorities, apparently without protest, treated the area as French, in particular in 1930, when a former Siamese Minister of the Interior was received by the French Resident with the French flag flying.

The essence of the Cambodian case, as successor to France, was that the Annex I Map represented an authentic delimitation binding on both countries and establishing Cambodian sovereignty; Thailand had acquiesced in that delimitation and was estopped by consequent conduct from arguing the contrary.

The essence of the Thai case was that the survey of 1907 was incorrect; it incorrectly portrayed a particular watercourse; the watershed ran, in 1904 and later, to the south of the Temple, so giving it to Thailand; the Annex I Map was not an authentic delimitation; no subsequent acts estopped them from going behind the map and claiming a frontier on the watershed.

The Court, by a majority of nine to three,[26] held that the line drawn on the Annex I Map was the frontier binding on the parties. They did not find that this map was a document of the Commission, expressly made authentic by Article 3 of the 1904 Treaty. But they considered that, as it was officially communicated without objection to the Siamese authorities, including members of the former Mixed Commission, members of the Siamese Cabinet and the Governor of the relevant Siamese province, Siam accepted it in 1908 as the outcome of the work of delimitation and thus authoritative against both parties as to where the frontier lay. But, in addition, they considered that the failure by Siam to challenge the Annex I Map or Cambodian actions relating to the Temple, particularly the French Resident's reception of the former Siamese Minister in 1930, thereafter confirmed this acceptance.

Judges Alfaro and Fitzmaurice supported the view of the Court but added separate opinions dealing with additional matters. Judge Alfaro gave a full account, with many citations, of the recognition in international law of the principle of estoppel or preclusion. Judge Fitzmaurice did not substantially differ from the judgment of the Court but wished to develop certain points further and to deal with some additional matters.

The three dissenting Judges[27] refused to recognize authority for the Annex I Map. They each gave separate dissenting judgments, but with differences mainly of emphasis. These judgments rested firmly on the watershed line provided by Article 1 of the 1904 Treaty. Judges Moreno Quintana and Spender (with Judge Fitzmaurice of the majority) considered that Thailand had proved that the watershed line ran along the outer edge of the spur on which the Temple lies, though Judge Wellington Koo thought that this question should be left for further expert inquiry. They considered that the manner of production and of acceptance of the Annex I Map were not such as to render it binding on Thailand. The Thai administrative acts were at least as good as the French acts to sustain a title to the area, and the Thai explanations of any inconsistencies were adequate.

The argument on this case begins and ends with the Annex I Map. Was it accepted on receipt as an authentic delimitation or was it not? If not, did Thailand act thereafter, especially by not objecting, in such a manner as to preclude her from attacking the map?

The two points have this in common. On the thesis supported by the Court, the Siamese at the time of their acceptance, or perhaps on later occasions, should have indicated their dissent from the map. In fact in 1908 they could only presumably have declared that they did not regard the line in the map as authoritative, since they had then no survey service and made no independent survey until 1934. The matter can be well analysed in terms of the maxim invoked by the Court, *Qui tacet consentire videtur si loqui debuisset et potuisset.*[28] Siam could not speak authoritatively against the map until its own survey was made in 1934–35; but could it rely on its own failure to survey? More important, ought it to have spoken? Ought a state receiving maps in the circumstances of this case to enter a reservation?

This may in part depend on the consequences. It is generally an element in estoppel, in this case acknowledged as part of the international law of preclusion, that a state can only go against its past statements if the other side has relied to its disadvantage on those statements. In the present instance, it is said in the judgment[29] that Thailand, having taken the benefit of the maps as a factor leading to certainty and stability, must abide by them.

The circumstances of this case were complex and peculiar. But, behind all the detail, the central issue in the policy of the law, and the related social and moral value, is clear. Is it preferable to achieve a solution, and an end to the argument, by a line on the map, ill- or well-founded, which was, to use a neutral word, passed between the parties? Or does one allow the reopening much later of this solution by going behind the map to the general criterion of the watershed which was specifically agreed, possibly thereby ignoring other results and benefits flowing from the map? Those who argue for the former will put a high duty on the dissenter to express his dissent, and did not find that duty met in the present case. Those who argue for the latter will be slow to impute to the parties a line other than one clearly and expressly and explicitly agreed.

III THE FRONTIER LAND CASE

The case concerning Sovereignty over certain Frontier Land[30] is a remarkable instance of the difficulty of frontier disputes arising out of a confused historical course of events. Essentially, it concerned sovereignty over two small plots of land totalling 14·378 hectares, less than thirty acres, in area.

The lands of the Belgian commune of Baerle-Duc include separate enclaves within the Netherlands commune of Baarle-Nassau. The question before the Court was whether the land in Plots Nos 91 and 92, Section A, Zondereygen was such an enclave and thus whether it was part of Belgium or the Netherlands.

In 1836 the Burgomasters of the two communes drew up a Procès-Verbal called in the Judgment the 'Communal Minute' but it was not finally signed till 1841. A copy of this was produced by the Netherlands without challenge and it states at the material point, 'Plots Nos 78 to 111 inclusive belong to the commune of Baarle-Nassau,' thus recognizing Plots 91 and 92 as part of the Netherlands.

In 1843 the two countries entered into a Boundary Treaty which said in Article 14, 'The status quo shall be maintained both with regard to the villages of Baarle-Nassau (Netherlands) and Baerle-Duc (Belgium) and with regard to ways of crossing them.' The Treaty also created a Boundary Commission which was to draft a Boundary Convention. This Convention, ratified in October 1843, provided maps and a 'Descriptive Minute' (Procès-Verbal Descriptif). But, in referring to Baarle-Nassau and Baerle-Duc, the Convention recalled that the status quo was to be maintained in accordance with the earlier treaty. Article 90 of the Descriptive Minute referred to the agreement of the local authorities in 1836 and set out the Communal Minute, as already referred to, with one vital difference. Where the Communal Minute produced by the Netherlands gave Plots Nos 78 to 111 to the Netherlands, this version of the Communal Minute gave Plots Nos 78 to 90 to the Netherlands, Plots Nos 91 and 92 to Belgium and Plots Nos 93 to 111 to the Netherlands.

Belgium relied on the text of the Communal Minute incorporated in the 1843 Convention. The Netherlands relied on the wording in the Convention referring to the status quo and invoked the Communal Minute, as produced by them in original, as authentic evidence of this. Alternatively, they pleaded that the 1843 Convention was vitiated by mistake; or, thirdly, that its ruling on sovereignty had been displaced by subsequent administrative acts of the Netherlands.

The Court, by ten votes to four,[31] held that Plots Nos 91 and 92 were Belgian. They held that the 1843 Convention was intended to dispose of the matter and not merely to hold in suspense the status quo, and thus the attribution of the Plots in Article 90 of the Descriptive Minute must prevail over the earlier Communal Minute.

The Court also rejected the Netherlands plea of mistake. The correspondence in 1841 showed that two versions of the Communal Minute were already in circulation and the maps used by the Commission for incorporation in the Convention showed them clearly as Belgian. The Court did not accept the historical hypothesis advanced by the Netherlands to establish and explain how the text, erroneous in its view, had been used in the Descriptive Minute. The Court rejected the argument based on Netherlands administrative acts, on the ground that these related to an enclave, and were frequently unknown to Belgium. Belgium had also done administrative acts and the Netherlands had not challenged its sovereignty until 1922 or repudiated Belgian assertions of sovereignty.

The dissenting declarations and opinions assigned the Plots to the Netherlands for different reasons. Judge Lauterpacht thought that it was impossible to settle the case either on the basis of the copy of the Communal Minute, whose authenticity could not be proved, or the Convention, since the latter was supposed only to record the status quo. He preferred to base the decision on the uninterrupted exercise by the Netherlands of administrative acts relating to the Plots, which resulted from their position as an isolated enclave; and in his view these local conditions provided an additional reason why, in the absence of clear provision in a treaty, there was no reason to disturb the existing state of affairs. Judge Spiropoulos thought the Belgian hypothesis that an error had somehow crept into the copy of the Communal Minute produced by the Netherlands was more speculative than the Netherlands hypothesis that an error had crept into Article 90 of the Descriptive Minute.

Judges Armand-Ugon and Moreno Quintana in their two dissenting opinions followed substantially similar lines of argument. They considered that Article 90 of the Descriptive Minute meant to incorporate an authentic Communal Minute. As the text which it in fact incorporated was inaccurate, that text had no legal effect and could not be invoked by Belgium. Furthermore the great preponderance of the administrative acts were by the Netherlands.

In this case, the Court was faced with a simple but difficult question. The Communal Minute and Article 90 of the Descriptive Minute, as the latter purports to incorporate the former, ought clearly to have been the same. Since they were not, the Court had to make an exhaustive examination, as far as the available documents allowed, of the course of events leading up to the establishment of the Descriptive Minute. But no overwhelmingly convincing argument emerges. The case can only be decided on the balance of hypotheses in the light of this intricate history. The Court, in the judgment, tended to give credit to the more solemn document, the Convention and its annexed Descriptive Minute, especially as the copy of the Communal Minute available to it, though apparently wholly in order and not open to specific challenge, was not automatically self-authenticating, and because there was some indication that, even at the time when the Descriptive Minute was being drawn up, variant versions of it existed. But the dissenting views are worthy of respect and understanding, for they preferred to follow the older version of the status quo as recorded in the Communal Minute as more authentically established.

As the relevant instruments did not determine the matter with overriding cogency, and because the parties advanced arguments based on them, the Court had also to review the administrative acts. These were the wide gamut of dealings to be expected in a history of a piece of land over nearly a century, including sale, the levying of taxes, registration of sale, inclusion in surveys and maps, an order for compulsory acquisition, and even one international act. This was the signed but unratified Boundary Convention of 1892 by which Belgium would have ceded the Plots to the Netherlands.

But administrative acts were carried out from each side, and many were unknown to the other side. It is not surprising that the Judges, whether they accepted the Belgian or the Netherlands respective arguments on the documents, tended to find that the administrative acts of the favoured party prevailed over those of the other party or at least that the latter did not displace the title based on the documents.

IV THE AWARD OF THE KING OF SPAIN

The case concerning the Arbitral Award made by the King of Spain on 23 December 1906 (Honduras and Nicaragua)[32] concerned a frontier dispute at second remove.

The Gámez–Bonilla Treaty of 7 October 1894 provided for the settlement of all outstanding disputes concerning the boundary between Honduras and Nicaragua. A Mixed Commission to do the detailed work was unable to reach agreement on a section of the frontier ending at the Pacific coast. The Treaty provided for this possibility by foreseeing an arbitral tribunal of three members, whose decisions 'shall be held a perfect, binding and perpetual treaty between the High Contracting Parties and shall not be subject to appeal'. One member of the Tribunal was to be appointed by each of the two countries. The third place was to be offered to members of the Diplomatic Corps of Guatemala City and, when the number of these was exhausted, the decision should be put to the Government of Spain, or by agreement, to another South American government. The third place was in fact offered to two Mexican members of the Diplomatic Corps but they left Guatemala before anything was done. After the two national Arbitrators had met the Spanish Minister to Central America, the post of Arbitrator was offered to the King of Spain and accepted.

The King of Spain, apparently a sole arbitrator, made his Award on 23 December 1906 defining the line in the unsettled section. Both governments welcomed it, though the Foreign Minister of Nicaragua in a Report to the National Legislative Assembly suggested that it needed clarification.

In a Note dated 19 March 1912, the Foreign Minister for Nicaragua raised the question of the validity of the Award for the first time.

The matter remained in dispute until, after action in the Organization of American States, the parties agreed on 21 July 1957 to submit 'the disagreement existing between them with respect to the Award' to the International Court of Justice.

The International Court, by fourteen votes to one,[33] rejected the contention of Nicaragua that the Award was invalid. Judge Moreno Quintana appended a separate declaration and Judge Spender gave a separate opinion; Judge *ad hoc* Urrutia Holguin gave a dissenting opinion.

Nicaragua argued first that the Award was invalid as the Treaty, which was of ten years' duration, had lapsed by efflux of time and that the appointment of the King of Spain was irregular under the terms of the Treaty. The Court rejected these allegations, both as unsubstantial on the merits, and on the ground that, as the parties had gone through with the arbitration they could no longer base objections on them. But it is noticeable that the Court[34] relied on this ground of preclusion in addition to their grounds based on the merits. Judge Spender indeed expressly said that he relied solely on the ground of preclusion, and that the appointment of the King of Spain was probably irregular.[35]

Nicaragua further argued that the Award was a nullity as vitiated by:

(*a*) excess of jurisdiction,
(*b*) essential error,
(*c*) lack or inadequacy of reasons in support of the Arbitrator's conclusions.

It is this part of the case which bears more closely on the question of frontier disputes.

The Rules set out in Paragraphs 1 to 7 of Article II of the Gámez–Bonilla Treaty are here relevant:[36]

1 Boundaries between Honduras and Nicaragua shall be those lines on which both Republics may be agreed or which neither of them may dispute.
2 Those lines drawn in public documents not contradicted by equally public documents of greater force shall also constitute the boundary between Honduras and Nicaragua.
3 It is to be understood that each Republic is owner of the territory which at the date of independence constituted, respectively, the provinces of Honduras and Nicaragua.
4 In determining the boundaries, the Mixed Commission shall consider fully proven ownership of territory and shall not recognize juridical value to de facto possession alleged by one party or the other.

> 5 In case of lack of proof of ownership the maps of both Republics and public or private documents, geographical or of any other nature, which may shed light upon the matter, shall be consulted; and the boundary-line between the two Republics shall be that which the Mixed Commission shall equitably determine as a result of such study.
> 6 The same Mixed Commission, if it deems it appropriate, may grant compensations and even fix indemnities in order to establish, in so far as possible, a well-defined, natural boundary-line.
> 7 In studying the plans, maps and other similar documents which the two Governments may submit, the Mixed Commission shall prefer those which it deems more rational and just.

The main contention of Nicaragua which is of interest here is the suggestion that the King of Spain had departed too lightly from historical factors, and in particular was not entitled to have recourse to Paragraph 6 quoted above. In the general view recognized by the Treaty, the principle applicable to Spanish American frontier determination was *uti possidetis juris*.[37] The frontiers should follow the historical boundaries dividing the former administrative districts of Spanish America, before their independence. Nicaragua considered that the Award had improperly diverged from this principle and had paid too much regard to actual occupation (contrary to Paragraph 4) and had fixed a 'natural boundary-line' without regard to historical factors. These arguments were supported by precedents of other arbitrations where either the Boundary Treaty or the Arbitrator was restrictive in allowing recourse to other than historical factors.

Nicaragua also advanced more detailed pleas suggesting that the Award was vitiated by 'essential error in that it failed to appraise correctly certain legal documents and failed properly to give reasons for its finding'.

The Court first held that by its express declarations and by conduct Nicaragua had recognized the Award as valid and that it was no longer open to it to challenge the validity of the Award. But the Court went on 'very briefly' to indicate that, even if complaint had been made in good time, the Award would still have been regarded by it as valid. The Court considered that it paid due account to historical and legal considerations (derecho historico). The evaluation of documents was within the Arbitrator's competence and his Award sufficiently reasoned.

In the Gámez–Bonilla Treaty and even more in the Nicaraguan arguments concerning the competence of the Arbitrator, we see an extreme respect for historical lines as a basis for settlement. There is a depreciation of other factors which are sometimes invoked in the settlement on legal grounds, whether by judicial or arbitral means. This follows from the circumstance of Spanish American independence where these lines were the most easily available basis and where ethnic and other considerations did not predominate. The acceptance in Latin America of lines drawn during the preceding rejected period of Spanish colonialism has interesting parallels in the present widespread reluctance in Africa to reopen frontiers inherited from the colonial period.

In this case again, the importance of arguments from preclusion is evident. The Court took this as its first ground, and Judge Spender in his separate opinion took it as the only available ground. Judge Moreno Quintana accepted this basis though he would have preferred to base the judgment on an analysis positively establishing the regularity of the Award rather than relying on the parties' acquiescence in it.

But, in the last resort, this case only concerns frontier disputes in the second remove. It concerns primarily the arbitral settlement of disputed frontiers and possible allegations of nullity in awards so arising. Much of the difficulty in the case arose from the less than perfect co-ordination of Article II as it applied to the Mixed Commission and arbitrations as well as the circumstances of the appointment of the King of Spain. But in all the circumstances, it is not surprising that the Award was upheld. The International Court of Justice, like other Courts, is right to be reluctant to substitute its own judgment for that of arbitral and other instances whose acts it may have to consider.

Finally it may be useful to review the criteria and methods applied by the Court.

Frontier lines can be drawn in reliance on varying factors and some of these factors have been discussed in the cases here under consideration.

A frontier may be drawn on ethnic grounds where two adjacent states represent different nations. This factor came up, but only in a negative way, in the Temple case, where it appears that the population on each side of the frontier was Khmer.[38] Even though the area involved in the dispute was important for symbolic reasons rather than for its population, the access to the Temple could have been important if it had not apparently been from both sides.[39]

The ethnic criterion could become of special interest in connection with frontier disputes if ever the asserted right of self-determination of peoples were applied by legal adjudication. If so, presumably if a people, whatever that may mean, chooses independent statehood, the boundary of the people often forms the frontier of the state. And indeed this was the principle which animated the decisions of the organs of the Allies in the frontier settlements for the new states in Europe created after the Great War of 1914–18. It was a line such as this which it was intended to reopen in the Jaworzina case,[40] briefly mentioned above.

So far this criterion has not been at issue in any case before the two International Courts. It has of course on occasion been one aspect of disputes brought to arbitration. Thus, in the Buraimi arbitration, the Tribunal was directed, by Article IV of the Arbitration Agreement of 30 July 1954, to take into account, among other factors, 'the traditional loyalties of the inhabitants' and 'the tribal organization and way of life of the tribes in the area'. In addition, resting on the not entirely cogent assumption that any section of a people will wish to join the remainder, a plebiscite, rather than an adjudication, is a means occasionally used for settling the question.

Natural features may also be the basis of a frontier, such as the watershed line in Article 1 of the Treaty of 13 February 1904 which was in issue in the Temple case.

Historical lines, i.e. those which have no ethnic or natural basis but antedate the establishment of the states, figured in the Award made by the King of Spain. There the frontier was based on the pre-existing Spanish colonial frontiers.

Arbitrary lines without any of the bases already mentioned can of course also arise from pure compromise or convenience. But usually an attempt is made to rest them on some justification.

A treaty, however, is normally required to establish a firm boundary, and the cases in court have tended to concern themselves mostly with the relevant treaties, whatever may be the factors on which the line is based. And, since frontier treaties tend to involve describing a line and also actual demarcation, either part of the process can give rise to subsequent disputes.

The problems in two cases studied at some length here arose simply because the process went wrong. In the Temple case, the Delimitation Commission never concluded its work by drawing up maps and authenticating them. In the Frontier Lands case, the text of the Communal Minute, as produced by the Netherlands, ought to have accorded with the text transcribed into the Boundary Convention. So also in the Rio Encuentro arbitration the line laid down in the 1902 Award could not be applied with certainty on the ground.

To settle the question the Court has available to it the whole gamut of legal arguments. In particular, the principles for interpretation of texts have to be applied to uncertainties in boundary treaties. But, in addition, the Court has perhaps been more willing to overcome defects in form than a national tribunal would.

As there is often long delay before frontier disputes come to adjudication, it is frequently impossible to disentangle at least in full the true course of events, and the Court has therefore had to place much reliance on the degree of administration one or other of the parties has actually exercised over the area in dispute. But the value to be attached to these acts depends in part on the extent to which they are known to the authorities of the other side and also the administrative level at which the acts are done and are known to the other side. And it must be confessed that the views taken by the judges frequently diverged as to where the preponderance of the administrative acts lay.

The most significant feature is, however, the reliance which the Court placed on the doctrine of preclusion or estoppel to facilitate its decision and to supplement the other material available to it. The principle prevents a state from going back on assertions by statement or by conduct or even by silence in the face of counter assertions.[41] As it rests on good faith and tends to reduce the scope of disputes, it seems to play a useful role.

But the main impression which results from a study of the cases which have come to court is how few the cases are and how small the areas of territory involved. States are reluctant to put at risk existing positions, whether their possession is the territory or only an unsatisfied claim to it. It is hard to escape the conclusion that this reluctance stems from a strong political sentiment and even perhaps a psychological instinct about national territory, whether actual or potential. The International Court is well equipped to settle conflicting legal claims to territory and it is the states which are slow to use it. If future developments of the international order can moderate national sentiment and strengthen a desire for settlement, the Court will find useful work to do in this field, and this will in turn advance those developments.[42]

TEXT REFERENCES

1. *ICJ Reports*, 1960, p. 192, discussed at greater length in Section IV of this Chapter.

2. The Case concerning Sovereignty over certain Frontier Land, Belgium and Netherlands: *ICJ Reports*, 1959, p. 209, also discussed in Section III.

3. E.g. The Tacna-Arica Question, Chile and Peru, which concerned a frontier plebiscite: Arbitral Award of 4 March 1925. Honduras Borders, Guatemala and Honduras: Arbitral Award of 23 January 1933. And the Chaco

Case, Bolivia and Paraguay: Arbitral Award of 10 October 1932. These cases are all reported in *UN Rep. of Int. Arbit. Awards*, vol. 2, p. 923, vol. 2, p. 1309 and vol. 3, p. 1819.

4. The Arbitral Award of the India–Pakistan Western Boundary Case Tribunal was announced on 19 February 1968; see pp. 191–92 above.

5. Arbitration Agreement of 30 July 1954, Treaty Series No. 65 (1954).

6. Kelly, *Eastern Arabian Frontiers*, New York, London 1964, p. 203.

7. Agreement (Compromiso) determined by the Government of the United Kingdom on 1 April 1965, Misc. No. 17 (1965), Cmnd 2682, and Award of HM Queen Elizabeth II of 9 December 1966, published for the Foreign Office by HMSO, 1966. This case is discussed in Chapter 6.

8. Antarctica case, United Kingdom and Argentina: Order of 16 March 1956, *ICJ Reports*, 1956, p. 12, and the similar case against Chile, ibid., p. 15. Both cases were removed from the list when the respondents did not accept the jurisdiction of the Court.

9. Declaration of the United Kingdom of 13 February 1946, *UNTS*, vol. 1, p. 3.

10. See note 41 below.

11. Temple of Preah Vihear, Cambodia and Thailand: Preliminary Objections, Judgment of 26 May 1961, *ICJ Reports*, 1961, p. 17.

12. Right of Passage over Indian Territory, Portugal and India: Preliminary Objections, Judgment, *ICJ Reports*, 1957, p. 125.

13. *ICJ Yearbook*, 1968–69.

14. The Temple of Preah Vihear, Cambodia and Thailand: Preliminary Objections, Judgment of 26 May 1961, *ICJ Reports* 1961, p. 17.

15. *ICJ Reports*, 1960, p. 6.

16. *PCIJ Reports*, Ser. B., No. 5.

17. *PCIJ Reports*, Ser. A., Nos 22, 24, and Ser. A/B, No. 46.

18. *ICJ Reports*, 1953, p. 47.

19. *PCIJ Reports*, Ser. A/B, No. 51.

20. *PCIJ Reports*, Ser. A/B, No. 53.

21. *PCIJ Reports*, Ser. B. No. 8.

22. *PCIJ Reports*, Ser. B., No. 8 at p. 57.

23. *PCIJ Reports*, Ser. B., No. 9.

24. *PCIJ Reports*, Ser. B., No. 12.

25. The Temple of Preah Vihear, Cambodia and Thailand: Judgment of 15 June 1962, *ICJ Reports*, 1962, p. 6.

26. *Per* Judges Winiarski (President), Alfaro (Vice-President), Basdevant, Badawi, Fitzmaurice, Koretsky, Tanaka, Bustamante y Rivero and Morelli.

27. Judges Moreno Quintana, Wellington Koo and Spender. Judges Tanaka and Morelli who supported the view of the Court on the main issue did not vote for an ancillary finding of the Court that Thailand must restore certain objects which may have been removed from the Temple. They held that this point was introduced too late in the proceedings.

28. *ICJ Reports*, 1960, p. 23.

29. *ICJ Reports*, 1960, p. 34.
30. Judgment of 2 June 1959, *ICJ Reports*, 1959, p. 209.
31. Judges Klaestad (President), Zafrullah Khan (Vice-President), Basdevant, Hackworth, Winiarski, Badawi, Kojevnikov, Cordova, Wellington Koo, and Spender.
32. Judgment of 18 November 1960, *ICJ Reports*, 1960, p. 192.
33. Judges Klaestad (President), Zafrullah Khan (Vice-President) Hackworth, Winiarski, Badawi, Armand-Ugon, Kojevnikov, Moreno Quintana, Cordova, Wellington Koo, Spiropoulos, Spender, Alfaro and Judge *ad hoc* Ago.
34. *ICJ Reports*, 1960, p. 209.
35. *ICJ Reports*, 1960, p. 220.
36. *ICJ Reports*, 1960, p. 199.
37. In his separate opinion, Judge Moreno Quintana, speaking as a representative of a Spanish American legal system, wished to rest the whole decision on a legal analysis showing the substantive regularity of the Award from this point of view.
38. See the Separate Declaration of Judge Fitzmaurice, the Temple case, *ICJ Reports*, 1962, p. 54.
39. Ibid., p. 54.
40. *PCIJ Reports*, Ser. B, No. 8.
41. For statements on the wide range of this doctrine see the separate opinion of Judge Alfaro in the Temple Case, *ICJ Reports*, 1962, p. 39 and McGibbon, 'Estoppel in International Law' in *International and Comparative Law Quarterly*, July 1958. The classical instance of this is in the Eastern Greenland case, *PCIJ Reports*, Ser. A/B, vol. 53, especially at p. 71.
42. An account of the cases involving frontier disputes considered by the International Court is in Chapter IV of Mme Bastid's lectures at the Hague Academy, *Receuil des Cours*, 1962, III, vol. 107 at p. 452.

8 CONCLUSIONS

Evan Luard

What conclusions can be drawn from the preceding studies?

If one looks at the history of territorial disputes over the last century or two, one might find some slight cause for optimism over the trend revealed. In general, the areas that have been the subject of dispute have become smaller and more marginal in importance. And, especially in the last twenty years or so, the armed conflict resulting has been on a lesser scale. Policies of systematic conquest, such as those of Prussia and Russia in the nineteenth century, or of the imperialist powers generally in Asia and Africa, are no longer pursued. As administration has penetrated to regions once scarcely governed at all, and so reduced the area of uncertainty, the general lines of the atlas have become clearer, firmer and more universally recognized. The Rann of Kutch, and the oasis of Buraimi can scarcely be compared with Poland, Alsace-Lorraine, Bessarabia, Korea or Mongolia as objects of dispute. The only areas today which could conceivably become the subject of territorial conflict of comparable size to those of earlier generations are the areas from time to time claimed by China in Siberia and central Asia; and even in this case China has so far given little indication of wishing to pursue such claims seriously, except in so far as the details of demarcation are concerned.

But the fact that the areas disputed are comparatively small does not prove that they may not be the cause of bitter conflict, and even of large-scale war. Though none of the frontier conflicts of the past twenty-five years have been very large in scale, this does not prove that this will be true in the future. Some of the remaining disputed areas, though not great in size, are large in importance. At the very least they may be thought to be so, and this is what counts. In a significant number of cases important raw materials have been involved. Oil in particular, which may be the source of huge revenues to the sovereign power, representing much of its national income, is frequently the prize in such disputes: this has almost certainly been a significant factor in the disputes over Kuwait, over Buraimi, that between the Trucial Sheikhdoms, and perhaps in the Sabah conflict between the Philippines and Malaysia. In other cases the area in question, even if unproductive, may be strategically significant: this was the case with the territories disputed between India and China. Finally, it is a commonplace that even territory that has little intrinsic value may be of great psychological importance to the nations concerned. Thus the fact that the remaining territories disputed today are relatively small in extent is not in itself a significant indication of whether they may become the cause of armed conflict in the future.

Certainly, as we saw in the first chapter, the total *number* of these disputes is very large indeed. If only a small proportion were finally to erupt in war, they could still be the cause of bloodshed and loss of life on a massive scale. The fact that the conflicts of this type that have occurred in the last twenty-five years (see the list on p. 8) have so far been on a comparatively small scale is therefore little assurance that the same thing will remain true in the future.

It is thus important to consider and assess the procedures available to the international community to contain, and where possible to resolve, such disputes. Do the accounts in the preceding chapters provide any useful conclusions about their relative effectiveness?

There is one distinction that it is important to make clear from the outset. International action in such questions may be designed to achieve two quite different things, and may be assessed in relation to either. It may be designed to *pacify* the dispute in question: to stop the fighting, if it has already broken out, or to prevent it if it has not. Or it may be designed to *resolve* the dispute: to bring a final settlement which both parties will accept, and which may prevent similar conflicts breaking out again in the future. It goes without saying that the second objective is the more desirable and the more important. It goes equally without saying that it is also far more difficult to achieve.

There is one further preliminary point, equally obvious but equally necessary to clarify. Disputes obviously differ greatly in the extent to which they are susceptible of either pacification or resolution by *any* method, whether political or legal, bilateral or international. Thus the fact that a particular procedure has failed in one case does not mean that any other would have succeeded any better. And the fact that one method has been successful, over one or a number of issues, gives no indication how suitable it would be to other cases of quite a different character; or that some other method might not have succeeded equally well.

If one takes, first, the less important task of *pacifying* disputes of this kind, it is clear that for this the political forms of procedure are more likely to be suitable than the legal ones. Even the looser legal procedures, such as mediation, take time to set in motion. Once tempers are already roused, they may be quite ineffective, and indeed merely arouse impatience. This is not always so: in the Cambodia–Thailand case, the appointment of a special representative by the Secretary General may well have done something to cool things down in a difficult period. Similarly, the Secretary General's mediator on Kashmir, together with the UN observers, may have helped to keep incidents to a minimum between 1950 and 1965. But normally in these situations it will be immediate first aid, rather than a final cure, that is required. And the political procedures, such as resort to the UN, are more likely to provide this.

Among these political procedures it can be argued that the

regional organizations have a record as good as, or better than, the UN. The OAU established procedures which restored stability fairly quickly over the Algeria–Morocco dispute (though they have not finally resolved it). Somalia's conflicts with her neighbours have been successfully contained by an African initiative, though in this case not by the OAU itself. ASEAN has played a significant role in reducing the temperature of the Philippines–Malaysia dispute. And the OAS has several times taken action successfully on questions of this kind. Over the Honduras–Nicaragua dispute in 1957, an investigating committee, and later an ad hoc committee, secured a cease-fire, withdrawals and a reference to the International Court. And when the same dispute broke out again in 1961 the Inter-American Peace Committee mediated successfully. The Organization also effectively calmed disputes over the Equador–Peru border in 1955, between Nicaragua and Costa Rica in 1949 and 1955, between Bolivia and Chile over the waters of the Rio Lauca in 1962, and over the Panama Canal in 1964 (though the last two cannot properly be considered as frontier disputes).

This conclusion is scarcely surprising. What is above all required in these cases is effective *influence* in favour of restraint. It is not astonishing that friends and neighbours may be more capable of exercising such influence in times of trouble than a remote organization, having nearly 130 members, many of them total strangers in ideology, outlook and geographical situation.

The UN, however, has also had some successes. Calls for a cease-fire were effectively followed by cease-fires (though they were not necessarily cause and effect) over Palestine in 1948, over Suez in 1956 and over Kashmir in 1965 (the first two were perhaps somewhat more than frontier disputes in the sense here discussed, but the conclusion still has validity). The UN resolution of 22 November 1967, on the Middle East, and the use subsequently made of it, represents precisely the type of international action to propose the terms of a settlement that may often be needed over such disputes. But a considerable proportion of the twenty frontier conflicts listed on pp. 8–11 – something like three-quarters – were not even substantively considered by the UN at all, let alone pacified. It can even reasonably be suggested that the League of Nations had a better record in dealing with frontier disputes than the UN though, as Mr Windass shows, its importance was rather in legitimizing situations that had come about already, than in imposing a settlement which would otherwise not have been achieved.

There is a further procedure for pacification that should perhaps be considered in this context, at least for comparison, though it is not strictly an international procedure of the kind examined in this book. This is bilateral negotiation between the two parties. For the pacification, as for the resolution, of disputes, it may be possible to achieve agreement without the interposition of any international body or procedure. The settlement of the confrontation between Malaysia and Indonesia took place in this way, though here a change of government in Indonesia was an essential factor. Pakistan and Afghanistan managed to halt open conflicts over their border by the same procedure. In the case of the Pakistan–India war in 1965, the mediation of the Soviet Union played an important part, as did UN action, but the effect was to bring the two sides together themselves to discuss a mutual withdrawal. Similarly Zambia's mediation over the Somali disputes had the effect of bringing about bilateral discussions.

Although bilateral talks sometimes calm things down, therefore, on the whole it cannot be said that they have played a large role in pacifying the various conflicts listed on pp. 8–11. In something like three-quarters of the cases no such negotiations, at least on the frontier itself, have taken place: and even when more normal relations have been restored, the frontier itself has often remained disputed.

This indicates that international action is often required at least to bring the two parties together. This has so far often been lacking. It may also impose restraint. The fact noted earlier, that few of the frontier conflicts of recent times have led to large-scale war has been at least partly due to the intervention of outside parties, either national or international, to urge moderation and to promote mutual withdrawals. Here the mobilization of world public opinion, for example in UN resolutions or OAU pleas, may be a form of pressure it is not easy to resist. Even Israel in 1957 felt ultimately obliged to withdraw, though no physical sanctions were brought to bear against her. We shall consider in a moment some of the ways in which international pressures of this kind might be made more effective. But it can be seen that the record of international organizations in securing a preliminary cessation of hostilities has not been totally without success.

It is when we turn to the more long-term task, the *resolution* of frontier disputes, that the legal procedures, as against the political, come more into their own.

There is a rough progression in the degree of formality of these procedures, political and legal, corresponding to the order in which they occur in this book. In general it can be said that the UN and regional organizations have almost never been involved to *settle* frontier disputes. Nor have they themselves normally sought to do so. They have had a fairly flexible range of procedures open to them in confronting such situations. They have sometimes sought to observe or control a frontier (as between Israel and her neighbours). They have sometimes asked to send someone to mediate (as over Kashmir). The Secretary General has appointed a representative (as over the Cambodia–Thailand dispute). They have sometimes requested a reference to the International Court of Justice (as the OAS did over the Nicaragua–Honduras dispute). But they have not generally tried to impose a settlement that could be regarded as final and beyond dispute. As Dr James puts it: '. . . the UN has achieved greater note as a prophylactic than as a patching-up agency. For, whereas it has made a significant contribution towards keeping violence in check in a number of dangerous areas, its endeavours to settle these, and other, problems have been markedly less successful.'

There are, however, occasions on which the task of pacification and that of resolution begin to merge into one. Again, the Arab–Israel dispute perhaps provides a suitable example. Under the resolution of 22 November 1967, Dr Jarring was set a task which involved both a withdrawal of forces and a permanent settlement which would involve general recognition of the frontiers so established. If his mission was successful, it would secure not just a temporary restoration of peace but the final resolution of the territorial problem. Similarly, it could be said that, in sending a new contingent of observers to patrol the Kashmir cease-fire line in 1965, the UN in practice confirmed that line as at least the provisional boundary to which all forces in the recent conflict must withdraw. In sending observers to confirm that the people of the Borneo territories of Malaysia wished to be part of Malaysia, and had been presented with this as the prime issue in elections, the UN was, in a certain sense, recognizing the legitimacy of the Malaysia–Indonesia boundary then in dispute. And in the cases where the UN Secretary General has appointed a special representative to mediate in disputes of this kind (as over Buraimi and the Cambodia–Thailand disputes), it must have been hoped that this would secure not only a cessation of hostilities and a withdrawal of forces, but the agreement of both parties to recognize that line as the final and permanent boundary (to some extent this did happen over Buraimi). In such cases therefore pacification automatically leads to resolution of the dispute concerned.

The cases where the UN has become involved, however, have normally been cases where violence had already broken out, and where the chief aim has been to bring about a halt to hostilities. Although the Charter lays emphasis on the need to bring 'disputes' to the United Nations before they have reached the point of conflict, by the parties themselves or by others, in practice this is very rarely done. Where there is a desire to seek a solution before any fighting has occurred, the dispute is not usually brought to the UN or to a regional organization. Whether one of the parties themselves takes the initiative, or a third party seeks to promote a settlement, they have more often turned to one of the legal procedures.

The first, and most informal of these has been some form of mediation. Mediation can indeed scarcely be regarded as a legal procedure at all. As we saw in the first chapter, it involves no obligation on the part of either party to accept the recommendations made. Nor is the proposed settlement necessarily to be based on legal grounds. For both these reasons it is normally the most attractive procedure to the parties, especially in cases where either attaches great importance to the territory in question, or is in some doubt about their legal title. It also has the advantage of flexibility, in that the mediator is not obliged to be ruled by the strictest interpretation of the law, nor indeed by legal considerations at all. He can thus assess precisely what are the interests felt to be most vital by each of the two parties, and devise a compromise that may best give some satisfaction to each. Especially if both parties are, at least privately, anxious to avoid open conflict, and would welcome some face-saving formula that will enable them to climb down, mediation may have a good chance of success.

Here too the line between pacification and resolution may become blurred. An act of mediation originally undertaken for the former purpose – because a conflict has reached a stage close to violence – may in practice, if successful, also produce something like a final resolution. The mediation of Mr Beck-Fries and Mr Gussing in the Thailand–Cambodia dispute (though it had little influence in causing the Temple dispute to be referred to the International Court of Justice) may have led the way to the resolution of other disagreements concerning the frontier between the two countries. The mediation by the Secretary General's representative over the Muscat and Oman question may have caused UN members to attach less weight to the ambitions and claims of the Emir of Oman, and so to resolve the purely territorial aspects. The recommendations of Mr Webster, the US mediator in the Guatemala–British Honduras dispute, though not fully accepted by any of those mainly concerned, may have done something to defuse the question in the period before independence, and so have encouraged a final acceptance by Guatemala of the status quo. Thus though, as Miss Schwiesow points out, none of the recent cases of mediation have led to a final resolution of the disputes concerned, they may have done something at least to reduce disagreement on them.

When we turn to cases of arbitration, resolution is normally the object of the exercise. Here the very fact that arbitration is accepted will usually mean that the parties are willing to accept some final solution of the problem. This means either that they feel considerable confidence in their own case; or that the territory is one that they do not care a great deal about. For this reason Mrs Fox even concludes that 'to expect arbitration to solve a major political issue is to exaggerate its importance as a procedure of peaceful settlement of international disputes'. This may sound a somewhat pessimistic verdict – it is certainly more pessimistic than the optimistic hopes of some international lawyers in the past – but it is probably realistic. It is significant, for example, that over the question which she principally discusses in her chapter, the Argentina–Chile dispute, the section that *both* parties agreed to submit to arbitration was the section that was of least economic or strategic value. Over a further stretch, which may possibly contain important resources, including oil, only one party, the party not in control, was willing to risk such a reference. Similarly, the Indian and Pakistani governments were able to agree to arbitration over the Rann of Kutch, which was not in itself intrinsically very valuable. But the same is never likely to be true of Kashmir, which is strategically, economically and psychologically of great importance to both countries. Finally, the breakdown of the attempt to arbitrate the Buraimi dispute can no doubt be partly attributed to the importance to both parties of the territory with its reputed oil resources, and the subsequent strong-arm tactics employed by both sides to keep it under their own control. This no doubt accounts for the fact that so few disputes are submitted to arbitration: it is interesting that such submission was far more common in the nineteenth century, but even then the territories concerned were not mainly very large or important.

These considerations apply of course even more strongly to judicial settlement, where the powers concerned have no control even over the choice of judges. As Mr Darwin points out: 'The main impression which results from a study of cases which have come to court is how few the cases are, and how small the areas of territory involved.'

There have only been three or four cases altogether since 1945. And they have concerned such esoteric and marginal areas as the Minquier and Ecrehos Islands, the Pays de Gex, two villages on the border between Belgium and the Netherlands, the Temple of Preah Vihear and so on. In such cases it may be a convenience to both parties to have some final determination of the frontier. This will in no way damage national interests: on the contrary it may provide an opportunity to show a magnanimous spirit of internationalism and goodwill, without any genuine risk to real national interests. There are some cases, also, where the party which believes its own case to be legally sound will agree to submit the case, but be resisted by the other, which bases its case on ethnic, historic or geographical, rather than legal grounds. This has been the case over the Antarctica, Gibraltar and British Honduras disputes, on each of which Britain was ready to accept arbitration and proposed this; and in each case was resisted by its opponents. But, except perhaps for the pre-war case of the dispute between Denmark and Norway over Greenland, it is difficult to point to any case of judicial settlement of a territorial dispute that has had any major importance, or that has altered the map in any significant way. This does not mean that it is of no account. It may be important, or even essential, to have some convenient mechanism for determining finally the details of national frontiers which are uncertain. But it is unlikely to provide, as international lawyers have sometimes hoped in the past, the means by which, in resolving international disputes, 'war might be replaced by law'.

There are one or two more general conclusions which might be drawn in considering these various procedures.

First, they have almost all of them, whether political or legal, been used almost exclusively for the *confirmation* of the status quo, rather than for changing it. The only exception to this is that in one or two cases strictly legal decisions, arbitration and judicial decision, have involved the marginal revision of an already established frontier. This was the case over the Nicaragua and Honduras frontier, where Nicaragua actually had to withdraw from areas she previously administered; and over the Preah Vihear temple, where Thailand had to do the same. Even here, since the areas were remote and relatively small, there has not often been much disruption of administration or the removal of many homes and people. The post-war period (since 1946) has seen nothing like the massive removals of people that took place, for example, between Greece and Turkey after the First World War. The fact that usually the status quo has been confirmed does not in itself mean that the procedures have been valueless. There may be a positive, and indeed important, value in having an existing situation *legitimized*, and mutually acknowledged in this way. For at least it will mean that it may become far less likely that a dispute will break out again over the same territories in the future. A grievance that may have been harboured and nurtured for long may, as a result, eventually become forgotten.

Secondly, whether political or legal procedures have been used, they have inevitably been most successful where the territory concerned has not been of great value, whether economic or strategic. In other words, though it is certainly true that a territory may have a psychological value for the populations quite out of proportion to its intrinsic value, so far as *government* decisions are concerned it is the intrinsic value which seems to count. If important economic resources are concerned, there is not usually any readiness to allow peaceful procedures to resolve the question of sovereignty. We have already recounted a number of cases where the presence of oil has prevented any amicable settlement.

On the other hand where the territories have been of little value, as in the Argentina–Chile and Belgium–Netherlands cases, agreement has been far easier.

There seem also to be some possible conclusions to be drawn about the regional distribution of these cases. It is scarcely surprising that there have been a fairly large number of disputes among the newer countries of the world. The receding of colonialism from Africa and Asia has inevitably left some unresolved, or newly reawakened, disputes behind; and we examined some of the forms these could take in the first chapter. Indeed, given the totally illogical nature of the colonial boundaries, whether from an ethnic, historical or a geographical viewpoint, it is a tribute to the wisdom of the successor governments that disputes have not been far more frequent. The OAU explicitly adopted the principle that its member governments should accept the inherited boundaries, and should undertake not to seek to overturn them by force. The Latin American countries, a century and a half earlier, had adopted a somewhat similar principle in the doctrine of *uti possidetis*. This has itself done much to reduce the difficulties. But it has not prevented all disputes. There have been those, such as that between Indonesia and Malaysia, or between Morocco and Mauritania, where one ex-colony has claimed the whole of another, as being traditionally its own territory. There have been those where two or more countries have laid claim to some colony at the point of independence, such as the claims of Morocco and Mauritania to Spanish Sahara, or Guatemala and Mexico to British Honduras. There have been those where a newly independent country has refused to accept the whole logic of the colonial boundaries, since they deprive them of a considerable part of their own peoples: this has been the not unnatural cause of Somali claims against their neighbours. For all these reasons, a considerable proportion of the remaining territorial disputes concern ex-colonial countries or territories. In Latin America, though a few historical grievances remain, on the whole the borders are more accepted now than they have ever been. And in Europe there has probably never been a time when the continent was so stable, and when there has been so little challenge to the existing territorial disposition: probably the only serious dispute of this type also concerns a colonial territory, Gibraltar, since it is doubtful whether the various territorial grievances in the Balkans, or the West German claim to the former Eastern territories are pursued for anything other than bargaining or pin-prick purposes. This development of territorial stability in Latin America, North America and Europe, gives some grounds for hope that territorial disputes are not an inherent feature of international life, and that it may not be over-optimistic to look to a day when all territories everywhere might be generally acknowledged and respected, at least in practice if not in theory.

Let us, finally, see if there are any practical conclusions to be drawn from this survey. Are there any ways in which the available procedures for resolving disputes of this kind might be extended or improved?

It is sometimes suggested that the UN has been more effective in restoring peace after conflict has already broken out than in preventing it arising in the first place: better at peace-keeping than in peace-making. There is, as we have seen, something in the view that international procedures in recent years have done more to pacify disputes than to resolve them. But it does not follow from this, as is sometimes suggested, that if new and better procedures for settlement could be devised fighting might be prevented from arising in the first place. For one thing, when a dispute has not given rise to open conflict at all, nations may have little wish, and no inclination, to submit it to mediation or arbitration, whatever procedures are available. This may gratuitously risk the loss of a territory that is now held without risk or difficulty. It is usually only the shock of open conflict that precipitates the will to submit, as occurred in the Nicaragua–Honduras and Thailand–Cambodia cases. Conversely, where the will to resolve exists, plentiful procedures and facilities for resolving such questions are available.

Besides those already mentioned – mediation, arbitration and judicial settlement – which may be invoked by any party at any time, there has existed for fifty years a permanent Court of Arbitration which is available for use in disputes of this kind, but has scarcely been used. In addition, the UN established in 1948 a Panel of Arbitration and Conciliation, for the same purpose: and this too has been almost unused ever since. Whatever has prevented the resolution of such disputes, therefore, it has not been the lack of available procedures for settlement.

It is true that the UN and other bodies could have more frequently, and more insistently, *demanded* recourse to these bodies than they have done. This might indeed have been desirable. It is certainly true that in general UN bodies have tended to wait until a dispute has reached the stage of open war before confronting it effectively. Sometimes it might have been more valuable to seek to bring outside pressures to bear at an earlier stage (as the Charter lays down: for example in Article 33). But it is by no means sure that there would normally be sufficient incentive for the parties to such a dispute, or sufficient urgency in the outside pressures, to produce much effect in those circumstances.

Partly for these reasons, as with pacification, in a number of cases, bilateral negotiations were the instrument which brought agreement on such questions. The boundaries between China and five of her neighbours (Burma, Nepal, Pakistan, Afghanistan and Mongolia) have been settled and agreed in this way. In Europe, bilateral negotiations between the Netherlands and West Germany, and between Belgium and the Netherlands, have tidied up small unresolved sections of the boundary previously in dispute. Negotiations between Iran and her neighbours in the Persian Gulf have at least moderated, and perhaps finally resolved, a number of territorial disputes in that area. But there have been a number of other cases where negotiations have led nowhere (India–Pakistan, Afghanistan–Pakistan, Philippines–Malaysia, Spain–Gibraltar, Argentina–Falkland Islands, Guatemala–British Honduras, Venezuela–British Guiana). In some cases, even where peaceful and amicable relations have been restored, the territorial issue has not been resolved (Malaysia–Indonesia, Morocco–Algeria, Argentina–Chile). And in very many cases bilateral negotiations have not even been attempted. One effective course, therefore, might be for the UN or regional organizations to urge governments (for example under Article 33 of the Charter) to seek bilateral solutions over such disputes, and to go on nagging until these are started. Something of this sort has happened over Gibraltar and the Falkland Islands, but it would be more effective over such issues as Morocco–Algeria, Argentina–Chile, where the difference is over the *situation* of a line, and is not a basic one of principle. And in certain cases, for example where negotiations are running into difficulties, or have broken down, or where friction has become acute, the appointment by the UN of a mediator, or a representative of the Secretary General, to help to find a compromise can be useful.

There are, however, other ways in which the UN might promote the resolution of frontier disputes. The League of Nations Council of Ambassadors set up a delimitation commission to determine the frontiers between some of the states of Europe after the Treaty of Versailles. This was admittedly a somewhat special situation, after the map of Europe had just been completely redrawn, and a treaty for this purpose, ambiguous or incomplete in some respects, recently signed. But it is not altogether impossible that a delimitation commission of this kind today, which would examine disputed frontiers and attempt to define and demarcate them more accurately, might have some value. In suitable cases it could approach the parties to see whether they would be willing to have the frontier defined, either by some particular procedure, or by the commission itself, which could recommend the terms of settlement. No doubt, in a number of cases such an approach would be refused by one party or the other, since the existing situation might be more favourable to them than any other. But in this way outside pressure would be brought to bear. In some cases at least, especially where the dispute was the source of real damage to the interests of both parties, it might be possible to bring about a settlement by these means. At the very least such a commission might be able to *demarcate* boundaries at present not demarcated at all, or only inadequately so: for example in the Persian Gulf.

Possibly even better than a UN commission would be action by regional organizations to the same end. As we have already seen, some of these organizations, such as the OAS and the OAU, already have quite a good record in this field. This has the advantage that each dispute is heard by those who are close neighbours, and perhaps able as a result to exercise a more effective influence than could any world body.

Finally there is also the possibility of setting up bilateral commissions to examine mutual frontiers. This proved a successful means of delimiting three or four thousand miles of the frontier between the US and Canada over a period of more than a century. Bilateral commissions have just been set up to keep the frontiers between Venezuela and Guyana and Austria and Hungary under review. In a few cases, therefore, this too might be a suitable alternative.

Such measures are particularly valuable in cases where the frontier is uncertain rather than disputed; or where the territory is not of great intrinsic value; or where some bargain or quid pro quo may be struck. Where the conflict is more acute, there is a danger that approaches from the outside may only evoke stubborn opposition from both sides, or even reawaken disputes that were previously quiescent and might have died away altogether. Sometimes a government is quite relaxed about a particular dispute, but may be compelled to respond to popular pressures when these are reawakened. For this reason, what is needed in the case of many frontiers is not so much to devise 'solutions', but measures designed to stabilize the existing situation, and reduce the risks of conflict arising. As we have seen, there are now very few areas where there does not exist at least some de facto border. The usual situation, therefore, is not of an uncertain and undemarcated frontier in dispute between two powers, but of one power in possession and under challenge from another.

In this situation there is considerable value in some objective and accurate record of where the existing administrative frontier lies, at least for the knowledge of international bodies. In many cases, where conflict over a frontier arises, the only effective response of international organizations will be to demand a return to the status quo ante. This is what the UN in fact did, with some success, over Suez, the India–Pakistan war of 1965, and other cases. In this case it is vital to know exactly what the status quo ante was. There could thus be great value if the UN could have at its disposal some kind of UN atlas, recording in precise terms the situation of existing administrative frontiers, even if it was clearly recognized that this was quite without prejudice to sovereign rights on either side. Though not all powers would be expected to acknowledge this as having any validity at all, most might be persuaded to undertake that they would at least not seek to overthrow the recorded frontiers by force. Certainly all who were not themselves involved could undertake to use their influence to the same end. And at the very least, such an atlas would serve as a record of the status quo, which could be used by the UN and other outside powers as a record of the situation to be restored where conflict had broken out.[1]

Finally, international action taken in crisis situations may have a long-term importance in resolving these disputes. As we have seen, measures taken in the first place to restore stability may in practice bring a relatively permanent settlement. The establishment of observers, or even of a peace-force, on a frontier over a considerable period of years may lead to such a stabilization that the line is unlikely finally to be overthrown. The UN may appoint a mediator, or commission, to examine a situation on the spot, and its conclusions may be difficult for either party to defy except at unacceptable cost in relation to world opinion. Here normally the task will be to suggest the ways in which the 'have' power can take certain steps to appease the pride of, or reduce inconvenience to, the 'have-not' power, without seriously damaging the status quo: this was the basis of recommendations made over the Guatemala–British Honduras, and the Venezuela–British Guiana disputes. Here too the international community may in effect give a kind of endorsement to the status quo, which may serve in the long run to stabilize and strengthen it.

Thirty or forty years ago, writers on peace and war wrote much of the problem of 'peaceful change'. This was supposed to be necessary to prevent change through war. It may be that this remains an equally important task today in relation to many aspects of the international order, above all perhaps over the economic relations of states: today it is here especially that peaceful change may be the necessary condition of preventing war-like change. But it is not self-evident that the *territorial* status quo must be subject to change to avoid conflict. Frontiers are partly arbitrary collections of lines anyway, and nations may be finally conditioned to accept them. Here, as over other disputes, time may be the best healer: the means of settlement most required. Certainly it is very difficult to conceive of any international procedures today that are likely to induce 'have' powers to relinquish important disputed territory to 'have-not' powers; unless, conceivably, through some exchange of territory. Especially where posession has become hallowed with time, it will not be easily surrendered.

The situation is different from thirty or forty years ago in that there are now, with the dubious exception of China, no major revisionist powers seeking to alter the status quo in this territorial sense. The main challenges to the international order are rather those which demand *internal* change, within existing borders. And the forces that demand this do not normally demand any change in the territorial status quo. It certainly seems likely that, as many of the foregoing studies imply, the international procedures likely to be most effective are those that seek to induce wider acceptance of *existing* territorial borders, rather than those that seek to devise new and ideal settlements to replace them. The importance of the various international procedures we have examined may be precisely that they can mobilize external pressures, usually backed by world public opinion, in favour of such an acceptance. In this way they may assist governments to justify to their own more militant public opinions (often the principal challenge to existing borders) accommodations to an existing reality, and convenient rationalizations for accepting them.

TEXT REFERENCE

1. The UN has in fact been engaged over the past five years in compiling a Map of the Millionth scale. Though primarily designed to record physical features, it could be used for this purpose.

A device that could be of particular value in situations of this kind is a 'freeze' of claims: an agreement between the parties not to pursue them for the moment. This has been done on a multilateral basis in Antarctica, where there exist a large number of mutually conflicting claims, and this agreement has been made explicit in the Antarctica Treaty. Similarly, pairs of countries have sometimes agreed not to pursue claims. Indonesia and the Philippines have each agreed to put aside their claims against Malaysia without formally renouncing them. There have been discussions of similar renunciations of Guatemala's claim against British Honduras and West Germany's against Poland. This might prove the most sensible way of dealing with rival claims to Kashmir, the remaining territorial disputes among the Persian Gulf Sheikhdoms, or with the various Saharan claims of Libya, Algeria, Morocco and Mauritania. Such 'freeze' agreements could be encouraged by regional bodies or the UN. Even such disputes as that over Gibraltar might be solved in this way: in return for certain concessions in Gibraltar, Spain might, without abandoning its claim to sovereignty, agree not to pursue it in an active form.

Again, in some cases, as we saw, what is required is *legitimation* of the status quo, to allow one side to climb down without loss of face. Here the UN can help. It was used for this purpose over the Indonesian claim to Sabah in 1963 (though here the claimant declined the opportunity afforded to climb down). There have been suggestions the UN could help in the same way over the Iranian claim to Bahrain: if a mission could show that the people of Bahrain did not want Iranian rule, it could help Iran to abandon the claim. This important function of providing confirmation and justification of the status quo might be provided in other cases by the UN or a regional organization.

BIOGRAPHICAL NOTES

HENRY DARWIN Born 1929. Called to the Bar by Lincoln's Inn in 1953. Member of the Legal Branch of HM Diplomatic Service since 1954. At present Legal Counsellor in the United Kingdom Permanent Mission to the United Nations, New York, and has represented the United Kingdom in legal committees of the United Nations and at international conferences. In addition to articles in legal periodicals, he contributed studies on certain aspects of the peaceful settlement of international disputes for the Report of the Study Group of the David Davies Memorial Institute on this subject.

HAZEL FOX MA Oxon. Barrister at Law, formerly Lecturer in Law, Somerville College. Tutor, Council of Legal Eucation. Publications: Simpson and Fox, *International Arbitrations*, London 1959, and various articles.

ALAN JAMES Senior Lecturer in International Relations at the London School of Economics and Political Science. Rockefeller Research Fellow in International Organization at the Institute of War and Peace Studies, Columbia University, New York during 1968. Author of *The Politics of Peace-keeping*, London, 1969.

PETER LYON Senior Lecturer in Commonwealth Studies in the University of London. He has taught at the London School of Economics and the University of Leicester. He was Visiting Associate Professor of Political Sciences at the University of California in 1967. He is author of *Neutralism*, Leicester 1963, and *War and Peace in South-East Asia*, London: OUP for RIAA, 1969, and many articles in scholarly journals.

NAOMI SCHWIESOW Received a Bachelor of Arts degree in philosophy from the University of Chicago in 1963. She has pursued graduate studies in political philosophy and international politics there and is at present a student at the Johns Hopkins University School of Advanced International Studies. She is also research assistant at the Washington Center of Foreign Policy Research.

STANLEY WINDASS Born 1930. Oxford University, First-Class Honours Degree in English, 1952. Teacher and Lecturer in English till 1962. At present employed by the Catholic Institute for International Relations and in the Sub-Department of Ethology at the University of Birmingham, on a research topic relating to Ethology and Culture. Publications include: *Christianity versus Violence*, London 1964, *A Blow for Peace*, London 1967, *Man Divided*, London 1969.

EVAN LUARD Member of the Foreign Service from 1950–56, serving in Hong Kong, Peking and London. Research Fellow of St Antony's College, Oxford, 1957–66, working on international affairs, and especially international institutions. 1966–   , MP for Oxford. Author of: *Nationality and Wealth*, London 1964, *Conflict and Peace in the Modern International System*, Boston 1968.

INDEX

Index

Index